THE COMPLETE
Sun Tzu
FOR
BUSINESS
SUCCESS

USE THE CLASSIC RULES OF *THE ART OF WAR*
TO WIN THE BATTLE FOR CUSTOMERS
AND CONQUER THE COMPETITION

GERALD A. MICHAELSON AND **STEVEN MICHAELSON**

Avon, Massachusetts

Published by Adams Business, an imprint of Adams Media,
a division of F+W Media, Inc.
57 Littlefield Street, Avon, MA 02322. U.S.A.
www.adamsmedia.com

Contains material adapted and abridged from *Sun Tzu: The Art of War for Managers, 2nd Edition,* by Gerald A. Michaelson and Steven Michaelson, copyright © 2010 by Steven Michaelson, ISBN 10: 1-60550-030-5, ISBN 13: 978-1-60550-030-0; *Sun Tzu for Execution,* by Steven W. Michaelson, copyright © 2007 by Steven W. Michaelson, ISBN 10: 1-59869-052-3, ISBN 13: 978-1-59869-052-1; and *Sun Tzu for Success* by Gerald Michaelson with Steven Michaelson, copyright © 2003 by Gerald Michaelson with Steven Michaelson, ISBN 10: 1-58062-776-5, ISBN 13: 978-1-58062-776-4.

ISBN 10: 1-4405-2880-2
ISBN 13: 978-1-4405-2880-4
eISBN 10: 1-4405-2893-4
eISBN 13: 978-1-4405-2893-4

Printed in the United States of America.

10   9   8   7   6   5   4   3   2   1

Library of Congress Cataloging-in-Publication Data
is available from the publisher.

This publication is designed to provide accurate and authoritative information with regard to the subject matter covered. It is sold with the understanding that the publisher is not engaged in rendering legal, accounting, or other professional advice. If legal advice or other expert assistance is required, the services of a competent professional person should be sought.
—From a *Declaration of Principles* jointly adopted by a Committee of the American Bar Association and a Committee of Publishers and Associations

Many of the designations used by manufacturers and sellers to distinguish their product are claimed as trademarks. Where those designations appear in this book and Adams Media was aware of a trademark claim, the designations have been printed with initial capital letters.

This book is available at quantity discounts for bulk purchases.
For information, please call 1-800-289-0963.

Contents

Part Three:
Sun Tzu for Success

Introduction

As I stood in the Great Hall of the People in Beijing, China, an entourage was approaching. The next thing I knew I was shaking hands with the premier of China—Li Peng. The personal introduction was part of a journey to China to present applications of Sun Tzu's strategies for business at an international symposium on *The Art of War*. Sun Tzu was a practical philosopher who wrote the 7,000-word *The Art of War* in about 500 B.C. I read it while researching my book *Winning the Marketing War* and found the content quite useful.

If you've read James Clavell's *Noble House* or seen the movie *Wall Street,* you've encountered some of the wisdom of this ancient Chinese strategist. In both the book and the movie, major characters quote from Sun Tzu as a foundation for their strategy.

The Art of War might be one of the oldest books you will ever read. Originally written on bamboo strips, this acclaimed work has achieved international recognition as *the* concentrated essence of winning strategy.

For centuries, *The Art of War* has held a pre-eminent position among both Chinese and Japanese strategists. Many of the sayings of Chairman Mao are simple restatements of Sun Tzu's philosophies.

When Chiang Kai-shek's military attaché advised British military strategist B. H. Liddell Hart that Chinese officers were trained from Hart's books, he replied it was time they went back to Sun Tzu:

> *Since in that one short book was embodied almost as much about the fundamentals of strategy and tactics as I [Hart] had covered in more than twenty books. In brief, Sun Tzu was the best short introduction to the study of warfare.*

Confirming again that *The Art of War* is *the* sound fundamental text on strategy.

EASTERN VERSUS WESTERN STRATEGY

The Art of War is the foundation of Eastern strategy. Sun Tzu's central thesis is that you can avoid fighting when you plan the right strategy before the battle. *On War* by Carl von Clausewitz, a German officer who wrote in Napoleon's time, is the foundation of much of Western strategy. Clausewitzian theory concentrates on the big battle as the way to win.

Readers will find *On War* filled with convoluted sentences and difficult to read. One English translation is over 600 pages long. Clausewitz's work expresses so many ideas that it can be used to justify any position. In contrast, *The Art of War* is a masterpiece of simplicity. When comparing Clausewitz and Sun Tzu, strategist Liddell Hart comments: "Sun Tzu has clearer vision, more profound insight, and eternal freshness." Although there is evidence that a translation of *The Art of War* could have been available to Napoleon, Sun Tzu's work has not generally been considered to contribute to Western military strategy.

Locked within Sun Tzu are secrets for business and personal success. Continued study and analysis of Sun Tzu yields new insights to unlock winning concepts.

A STRATEGIC MANUAL FOR BUSINESS LEADERS

Using Sun Tzu's strategies in business is nothing new. The existence of over 100 Japanese translations of *The Art of War* indicates it has served as a source of strategic thinking for many Japanese managers. In contrast, only a handful of English translations exist, but they are circulated throughout the business world.

There is much evidence that *The Art of War* is making significant contributions to the thinking of contemporary business leaders. Harvard Professor Michael Porter quoted from Sun Tzu when he lectured the National Football League owners on how they could defeat the now-defunct United States Football League. Venture capitalist Asher Edelman made *The Art of War* required reading for admission to his course on entrepreneurship at Columbia University. Quantity orders for *The Art of War* have been placed by business organizations, trade unions, and law-enforcement agencies. Western officers who laid plans for the first Gulf War were well versed in Sun Tzu; it would seem as though Saddam Hussein was not.

The Art of War is a classic not only of strategy but also of simplicity. There was nothing very complex about warfare in Sun Tzu's time. It involved land battles of large bodies of troops armed with personal weapons. The simplicity of *The Art of War* makes Sun Tzu's lessons readily transferable to business strategy and understanding the strategic rules of business in the new millennium.

The lessons of Sun Tzu are thousands of years old, and it is the test of time that makes the ancient lessons valuable to the business manager. Many business lessons have existed for such a short time that they have yet to crystallize as valid strategies. Evidence of respect for the passage of time to give veracity to lessons comes from a Chinese historian asked in 1925 to identify the lessons of the French Revolution. He replied, "I would love to, but it is still too early to tell."

STRATEGY AND TACTICS

The fundamental principles of strategy are the same for all managers, all times, and all situations. Only the tactics change, and tactics are modified to the times.

Strategy is best defined as "doing the right thing," while tactics is "doing things right." Where does strategy end and tactics begin? Admiral Mahan in his work on sea power said, "Contact is a word which perhaps better than any other indicates the dividing line between tactics and strategy." Strategy stops at the border in war and at the headquarters door in business; tactics begins with contact with the enemy in war and at the customer in business. Sun Tzu's *The Art of War* provides fundamental lessons for contemporary strategic thought and serves as a fertile source of ideas for tactics.

ABOUT THIS TRANSLATION

Because there are so few English language translations of *The Art of War*, the emergence of a new translation has special significance. I felt fortunate indeed when I received this translation in Beijing at a symposium sponsored by The Research Society of Sun Tzu's *The Art of War.* Translation of Chinese ideograms into English is a complex task because each character can have many different meanings. Consequently, the personal and professional backgrounds of the translators tend to determine the wording of the translation. The Chinese language scholars who undertook the difficult task of translating from the original documents concentrated on finding the most accurate interpretations of the ideograms.

Eastern and Western strategic writings exist as two distinct and separate sources of information, seldom communicating with each other. Western strategists build upon the strengths of previous Western strategists; Eastern strategists similarly reinforce each other. Neither builds on the strength of the other. An important contribution of this work is to provide a conceptual linkage between the fundamental lessons of the two. By analyzing key concepts from both Eastern and Western strategic thought, you gain an insight into how *both* can strengthen your strategy *and* tactics.

This book does not propose a short list of key strategies, but rather is formulated around the understanding that strategy is a mental process. The best strategy comes from the right mindset. Clausewitz said, "Theory can give no formula with which to solve problems. It lets the mind take a look at objects and their relations and then the mind goes to higher regions of action, there to act." This book provides a refreshing way to immerse oneself in the great strategic thinking which nurtures the mind.

This new translation of Sun Tzu is a joy to read—and read again. Sun Tzu's lessons can be applied to real-life situations and serve as an everyday resource for all kinds of strategic thought. For example, one version of *The Art of War* relates Sun Tzu's principles to winning in the stock market. An English translation, *The Art of Strategy,* is organized as a template for the strategies of life.

The strategic lessons in *The Art of War* have become a general construct to solve a variety of problems. Although the original text is founded in military strategy, the applications in this book focus on strategic issues for managers.

READER'S GUIDE

Because the content of the book flows from Sun Tzu's philosophy, it should not be considered a complete modern strategic manual. Instead, the value of this book is its ability to simplify the complexity of strategic thinking. While you may want to take the strategic wisdom of Sun Tzu seriously, do not take the modern translation of the ancient words too literally.

—Gerald A. Michaelson
March 1999

To my father, the Business Master I learned from. And to the successful future of Sue, K.T. Dannie, Jessica, and Nicholas.
—Steven Michaelson

PART ONE

Sun Tzu

THE ART of WAR FOR MANAGERS

Chapter 1

Preparing for the Battle Is Essential to Winning

LAYING PLANS

Management Rules

- Thoroughly Assess Conditions
- Compare Attributes
- Look for Strategic Turns

The vision of what the organization wants to be must be planned with an awareness of reality. That is why this chapter focuses on assessment.

The vision components articulate purpose, mission, guiding values, and a vivid image of the organization's future. From the vision, leaders can determine the strategy, set strategic initiatives, and align the organization.

The more sophisticated the planning process becomes the harder it is to introduce the flexibility to accommodate changes in the situation. In rigid systems, planning and obedience to the plan are regarded as the key to victory. Carefully laid plans rigorously implemented without deviation are regarded as the way to overcome the inevitable confusion. As ever-increasing time and attention are focused on "the process of planning," the successful execution of the plan can become secondary. However, any football coach can tell you that rigidity does not win games. Every coach has plans that allow for flexibility in formations to adapt to reality. It follows that it is not strategists who cause changes in the plan—it is reality.

A common mistake is to consider planning as only a mental process, an idea in our head that simply looks at the past and adjusts for the future. If your plan is not in writing, you do not have a plan at all. Instead, you have only a dream, a vision, or perhaps even a nightmare. The simple written plan works best.

Clearly define the problem before seeking a solution. Do not limit your planning horizon to what can be accomplished with existing tools. If the only tool you have is a hammer, everything will look like a nail.

THOROUGHLY ASSESS CONDITIONS—TRANSLATION

Sun Tzu says:

War is a matter of vital importance to the state; a matter of life and death, the road either to survival or to ruin. Hence, it is imperative that it be thoroughly studied.

Therefore, to make assessment of the outcome of a war, one must compare the various conditions of the antagonistic sides in terms of the five constant factors:

1. Moral influence
2. Weather
3. Terrain
4. Commander
5. Doctrine

These five constant factors should be familiar to every general. He who masters them wins; he who does not is defeated.

Business Parallels to Five Constant Factors

1. **Moral influence means a "spirit of mission."** The strength of belief that the purpose is morally sound rallies a fighting spirit and generates a firestorm of commitment.
2. **Weather equates to "outside forces."** Industry consolidation is an outside force, as is the emergence of world competition and the influence of environmentalism.
3. **Terrain is the "marketplace."** As the general must know the terrain, so the strategist must consider the scene of action—people, place, product, promotion, price, etc.

4. **Commander has an equivalent in "leadership."** The names keep changing, but the principles of leadership remain the same.
5. **Doctrine is comparable to "guiding principles."** Understand and apply the fundamental principles that determine success.

THOROUGHLY ASSESS CONDITIONS—MANAGER'S COMMENTARY

Good assessment is the foundation of a successful operation.

When the management of a major pharmaceutical company found that product development activity was decreasing, an assessment revealed the reason. Although senior managers claimed development was a team effort, analysis of their twenty-five most profitable drugs revealed that two people initiated ten of them. The reason product development declined was because both people had moved to positions where they were no longer in the development stream.

Every assessment must include a thorough analysis of how to increase business with existing customers. As proof, an Ogilvy & Mather analysis showed that the return on the marketing investment to existing customers can be many times greater than to prospective customers. The greatest source of increased sales and profits is from those who know you and are already purchasing your products.

In today's business world, the assessment before the plan is often ignored in the rush to action. When action is taken without a thorough assessment of the situation, too often people begin working on the wrong things. In these circumstances, the result will be a lot of effort expended with no gain.

Assessments are simply methodologies for gathering data in a structured process designed to elicit facts or perceptions. Assessments can be internal or external and they can be conducted by one or more individuals. Assessments can be surveys distributed to everyone or interviews conducted across a vertical slice of the organization.

Good assessments go beyond the current situation. They dig into underlying causes and search for new and better ways to achieve success. To achieve good results, ask questions in pairs so the first question determines the perception of the current status and the second reveals opportunities. For example, the first question might ask for a definition of an objective, while the second would ask for ideas about how the objective should be achieved.

When assessments are conducted by an external organization, respondents usually feel they have a better chance of giving anonymous input, which provides more accurate data. Internally, the assessment provides information on strengths and weaknesses that can energize and direct self-renewal. Externally, the assessment reveals threats and opportunities.

COMPARE ATTRIBUTES—TRANSLATION

Sun Tzu continues:
    Therefore, to forecast the outcome of a war the attributes of the antagonistic sides should be analyzed by making the following seven comparisons:

1. Which sovereign possesses greater moral influence?
2. Which commander is more capable?
3. Which side holds more favorable conditions in weather and terrain?
4. On which side are decrees better implemented?
5. Which side is superior in arms?
6. On which side are officers and men better trained?
7. Which side is stricter and more impartial in meting out rewards and punishments?

> By means of these seven elements, I can forecast victory or defeat. If the sovereign heeds these stratagems of mine and acts upon them, he will surely win the war, and I shall, therefore, stay with him. If the sovereign neither heeds nor acts upon them, he will certainly suffer defeat, and I shall leave.

A STRATEGIC MORAL

Following the success of the Prussian army in the Franco-Prussian War, the British General Staff sent a team of aristocrats to find out the secret of success. They reported the Prussian troops were all clean-shaven with short-cropped hair. The British Army copied this; it remains a law to this day.

The moral of the story is: Don't copy the wrong thing! (Or, don't send aristocrats to do competitive studies.)

COMPARE ATTRIBUTES—MANAGER'S COMMENTARY

Compare competitive strengths and weaknesses.

When Coke and Pepsi engage in competitive battles, or when P&G determines how to increase market share, these organizations use competitive marketing research as an input ingredient. When Xerox determined it wanted to be a world-class competitor, it benchmarked every process to determine how to make that process the best in its class.

Comparisons of attributes can be made by either a direct competitive comparison of strengths and weaknesses or benchmarking that studies comparable processes in any other organization. Benchmarking is a learning experience that "steals shamelessly" from friend and foe alike. When Ford benchmarked six other well-run companies, it found the following key attributes: executives spent time outside their offices communicating with employees; people and their skills were a competitive advantage; trust replaced controls; cross-functional teams developed cutting-edge products and services; bureaucracy was out and teams were in; authority was delegated; training was readily available; and each benchmarked company said it was customer driven.

As people on a benchmarking team observe successful new practices elsewhere, they become enthusiastic champions of change. For example, when an international electronics company benchmarked its plants by function, benchmarking teams found several plants had extremely efficient manufacturing processes. The people involved in the benchmarking activity championed the rapid acceptance of the more efficient processes throughout the organization.

A *Fortune* 500 company benchmarked attributes that other large organizations considered key to success. The best companies listed processes that achieved results as the keys to success, while less successful ones ignored processes and simply listed the results—as though each was unaware of the fact that process performance determines results.

Companies that compete using customer data, employing CRM (customer relationship management) techniques, are regularly benchmarking. This very accountable branch of marketing is constantly assessing the payout of a customer offer and evaluating each offer versus other inducements. The offer with the best payback is expanded or used again. These companies are continually testing offers at a small scale to evaluate their relative effectiveness. Online retailers like Overstock. com segment their customer base and benchmark offers against different groups of customers to build more refined targeting and even better results.

LOOK FOR STRATEGIC TURNS—TRANSLATION

Sun Tzu continues:

Having paid attention to the advantages of my stratagems, *the commander must create a helpful situation over and beyond the ordinary rules.* By "situation" I mean he should act expediently in accordance with what is advantageous in the field and so meet any exigency.

All warfare is based on deception. Therefore, when able to attack, we must pretend to be unable; when employing our forces, we must seem inactive; when we are near, we must make the enemy believe we are far away; when far away, we must make him believe we are near.

Offer a bait to allure the enemy, when he covets small advantages; strike the enemy when he is in disorder. If he is well prepared with substantial strength, take double precautions against him. If he is powerful in action, evade him. If he is angry, seek to discourage him. If he appears humble, make him arrogant. If his forces have taken a good rest, wear them down. If his forces are united, divide them.

Launch the attack where he is unprepared; take action when it is unexpected.

These are the keys to victory for a strategist. However, it is impossible to formulate them in detail beforehand.

Now, the commander who gets many scores *during the calculations in the temple* before the war will have more likelihood of winning. The commander who gets few scores during the calculations in the temple before the war will have less chance of success. With many scores, one can win; with few scores, one cannot. How much less chance of victory has one who gets no scores at all! By examining the situation through these aspects, I can foresee who is likely to win or lose.

LOOK FOR STRATEGIC TURNS—MANAGER'S COMMENTARY

Develop strategies that go beyond conventional rules.

When the Minutemen faced the Redcoats on the open battlefield of Concord in the traditional frontal confrontation of the time, the minutemen lost. Then, the minutemen made a fundamental shift in their battle tactics and fired on the redcoats from behind stone fences as they returned to Boston. This shift in tactics initiated a strategic turn in combat, as the new strategy of skirmishing contributed to the success of the American Revolution.

Externally Focused Strategic Turns: Wal-Mart's initial strategy focused on small towns. Wherever it invaded, competitive merchandising strategy was changed forever. The advent of mass merchants like Wal-Mart at one extreme of retailing, and specialty boutiques at the other, reshaped merchandising strategies across a wide variety of industries.

ESPN is an example of a cable network that heralded a new strategy in marketing. ESPN doesn't have viewers; it has fans that make it a competitive powerhouse. Originally a network with a lot of sporting events, ESPN has reshaped itself into a network for sports junkies. It supplies sporting news and events to every single continent including Antarctica.

Internally Focused Strategic Turns: At the Tactical Air Command during six and one-half years of General Bill Creech's leadership, dramatic improvements in combat readiness were made with no additional people or money. To achieve this awesome record, Creech changed the internal operating strategy to focus on decentralization of authority. His commanders immersed themselves periodically in operations—for example, spending a week with a night maintenance crew. Throughout his command, he applied the principles of quality management as outlined in his bestselling book *The Five Pillars of TQM* (product, process, organization, leadership, and commitment).

As a result, the combat capability of the Tactical Air Command doubled and billions of dollars were saved. Out-for-maintenance aircraft were reduced 71 percent, and monthly sorties increased 80 percent (the productivity bottom line). Fighter parts delivery time was reduced dramatically, and aircraft accident safety increased 275 percent.

Sometimes missed strategic turns become evident after business results deteriorate. For years, while Detroit automakers declined, Toyota grew. When the 2008 financial crisis hit and Detroit automakers tumbled, Toyota initially looked to be a beneficiary of U.S. automakers' continued troubles—it continued to grow and overtook GM to become the world's largest automaker. But less than a year later, the president of Toyota said his company was one step away from "capitulation to irrelevance or death." His words were reflective of the wrong strategic turn of his predecessors, who had pursued rapid growth as the auto business matured.

WAGING WAR

Management Rules

- Marshal Adequate Resources
- Make Time Your Ally
- Everyone Must Profit from Victories
- Know Your Craft

Since the ideal strategy is whatever works best, it follows that implementation is a powerful component of the strategic rollout. The tactical implementation plan is as important as the strategic plan because it takes the vision and strategy to the point of contact.

A European strategist, Captain Johnstone, wrote in 1916:

You do not know how the enemy is disposed? Fight and find out. The decisive attack can only be confidently fixed after some fighting. The tentative attack is not a separate fight, but the beginning of the battle. Launch a formation against the whole front and you learn the shape.

With the right strategy, the battle is only half won; the strategy succeeds only with professional execution of tactics. Problems arise when planning is separated from execution. This is like separating thinking from doing—it diffuses responsibility.

The important thing is to get started. Too much time spent in planning can breed indecisiveness and error. It is often better to engage in some form of simultaneous planning and implementation. This can be as difficult as changing a tire while the car is moving. Tactical plans must be shaped in relation to reality with the information learned from contact.

In every endeavor, the abnormal is normal and uncertainty is certain. A contingency plan should be prepared to allow for the abnormal. The exercise of preparing the contingency plan yields insights into threats and opportunities.

Close examination of companies with great reputations for long-range planning reveals they also focus on short-term gains. That is, they play for the championship one day at a time with a consistent focus on long-range direction.

MARSHAL ADEQUATE RESOURCES—TRANSLATION

Sun Tzu says:
Generally, operations of war involve one thousand swift chariots, one thousand heavy chariots and one hundred thousand mailed troops with the transportation of provisions for them over a thousand li. Thus the expenditure at home and in the field, the stipends for the

entertainment of state guests and diplomatic envoys, the cost of materials such as glue and lacquer and the expense for care and maintenance of chariots and armour, will amount to one thousand pieces of gold a day. *An army of one-hundred-thousand men can be raised only when this money is in hand.*

MARSHAL ADEQUATE RESOURCES—MANAGER'S COMMENTARY

Invest adequate resources so the operation can be sustained.

Home Depot, Best Buy, and other giant category killers in the retailing marketplace understand how to marshal enough resources to overwhelm the market. By combining the concentration of an overwhelming assortment of merchandise with the propaganda of everyday low prices, they suck up market share like crazy.

The cry from every business failure is, "We ran out of money," but the real problem was probably one or more of the following: not enough managerial talent or operational skill, wrong products or services, or one of myriad other inadequate resources required to make the organization successful.

The failure of many airline start-ups is an obvious business parallel to Sun Tzu's expressed need to have enough resources to survive. Often, these business failures are accompanied by an announcement that the organization ran out of capital before it could generate enough business to be profitable. So it is that all business problems eventually become financial problems. In every battle, the one with the most resources has the odds in his favor. As Damon Runyon said, "The battle may not go to the strong, or the race to the swift, but that's the way to bet."

The problem of adequate resources is especially critical in start-ups because they do not have the base of loyal customers that sustains mature businesses in an economic downturn. But all companies face choices. Paul Otellini, the current CEO of Intel, says, "Every Intel CEO makes at least one big bet." In Otellini's case, it was on the Atom mobile chip—their smallest chip ever.

To achieve success, you must have superiority. However, that superiority is always relative. It is only necessary to answer the question: What is the allowable limit of resources to allocate? If you are truly determined to win, there is no upper limit. However, this does not mean you should recklessly squander resources. When resources are depleted and cannot be replenished, the result will be bankruptcy.

MAKE TIME YOUR ALLY—TRANSLATION

Sun Tzu continues:

In directing such an enormous army, a speedy victory is the main object.

If the war is long delayed, the men's weapons will be blunted and their ardor will be dampened. If the army attacks cities, their strength will be exhausted. Again, if the army engages in protracted campaigns, the resources of the state will not suffice. Now, when your weapons are blunted, your ardor dampened, your strength exhausted and your treasure spent, neighboring rulers will take advantage of your distress to act. In this case, no man, however wise, is able to avert the disastrous consequences that ensue.

Thus, while we have heard of stupid haste in war, we have not yet seen a clever operation that was prolonged. There has never been a case in which a prolonged war has benefited a country. Therefore, only those who understand the dangers inherent in employing troops know how to conduct war in the most profitable way.

Hence, what is valued in war is a quick victory, not prolonged operations.

SPEED WINS

Throughout history, winning generals developed disciplines and systems for moving faster than their opponents. Napoleon's troops marched at 120 paces per minute while his opponents marched at 70 paces; speed alone gave Napoleon an advantage that contributed to his success.

Sun Tzu's point is not that speed can overcome stupidity. Operations must be completed rapidly because when actions take too long, the chance increases for errors and unforeseen events to contribute to failure.

MAKE TIME YOUR ALLY—MANAGER'S COMMENTARY

The key is to become rapidly effective and efficient.

Cisco and Salesforce.com are examples of fast-moving companies that won early strong positions in technology: computer networking and business-to-business CRM. Internally, cycle-time reduction and just-in-time systems have increased the effectiveness and efficiency of production.

Some businesses in traditional industries have used the Internet to dramatically change industry cycle times. Ponoko.com lets consumers order furniture and craft products over the Internet and doesn't begin production until someone orders one. Individual production is sourced, via the Internet, to a producer with the capability to manufacture the product and get it to consumers quickly.

A speedy victory is indeed the main objective, and the value of time, being a little ahead of your opponent, has contributed to many victories. Achieving this advantage involves both getting started quickly and rapidly attaining a position of strength.

Building strength rapidly is, in itself, a clever advantage either because you take the opponent unaware or because the swift concentration of multiple elements creates the force of simultaneous action. So it is that the first one to the river usually crosses without difficulty.

The speed with which a position is occupied is critical. Those who own a position early may need to expend fewer resources defending it than those who come later and must try to occupy that position. The defense of an occupied position is always less costly than the expenditure required to take that position.

Because the high cost of acquiring new customers depletes financial resources more rapidly than the cost of keeping existing customers, new business ventures must move rapidly to build a loyal customer base.

Here are a few key issues in making time an ally:

- As a rule, earliest is best. Time saved is time gained.
- The later you start, the more you require.
- The more urgent the need for a decision, the longer it takes.
- Rapid decision making produces rapid execution.
- Rapid action is simultaneous action.
- Delayed decisions inevitably lose their positive quality.
- All the positive consequences of speed accrue to the early offensive.
- The less you delay:
  the less apt you are to be surprised
  the less ready will be your competitor
  the greater the probability your time of attack will be earlier than expected

As a result, your opponent will be surprised and the consequences will accrue in your favor.

EVERYONE MUST PROFIT FROM VICTORIES—TRANSLATION

Sun Tzu continues:

Those adept in employing troops do not require a second levy of conscripts or more than two provisionings. They carry military supplies from the homeland and make up for their provisions relying on the enemy. Thus the army will be always plentifully provided.

When a country is impoverished by military operations, it is because an army far from its homeland needs a distant transportation. Being forced to carry supplies for great distances renders the people destitute. On the other hand, the local price of commodities normally rises high in the area near the military camps. The rising prices cause financial resources to be drained away. When the resources are exhausted, the peasantry will be afflicted with urgent exactions. With this depletion of strength and exhaustion of wealth, every household in the homeland is left empty. Seven-tenths of the people's income is dissipated and six-tenths of the government's revenue is paid for broken-down chariots, worn-out horses, armour and helmets, arrows and crossbows, halberds and bucklers, spears and body shields, draught oxen and heavy wagons.

Hence, a wise general is sure of getting provisions from the enemy countries. One zhong of grains obtained from the local area is equal to twenty zhong shipped from the home country; one dan of fodder in the conquered area is equal to twenty dan from the domestic store.

Now in order to kill the enemy, our men must be roused to anger; to gain the enemy's property, our men must be rewarded with war trophies. Accordingly, in chariot battle, when more than ten chariots have been captured, those who took the enemy chariot first should be rewarded. Then, the enemy's flags and banners should be replaced with ours; the captured chariots mixed with ours and mounted by our men. The prisoners of war should be kindly treated and kept. This is called "becoming stronger in the course of defeating the enemy."

EVERYONE MUST PROFIT FROM VICTORIES— MANAGER'S COMMENTARY

Strengthen human resources and material assets with each victory.

In companies funded through private equity that have not yet declared an Initial Public Offering, employees sign up for below-market salaries in the hope of large payouts when the company goes public. Most times, of course, these hopes end up dashed. But there are well-known stories of a few of these that worked: Google's IPO is one of the best known, enriching many early employees. The hope of large rewards motivates employees and aligns their personal financial well-being with the success of the company. In these organizations, attracting the best people depends on the ability of the company to convince prospective employees of the likelihood of the big payout.

While I was visiting the national headquarters of one of America's most successful companies, one of its major competitors announced it was going out of business. Within minutes, you could hear secretaries on the phone advising branch managers to immediately interview and hire the best of the now-defunct competitor's salespeople (who would also have contacts with the best prospects). As Sun Tzu says, "This is called 'becoming stronger in the course of defeating the enemy.'" What a loss of good fortune it would be to win the battle and not become stronger.

Too often, a corporate acquisition results in a "housecleaning" of very competent and experienced people. The people who are terminated in the interest of financial efficiencies are often those who really know the customers, the culture, and the subtle elements necessary for success. Because these experienced people are terminated, the acquired company becomes weaker before it becomes stronger, if it survives at all.

The acquisition strategy of many successful companies has been to keep the original owners and staff of acquired companies as active managers while providing the financial resources to power future growth.

The chairman of a successful business built on friendly acquisitions said, "One of the key objectives in an acquisition is to retain the existing management. They are the people who built the business, and if we are going to buy that business, it is important to utilize their strengths."

The opportunity to profit from victories also applies to internal recognition and reward programs. Think about providing opportunities for everyone to win. Make the award cycle short and issue rewards immediately after the event. Always gather an audience when you give recognition.

KNOW YOUR CRAFT—TRANSLATION

> *Sun Tzu continues:*
> And therefore the general who understands war is the controller of his people's fate and the guarantor of the security of the nation.

QUALITIES OF LEADERSHIP

Thousands of years ago, one of Sun Tzu's commentators, Ho Yen-hsi, wrote, "The difficulties in the appointment of a commander are the same today as they were in ancient times"—and that was said during what we consider ancient times.

Napoleon, in his maxims, said, "It is exceptional and difficult to find in one man all the qualities necessary for a great general. That which is most desirable, and which instantly sets a man apart, is that his intelligence or talent are balanced by his character or courage. If his courage is the greater, the general heedlessly undertakes things beyond his ability. If, on the contrary, his character or courage is less than his intelligence, he does not dare carry out his plans."

Mao Ze Dung wrote, "In actual life we cannot ask for an invincible general; there have been few such generals since ancient times. We ask for a general who is both brave and wise; who usually wins battles in the course of war—a general who combines wisdom with courage."

British Major General J. F. C. Fuller writes about a competitive quality: "Originality, not conventionality, is one of the main pillars of generalship. To do something that the enemy does not expect, is not prepared for, something which will surprise him and disarm him morally. To be always thinking ahead and to be always peeping round corners. To spy out the soul of one's adversary, and to act in a manner which will astonish and bewilder him, this is generalship."

Military writers also agree that an important quality of an ideal leader is a concern for people. In *On the Psychology of Military Incompetence,* Dixon points out that humanitarianism is a prerequisite for high morale and physical health.

KNOW YOUR CRAFT—MANAGER'S COMMENTARY

Master the expertise required to win.

When Fortune magazine lists the ten most admired companies, it generally recognizes the leadership of each. In general, the most admired companies have strong and stable leadership—people who know their business well. Look at the most recent top five companies on this list and the length of tenure of their CEOs.

1. Apple—Steve Jobs spent decades with Apple and has been CEO since 1997.
2. Berkshire Hathaway—Warren Buffett has been at the helm for more than forty years.
3. General Electric—Jeffrey Immelt's been CEO for almost a decade.

4. Google—Eric Schmidt has been CEO since 2001, but the company has only been around since 1998.

Many of the star executives of top companies are long-time experts in their craft; they have succeeded in their current roles as well as in other roles in their companies or industries.

When the early Romans built an aqueduct, the engineer who designed the structure stood under it when the scaffolding was removed. His expertise in his craft truly determined whether he lived or died.

Computer people should run computer companies (witness the disastrous, short term of John Scully when he moved from Pepsi to Apple); beverage people should run beverage companies; and airline people should run airline companies. The credentials of an industry expert are impressive: Who would argue about coffee with Starbucks founder Howard Schultz or motorcycles with Harley-Davidson turnaround leader Vaughn Beals?

The trio in Tampa who opened the first of over 500 Outback Steakhouses had years of restaurant experience with Steak & Ale, Bennigan's, and Chili's and at the New Orleans World's Fair. This Australian concept restaurant has become one of the most popular and profitable steakhouses of the 1990s.

Any venture capitalist will tell you that the background and character of the people is the most important factor in the success of a new venture.

ATTACK BY STRATAGEM

Management Rules

- Win Without Fighting
- Strength Against Weakness—Always
- Beware of "High-Level Dumb"
- Obey Fundamental Principles

At every level of any operation, strategy is indeed "war on a map"—it is the "plan on paper." Strategy deals with the allocation of resources to the battle. In *On War*, Clausewitz says that strategy sets the point where, the place when, and the force with which the battle is to be fought.

In his book *Strategy* B. H. Liddell Hart explains the objective of strategy: "The true aim is not so much to seek battle as to seek a strategic situation so advantageous that if it does not of itself produce the decision, its continuation by battle is sure to achieve this."

The first rule in strategy is to pay painstaking attention to the needs and wants of the customer, and your organization's ability to fulfill those needs. This analysis includes every step from design through delivery and after-sale service. Only after a thorough analysis of your ability to meet the customers' needs do you check with competitive realities to determine the viability of your strategy. Great strategy never reacts to the competitor; instead, strategy defines the opportunity in terms of the customer and then considers the situation in the competitive environment. Strategy must also consider the depth of corporate resources, effect of government regulations, environmental concerns, and currency fluctuations.

Strategy is not a competitive game. "Do more, better, faster" is not a strategy. Strategy focuses on adding real value to the customer. Strategy does not seek confrontation; instead, it seeks to achieve objectives with minimum combat.

Great strategies arise from intense discussion and deliberation that take into account internal strengths and weaknesses and external threats and opportunities. This thorough analysis provides insights that can identify important strategic opportunities.

WIN WITHOUT FIGHTING—TRANSLATION

Sun Tzu says:

Generally, in war the best thing of all is to take the enemy's state whole and intact; to ruin it is inferior to this. To capture the enemy's entire army is better than to destroy it; to take intact a battalion, a company or a five-man squad is better than to destroy them. Hence, to win one hundred victories in one hundred battles is not the acme of skill. To subdue the enemy without fighting is the supreme excellence.

Thus, the best policy in war is to attack the enemy's strategy. The second best way is to disrupt his alliances through diplomatic means. The next best method is to attack his army in the field.

The worst policy is to attack walled cities. Attacking cities is the last resort when there is no alternative.

It takes at least three months to make mantlets and shielded vehicles ready and prepare necessary arms and equipments. It takes at least another three months to pile up earthen mounds against the walls. The general unable to control his impatience will order his troops to swarm up the wall like ants with the result that one third of them are slain, while the cities remain untaken. Such is the calamity of attacking walled cities.

Therefore, subdue the enemy's army without fighting. They capture the enemy's cities without assaulting them and overthrow his state without protracted operations.

Their aim must be to take all under heaven intact through strategic superiority. Thus, their troops are not worn out and their triumph will be complete. This is the art of attacking by stratagem.

SUN TZU'S STRATEGY APPLIED TO BUSINESS

Subdue the enemy's army without fighting: Find a nonconfrontational strategy.

Capture the enemy's cities without assaulting them: Use an indirect approach.

Overthrow his state without protracted operations: Win without expending excessive time or resources.

WIN WITHOUT FIGHTING—MANAGER'S COMMENTARY

The ultimate victory is to win without conflict.

Alamo Car Rental's first market entry was in the least crowded (and least alluring) niche of tour operators who purchased auto rentals at wholesale rates. Enterprise Rent-A-Car found a different point of entry into the same business. Originally a leasing company, it began an entry into rental cars when an enterprising manager at one of its offices began picking up customers for the start of their lease. No one else did that, and that became Enterprise's point of entry.

Across the television spectrum are companies that carved out a niche where there was limited competition: CNN in news, HGTV in home and garden ideas, MTV in music for the younger generation, the History Channel in documentaries, and the list goes on. Everyone with a new product or business concept has rushed to expand rapidly and capture markets ahead of competition.

The concept of being victorious without engaging in conflict is fundamental to Sun Tzu's strategic thought. To apply this concept, it is necessary to seek victory before entering the competitive arena. Otherwise, you must fight in the hope of winning. This concept of winning before the battle applies to every situation. We so often find that the outcome has really been determined before the battle. This is expressed in the saying, "The side that wins will be the side that has already won."

Strategy is a *planning* process. It is war on paper. It is doing the right thing. It is seeking victory before the battle.

Tactics is a *contact* process. It is the action of the war. It is doing things right. It is the battle.

The best organizations develop win-win strategic initiatives. They do their planning (strategy) so well they are sure to win. When competitive forces are encountered, their implementation (tactics) is so good they win anyway.

STRENGTH AGAINST WEAKNESS—ALWAYS—TRANSLATION

Sun Tzu continues:
  Consequently, the art of using troops is this:
  When 10 to the enemy's one, surround him.
  When five times his strength, attack him.
  If double his strength, engage him.
  If equally matched, be capable of dividing him.
  If less in number, be capable of defending yourself.
  And if in all respects unfavorable, be capable of eluding him.
  Hence, a weak force will eventually fall captive to a strong one if it simply holds ground and conducts a desperate defense.

STRENGTH AGAINST WEAKNESS—ALWAYS— MANAGER'S COMMENTARY

Battles are won by concentrating strengths.

In America, Gillette will sell the most razor blades, Frito-Lay will sell the most potato chips, and Anheuser-Busch the most beer. The reason is they have more locations selling razor blades, potato chips, or beer. Their location strength is backed up with all the necessary strength of production and distribution.

Operations succeed because someone knows how to concentrate strengths against weaknesses. The rule of ratios of strengths is simple: If we do not have real superiority, we cannot win. The objective is not an equal match; seek an unequal advantage in your favor.

The issue is not one of raw numbers; superiority can be achieved in a variety of ways. In business competition, the superiority can be in elements of the marketing mix such as place (locations or shelf space), price, promotion, product, etc. Superiority can also be attained in the fighting spirit of the organization.

It is vital to know the strengths and weaknesses of our opponent in order to assess where the attack must be focused. Underestimate the opponent and the results can be disastrous.

The use of simple mathematical ratios to indicate when one should launch the offensive has a real application to every strategic situation. When you have overwhelming superiority, you will win. When the other side has overwhelming superiority, it will win. Between these two extremes are a variety of situations in which extended combat will be required.

Much of success in any endeavor can be achieved by focusing your resources where you can achieve decisive results profitably; you cannot be strong everywhere. This requires a careful analysis of both profit opportunities and market needs. The priority ranking is important. First, you must satisfy the needs of the market. Then, and only then, can you profit from your actions. When the profit requirements are first, you have the wrong decision sequence. The decision on the needs of the market is always made before the financial decision. It's done successfully no other way.

As you think about applying strength, think seriously about reinforcing your own strength. This is often the best way to win.

BEWARE OF "HIGH-LEVEL DUMB"—TRANSLATION

Sun Tzu continues:

Now, the general is the bulwark of the state:

If the bulwark is complete at all points, the state will surely be strong.

If the bulwark is defective, the state will certainly be weak.

Now, there are three ways in which a sovereign can bring misfortune upon his army:

1. By ordering an advance while ignorant of the fact that the army cannot go forward, or by ordering a retreat while ignorant of the fact that the army cannot fall back. This is described as "hobbling the army."
2. By interfering with the army's administration without knowledge of the internal affairs of the army. This causes officers and soldiers to be perplexed.
3. By interfering with direction of fighting, while ignorant of the military principle of adaptation to circumstances. This sows doubts and misgivings in the minds of his officers and soldiers.

If the army is confused and suspicious, neighboring rulers will take advantage of this and cause trouble. This is simply bringing anarchy into the army and flinging victory away.

ORDERS VERSUS INSTRUCTIONS

In the Prussian armies of the late nineteenth century, a system was instituted to clearly differentiate between orders and instructions:

- *Instructions* were an expression of the commander's wishes, not to be carried out unless manifestly practicable.
- *Orders* were to be obeyed instantly and to the letter.

However, orders could be issued only by an officer *actually present with the troops concerned and fully aware of the situation.*

This clear differentiation provides a methodology to ensure headquarters does not run operations by remote control.

BEWARE OF "HIGH-LEVEL DUMB"—MANAGER'S COMMENTARY

Avoid acting without full knowledge of the situation.

The financial collapse of 2008 was presaged by a naïve confidence in the financial system and the mechanisms to control risk. A few years before the almost-meltdown, Alan Greenspan, then head of the Federal Reserve, said, "I believe that the general growth in large [financial] institutions have occurred in the context of an underlying structure of markets in which many of the larger risks are dramatically—I should say, fully—hedged." We later learned the risk inherent in big financial institutions, particularly those deemed "too big to fail." The risks that remained in the system, despite Greenspan's reassurances, came close to creating a financial collapse.

In *The Reckoning,* David Halberstam's book on the auto industry, he articulates the problem of "men whose strength was that they could hear the truth in their own voices." Halberstam says, "There were, it was believed, few honest answers at Ford during McNamara's years because there were few honest questions." When managers do not ask the right questions, the answers do not make any difference, creating "high-level dumb" situations.

Do not sow the seeds of destruction by micromanaging. There are a variety of alibis for this behavior; none are valid! No subordinate can operate at a level of competency when the boss supervises every detail. More than 100 years ago, Marshal Saxe wrote about generals who wish to do everything on the day of battle and as a result do nothing. Saxe says, "If the general wishes to be a sergeant-major and be everywhere, he will act like the fly in the fable who thought it was he that was driving the coach."

When management is incompetent, good people simply "fire their boss" by leaving the organization. High turnover rates can be a signal of trouble.

In *On the Psychology of Military Incompetence*, author Norman Dixon cites anxiety as the most common cause of leadership failure. He theorizes that what has been taken for lack of intelligence was perhaps due to the crippling effects of anxiety on perception, memory, and thought.

Dixon identifies personal faults common to incompetence:

- A fundamental conservatism and clinging to outworn tradition
- A tendency to reject or ignore information
- A tendency to underestimate the opponent
- Indecisiveness
- A failure to make use of surprise
- A predilection for frontal assaults
- A failure to make adequate reconnaissance

Too often, incompetent leaders resist new information because it might cause them to change their course of direction. The greater the impact of the new information, the more strenuously it is resisted because if changes must be made, then they were wrong before.

OBEY FUNDAMENTAL PRINCIPLES—TRANSLATION

Sun Tzu continues:

Thus, there are five points in which victory may be predicted:

1. He who knows when to fight and when not to fight will win.
2. He who understands how to handle both superior and inferior forces will win.
3. He whose ranks are united in purpose will win.
4. He who is well prepared and lies in wait for an enemy who is not well prepared will win.
5. He whose generals are able and not interfered with by the sovereign will win.

It is in these five points that the way to victory is known. Therefore, I say:

Know the enemy and know yourself, and you can fight a hundred battles with no danger of defeat.

When you are ignorant of the enemy but know yourself, your chances of winning and losing are equal.

If ignorant both of your enemy and of yourself, you are sure to be defeated in every battle.

Sun Tzu's Fundamental Principles Adapted for Business

1. Understand when to launch the offensive. Good information sources will help you know when to take offensive action and when to withhold it.
2. Allocate resources. Use different strategies when inferior and superior.

3. Plan a united effort. Secure a common belief at all levels in a common vision.
4. Take advantage of opportunities. Be prepared to act when others are unprepared.
5. Decentralize. Each unit leader must know her area and be empowered with authority.

OBEY FUNDAMENTAL PRINCIPLES—MANAGER'S COMMENTARY

**The chances for failure are high when the rules
that ensure victory are ignored.**

Here are a few fundamental principles of business:

Organize an Intelligence System: Know your market as well as you know yourself. Decision making must be data driven.

Maintain Objectives: Determine a clear direction and keep a steady aim. Do not wander down side tracks.

Establish a Secure Position: Strengthen your core competencies. Occupy a position that cannot easily be taken by your opponent.

Keep on the Offensive: Being on the offensive preserves freedom of action and keeps you in control.

Plan Surprise: This is the best way to gain psychological dominance and deny the initiative to your opponent. Speed is an essential component of surprise.

Think Maneuver: Consider how to put yourself at an advantage and your opponent at a disadvantage. Find lightly defended or unoccupied competitive positions.

Concentrate Resources: Mass sufficiently superior force at the decisive place and time. Be a guerrilla when you can't be a gorilla. The strongest at any given time and place will always defeat the weakest.

Practice Economy of Force: When you concentrate somewhere, you will be weak in other areas.

Keep It Simple: The simple works best. Even the simplest plans can be difficult to execute.

These fundamental principles of business are guidelines that lead to success. Although principles can sometimes be violated, they must always be considered. To know the principles and violate them is to take risks. To ignore the principles is stupidity. Violate these principles only when you *know* you are violating them. The further you stray from the fundamental truths, the greater the risks.

Applying the principles is an art. It is in this art that judgment comes into play. Professionals are aware of the subtleties of business rules; amateurs too often ignore the rules. Both take risks; both win and lose. Only one has the odds in his favor. The greater the experience the professional manager has, the greater his understanding the risks of straying from the principles and the less his tendency to stray without a valid reason.

DISPOSITION OF MILITARY STRENGTH

Management Rules

- Be Invincible
- Attain Strategic Superiority
- Use Information to Focus Resources

In business discussions, the issue constantly arises: Does strategy determine tactics or is it tactics that determines strategy? Strategy always comes before tactics, just as thinking comes before doing. However, thinking can be the easy part; it's the doing that is difficult.

It is a business fundamental that the strategy must be correct for the tactics to succeed. There's no chicken-and-egg problem here; the strategy must be right first, you must be *doing the right thing.* Then the tactics can support the strategy by *doing things right.* Excellent strategy at higher levels can sustain many tactical failures at lower levels. The converse is rarely true. Sustained tactical success—even continuous brilliant execution of tactics—seldom overcomes an inadequate strategic posture.

A bad strategy supported by good tactics can be a fast route to failure as, for example, driving fast and skillfully in the wrong direction will not get you to your destination. Success requires a balance of strategy and tactics. History proves that the best strategy and tactics are achieved in areas fundamental to the core strengths of the organization.

Strategy must consider tactics, and successful tactical implementation requires an appreciation of strategy. Otherwise, the tactician will not understand why he is doing what. When we do not understand the underlying concepts, we do not have the ability to improve or improvise properly.

BE INVINCIBLE—TRANSLATION

Sun Tzu says:

The skillful warriors in ancient times first made themselves invincible and then awaited the enemy's moment of vulnerability. Invincibility depends on oneself, but the enemy's vulnerability on himself. It follows that those skilled in war can make themselves invincible but cannot cause an enemy to be certainly vulnerable. Therefore, it can be said that, one may know how to achieve victory, but cannot necessarily do so.

Invincibility lies in the defense; the possibility of victory in the attack. Defend yourself when the enemy's strength is abundant, and attack the enemy when it is inadequate.

Those who are skilled in defense hide themselves as under the most secret recesses of earth.

> Those skilled in attack flash forth as from above the topmost heights of heaven.
>
> Thus, they are capable both of protecting themselves and of gaining a complete victory.

BE INVINCIBLE—MANAGER'S COMMENTARY

Build strengths that can take advantage of opportunities.

The invincible awards in American business go to companies like Microsoft, with its take-no-prisoners attitude; McDonald's, which is everywhere; and Starbucks, which owns the high ground in gourmet coffee. They may have off years, but their industry leadership positions have yet to be seriously challenged.

A common characteristic of these premier organizations is a strong founding leader who set the direction and kept the organization on course. Strong companies are founded by strong individuals—when they leave, the stamp of their culture becomes the core of the organization's future.

At Ogilvy & Mather, founder David Mather established the practice of sending each new branch head a nested set of wooden dolls—each doll opens to reveal a smaller replica of the doll. Inside the smallest is a message: "If each of us hires people who are smaller than we are, we shall become a company of dwarfs; but if each of us hires people who are bigger than we are, Ogilvy & Mather will become a company of giants."

Personal leadership is where "art" takes over to control the application of "science." This does not mean that principles are ignored, but rather that the successful leader understands how to properly apply the principles.

No leader does it alone. As Manfred Kets de Vries points out in *Life and Death in the Executive Fast Lane:* "The derailment of a CEO is seldom caused by a lack of information about the latest techniques in marketing, finance, or production; rather, it comes about because of a lack of interpersonal skills—a failure to get the best out of people who possess necessary information."

Coca-Cola has a chief learning officer whose job is to figure out how to institutionalize the sharing of experiences between branch offices, countries, and people, and to turn Coke into a "learning organization." Google offers "20 percent time" to its engineers, company time that they can spend working on corporate projects they are personally passionate about. "The ability to learn faster than your competitors may soon be the only sustainable competitive advantage," says Arnie De Geus, head of planning at Royal Dutch Shell.

ATTAIN STRATEGIC SUPERIORITY—TRANSLATION

Sun Tzu continues:

To foresee a victory no better than ordinary people's foresight is not the acme of excellence. Neither is it the acme of excellence if you win a victory through fierce fighting and the whole empire says, "Well done!" Hence, by analogy, to lift an autumn hair [hare] does not signify great strength; to see the sun and moon does not signify good sight; to hear the thunderclap does not signify acute hearing.

In ancient times, those called skilled in war conquered an enemy easily conquered. Consequently, a master of war wins victories without showing his brilliant military success, and without gaining the reputation for wisdom or the merit for valor. He wins his victories without making mistakes. Making no mistakes is what establishes the certainty of victory, for it means that he conquers an enemy already defeated.

Accordingly, a wise commander always ensures that his forces are put in an invincible position, and at the same time will be sure to miss no opportunity to defeat the enemy. It follows that a triumphant army will not fight with the enemy until the victory is assured, while an army destined to defeat will always fight with the opponent first, in the hope that it may win by sheer good luck. The commander adept in war enhances the moral influence and adheres to the laws and regulations. Thus it is in his power to control success.

ATTAIN STRATEGIC SUPERIORITY—MANAGER'S COMMENTARY

A successful strategy achieves victory before the battle.

There is a long history of the successful entry of products where competition was minimal or nonexistent: Xerox into copiers, IBM into data analysis, Apple into home computers, and Crest with fluoride toothpaste. With this kind of superiority, the initial competitive battle was quite limited in scope.

Milwaukee-based Kohl's has cut a wide swath in soft goods retailing with a leadership dedicated to a carefully crafted strategy. A stock analyst says, "Kohl's combines the cost structure of a discounter and the brands of a department store. It straddles those worlds and takes share from both." The design and merchandising is not too upscale and not too low rent. The shopper finds a clean, bright store where everything is easy to find. The service is good and the perceived value is high.

The introduction of Tide detergent by Procter & Gamble involved a classic strategy of gaining brand-name superiority. When automatic washers first came to market, manufacturers were anxious to educate new purchasers to use detergent instead of soap, which would leave a scum in places that could not be cleaned. So P&G provided leading producers with free boxes of Tide to be packed in every automatic washer at the factory. The free trial experience convinced many to become repeat customers. And Tide became the leading detergent brand without engaging in a major conflict.

Although all conflict cannot be avoided, a well-planned strategy will nullify most opposition. Fighting and winning requires less strategic skill than winning without fighting.

Opportunities for attaining strategic superiority can be found in:

- The product or service that is so clearly unique and carefully targeted that it is has no competition
- The idea that is so completely researched and validated that no other seems viable
- The fundamental truth that is presented with such moral strength that any other approach appears immoral

The issue is always how one's strategy can win the customer and nullify the opposition. The offensive should never be aimed at the opponent's strengths. Strategies that focus on the customer's needs and consider the opponent's weaknesses have the best odds for winning.

USE INFORMATION TO FOCUS RESOURCES—TRANSLATION

Sun Tzu continues:
Now, the elements of the art of war are first, the measurement of space; second, the estimation of quantities; third, the calculation of figures; fourth, comparisons of strength and fifth, chances of victory.

Measurements of space are derived from the ground. Quantities derive from measurement, figures from quantities, comparisons from figures, and victory from comparisons.

> Therefore, a victorious army is as one yi balanced against a grain, and a defeated army is as a grain balanced against one yi.
>
> An army superior in strength takes action like the bursting of pent-up waters into a chasm of a thousand fathoms deep. This is what the disposition of military strength means in the actions of war.

USE INFORMATION TO FOCUS RESOURCES— MANAGER'S COMMENTARY

Use data to plan overwhelming advantages.

When Robert Nardelli was president of General Electric's power systems unit, he asked his top 100 customers about their most critical needs and how GE could provide solutions. The answers prompted the company to drastically reduce its response time for providing parts. It also opened the opportunity to advise utilities on the nuances of expanding into foreign markets that were new to them but not to GE.

Many online advertisers use customer data to present more relevant ads to prospects. Online search-engine marketing may be the most targeted marketing ever developed. In general, the more relevant the recommendations the higher the sales from those communications so the performance of the data to make decisions that drive sales is highly tracked and managed.

Organizations that have added only customer input to their historic financial measurements have not completed their system. Although the customer input adds another dimension, the financial measures only serve to keep score on what has happened. More is needed.

The solution is to focus on defining and aligning performance in several key areas: financial, customer, employee, process, innovation, and learning. With achievement of the corporate strategy as the main objective, supportive objectives are established for each key performance area at every level of the organization. Then, a measurement system to track performance is cascaded so that everyone is aligned to achieve the desired results. This cascading measurement system, often called a balanced or synchronized scorecard, encourages the kind of performance that achieves results in areas critical to success.

This balanced system of measurements is a dynamic, continuous activity where all processes are aligned with strategy. To put it simply, linking your vision to performance improves productivity and profit potential.

Chapter 2

You Must
Fight to Win

USE OF ENERGY

Management Rules

- Build a Sound Organization Structure
- Apply Extraordinary Force
- Coordinate Momentum and Timing

There are two basic command systems for the use and control of energy in the attack:

Centralized control—Reinforcing weakness: Imagine a field of battle where the commander monitors the front line to see where he is winning and losing. When he sees that one of his units is losing, he sends in reserves to strengthen the weakness. This system of reinforcing weakness requires a high degree of control.

Decentralized control—Reinforcing strength: In this situation, as offensive forces move forward, they attempt to bypass strengths instead of engaging in battle. If the offensive forces meet opposition, they go around again and again until they find a place they can penetrate. The front-line commander does not ask for permission to advance; he merely reports while the senior commander and his staff monitor and support the advance. This decentralized control reinforces strength.

The decision to use a system of centralized or decentralized control depends on the mental set of the senior officers and the corporate culture. Whether the culture tolerates one system or the other has a great deal to do with success.

Someone must be in charge. Where everyone decides everything, no one decides anything. Rule by committee can become rule by mediocrity. Chaos is the inevitable result when decisions are made by everyone. Clearly expressing his views on command, Napoleon wrote to the National Assembly stating that one bad general is preferable to two good ones.

Be careful! The ability of modern communications to reach everywhere can make it too easy to concentrate all power in a single person, who through overwork is often in over his head.

No one command system is best. Command systems radically different from each other have led to equally good results.

BUILD A SOUND ORGANIZATION STRUCTURE—TRANSLATION

Sun Tzu says:

Generally, management of a large force is the same in principle as the management of a few men: it is a matter of organization. And to direct a large army to fight is the same as to direct a small one: it is a matter of command signs and signals.

ORGANIZATIONAL WARNINGS

In 210 B.C., Petronius Arbiter wrote: "We trained hard, but it seemed that every time we were beginning to form up in teams we would be reorganized. I was to learn later in life that we tend to meet any new situation by reorganizing, and a wonderful method it can be for creating the illusion of progress while producing confusion, inefficiency, and demoralization."

Over 100 years ago, a French officer, Ardant du Picq, warned:

Note the army organizations and tactical formations on paper are always determined from a mechanical point of view, neglecting the essential coefficient, that of morale. They are almost always wrong . . . . Mental acquaintanceship is not enough to make a good organization. A good general esprit is needed.

In his book *Generalship: Its Diseases and Their Cure*, J. F. C. Fuller wrote: "The horde army paralyzed generalship, not so much because it changed tactics, but because it prevented tactics changing."

Discussing the resulting staff structure, he said, "The general alone is responsible, therefore the general alone should and must decide and must elaborate his own decisions and not merely have them thrust on him by his staff like a disc upon a gramophone."

BUILD A SOUND ORGANIZATION STRUCTURE— MANAGER'S COMMENTARY

The organization exists so that tasks can be managed, people supported, and results achieved.

At Harley-Davidson, the organization chart has been described as three overlapping circles: a Create Demand Circle responsible for marketing and sales; a Produce Products Circle for engineering and production; and a Support Circle for all other functions. In the middle, where the circles intersect, is a Leadership and Strategy Council that oversees general management functions like planning, budgeting, and human relations. The overlapping of the circles emphasizes the interdependence between areas and encourages participation and collaboration.

No single organization structure works everywhere.

Change management consultant Gerald Sentell says, "Structure is to an organization as channels are to river systems. They direct and control flows of human interaction and activity . . . . When the structure can contain and direct the flows of behavior, the system functions. When the flows jump out of the structured channel, the results can create great change."

When organizations are structured to maximize strengths within departments, the result can disrupt the overall optimization of the organization. When departments are organized to serve themselves, the sum total of these departmental kingdoms is not maximized to serve the customer, and business is lost to competitors who know how to focus strengths on the customer.

Systems and processes should not be designed to accommodate the strengths and weaknesses of individuals. Instead, the requirements of the system determine where people are placed in the structure.

Structure follows strategy, always. First determine the strategy to achieve your vision and then develop the organization structure. Finally, put the best people in place.

APPLY EXTRAORDINARY FORCE—TRANSLATION

Sun Tzu continues:

That the whole army can sustain the enemy's all-out attack without suffering defeat is due to operations of extraordinary and normal forces. Troops thrown against the enemy as a grindstone against eggs is an example of the strong beating the weak.

Generally, in battle, use the normal force to engage and use the extraordinary to win. Now, to a commander adept at the use of extraordinary forces, his resources are as infinite as heaven and earth, as inexhaustible as the flow of the running rivers. They end and begin again like the motions of the sun and moon. They die away and then are reborn like the changing of the four seasons.

There are not more than five musical notes, but the various combinations of the five notes bring about more melodies than can ever be heard.

There are not more than five basic pigments, yet in blending them together it is possible to produce more colors than can ever be seen.

There are not more than five cardinal tastes, but the mixture of the five yields more flavors than can ever be tasted.

In battle, there are not more than two kinds of postures—operation of the extraordinary force and operation of the normal force, but their combinations give rise to an endless series of maneuvers. For these two forces are mutually reproductive. It is like moving in circle, never coming to an end. Who can exhaust the possibilities of their combinations?

APPLY EXTRAORDINARY FORCE—MANAGER'S COMMENTARY

Use the normal to engage, the extraordinary to win.

Frito-Lay knows how to apply extraordinary force at the point of sale with drivers who restock customers' shelves with uncommon frequency. With the extraordinary force of over 2 million agents knocking on doors, Avon is the world's number-one direct seller of cosmetics. Cyberspace is turning storefront retailing into the normal force and Internet retailing into the extraordinary.

Virgin and its founder, Richard Branson, are masters of the extraordinary. From the publicity generated by luxurious airport lounges and comfortable airplane seating to headline-grabbing stunts like hot-air ballooning, Branson knows how to use the extraordinary to build a brand image and extend it to music, airlines, mobile cellular service, vodka, financial services, and tourist space travel.

This powerful idea of moving from the normal to the extraordinary achieves results at every level and in every situation. The classic human relations case study occurred years ago at the Bell Lab Hawthorne plant when researchers determined that giving extraordinary attention to a small group of workers increased production. This study concluded that production went up regardless of whether working conditions were enhanced or made worse. The key was the extraordinary attention. Today, results are being achieved by people-oriented activities that apply the extraordinary. It may be as simple as applying teamwork to problem solving, finding new ways to get commitment, or initiating training programs.

The idea of using the extraordinary is an extremely simple concept that clearly identifies what must be done to win. Too often, our plans are based on using only the normal force and the result is that only "normal" results are achieved. Every annual plan that simply adds "some effort" to what was done last year is only another plan. It takes the force of extraordinary effort to achieve extraordinary results.

The idea of using extraordinary force does not mean more of the same effort. Extraordinary action results from out-of-the-box thinking. Major General J. F. C. Fuller writes, "If we wish to think clearly, we must cease imitating. If we wish to cease imitating, we must make use of our imagination. Audacity and not caution must be our watch word."

COORDINATE MOMENTUM AND TIMING—TRANSLATION

Sun Tzu says:

When torrential water tosses boulders, it is because of its momentum; when the strike of a hawk breaks the body of its prey, it is because of timing. Thus, in battle, a good commander creates a posture releasing an irresistible and overwhelming momentum, and his attack is precisely timed in a quick tempo. The energy is similar to a fully drawn crossbow; the timing, the release of the trigger. Amid turmoil and tumult of battle, there may be seeming disorder and yet no real disorder in one's own troops. In the midst of confusion and chaos, your troops appear to be milling about in circles, yet it is proof against defeat.

Apparent disorder is born of order; apparent cowardice, of courage; apparent weakness, of strength. Order or disorder depends on organization and direction; courage or cowardice on postures; strength or weakness on dispositions.

Thus, one who is adept at keeping the enemy on the move maintains deceitful appearances, according to which the enemy will act. He lures with something that the enemy is certain to take. By so doing he keeps the enemy on the move and then waits for the right moment to make a sudden ambush with picked troops.

Therefore, a skilled commander sets great store by using the situation to the best advantage, and does not make excessive demands on his subordinates. Hence he is able to select the right men and exploits the situation. He who takes advantage of the situation uses his men in fighting as rolling logs or rocks. It is the nature of logs and rocks to stay stationary on the flat ground, and to roll forward on a slope. If four-cornered, they stop; if round-shaped, they roll. Thus, the energy of troops skillfully commanded is just like the momentum of round rocks quickly tumbling down from a mountain thousands of feet in height. This is what "use of energy" means.

COORDINATE MOMENTUM AND TIMING—
MANAGER'S COMMENTARY

Momentum provides force; timing applies strength at the right moment.

Subway opened over 10,000 stores in the 1980s and '90s in the United States. It maintained its momentum and a high rate of franchisee growth by shifting to an international focus in the '90s and the first decade of this century, and now has more than 33,000 stores worldwide. In fact, it now operates more outlets than McDonald's.

Nothing succeeds like success, and success generates its own momentum. Even in the difficult recession economy of 2009, Toyota maintained the momentum of its pioneering hybrid Prius with an aggressively marketed introduction that created waiting lists while other car companies saw double-digit declines of all their models.

Just as volume sales create momentum and enthusiasm, obsolete inventory stifles innovation and growth. When the cash register rings, it seems like you are doing everything right; when it doesn't ring, the mistakes are very visible.

Successful strategic thrusts are achieved by rapidly accumulating power (momentum) and releasing that power when it will have the most desirable effect (timing). A typical business application would be the introduction of a very competitive new product or the implementation of a major change in warranty or pricing at a major trade show, when it would be most disruptive of a competitor's plans.

Momentum and timing are most often combined in advertising campaigns where massive expenditures are timed with seasonal demand. Or as an associate often said when we discussed timing of a major event, "Let's go hunting when the birds are flying."

The simultaneous use of multiple principles or techniques, a concept the military refers to as force multipliers, can apply a lot of pressure. It is not that victory is achieved with the application of a single principle, but rather the use of multiple principles achieves a reinforcing momentum. The cumulative effort of doing a lot of right things right multiplies into awesome power! This happens when retailers move into a new market with multiple locations featuring extensive selections and engage in enough advertising to make them a super power in the media.

WEAKNESS AND STRENGTH

Management Rules

- Take the Initiative.
- Plan Surprise.
- Gain Relative Superiority.
- Seek Knowledge.
- Be Flexible.

Achieving real superiority is fundamental to the concept of strength against weakness. Your strategy and tactics must be designed with the idea that your competitor will not have anywhere near an equal chance to win. Strategically, the concentration of strength against weakness is a mental process. Tactically, this concentration is a physical act.

Here are key methodologies for concentrating strength against weakness:

Flank: Concentrate strength against weakness by launching an end run around strong points to a lightly defended or unoccupied position. In your search for weakness, consider these two key elements:

1. Look for weakness at a junction. It can be between geographic locations or product lines. Also explore going around the extreme low end or high end of a product category.
2. Since every strength has a corresponding weakness, look for the weakness of the opposition's strength.

Segment: This is concentrating strength in a specific area. The small can never equal the big everywhere, but anyone can be strong somewhere. As markets have been segmented and resegmented, marketers discover new ways to concentrate against weakness and then concentrate again into a smaller niche or particle market.

Overwhelm: Any initiative can be achieved if enough strength is concentrated to support it. Conversely, any initiative can be defeated if enough strength is focused against the weakness of that initiative.

Reinforce: The best odds for success are achieved by spending time, money, and energy reinforcing what is working. Then you are leveraging off what you do well.

TAKE THE INITIATIVE—TRANSLATION

Sun Tzu says:

Generally, he who occupies the field of battle first and awaits his enemy is at ease; he who arrives later and joins battle in haste is weary. And, therefore, one skilled in war brings the enemy to the field of battle and is not brought there by him.

One able to make the enemy come of his own accord does so by offering him some advantage. And one able to stop him from coming does so by inflicting damage on him.

Therefore, on the day the decision is made to launch war, you should close the passes, destroy the official tallies, and stop the passage of all emissaries. Examine the plan closely in the temple council and make final arrangements.

If the enemy leaves a door open, you must rush in. Seize the place the enemy values without making an appointment for battle with him. Be flexible and decide your line of action according to the situation on the enemy side.

At first, then, exhibit the coyness of a maiden until the enemy gives you an opening; afterwards be swift as a running hare, and it will be too late for the enemy to oppose you.

SEIZE AND MAINTAIN THE INITIATIVE

Mao Ze Dung wrote, "No military leader is endowed by heaven with an ability to seize the initiative. It is the intelligent leader who does so after a careful study and estimate of the situation and arrangement of the military and political factors involved."

In *The Foundations of Strategy,* Captain Johnstone warned, "The initiative, once handed over to the enemy, is hard to regain: Ward off blows for a week and your hands are full of defensive details, you begin to be apprehensive of the unseen work of the enemy, and you abandon your plan on small provocation."

TAKE THE INITIATIVE—MANAGER'S COMMENTARY

By its very nature, the offensive offers an advantage for gaining superiority.

Minnesota Mining & Manufacturing (3M) strives to generate one-third of its sales revenues from new products that did not exist four years ago. In a single year, 3M received over 500 U.S. patents for new products. It accelerates sales with a Pacing Plus initiative that rapidly develops and markets the most promising new products aimed at high-growth industries.

In a relatively short time, Wal-Mart has become the world's largest retailer. Its low-price, low-cost model allowed Wal-Mart to first take the initiative in the United States and later in overseas markets. The company first entered the mass-market channel, then added food and built the first national chain of Supercenters. Recent initiatives include a strong dot. com presence and Hispanic-format stores.

The most effective and decisive way to reach the objective is to seize, retain, and exploit the initiative. Being on the offensive puts you in control and forces the opponent to react.

Taking the initiative is first a strategic mental process followed by real tactical action. By acting first, we preserve freedom of action. If our opponent moves first, our only choice may be to react.

The attack has the advantage of initiative. It often forces action on our opponent and relegates him to second place. Initiating the offensive adds positive morale to our side.

The keys to the successful initiative are skill, preparation, and information. The norm is not enough time, not enough resources, not enough information. Consequently, the initiative often requires that "great mental leap in the dark."

Only rarely will exact details be known. While the attempt to get more information is made as a matter of course, waiting for news in a difficult situation is a bad error. While data is needed to launch the offensive, normally the sooner that something is done the better the odds in your favor and the better the results.

Beware! The offensive does not offer a solution to all problems. Your desire for action must be matched by wisdom.

PLAN SURPRISE—TRANSLATION

Sun Tzu continues:

Thus, when the enemy is at ease, he is able to tire him; when well fed, to starve him; when at rest, to make him move. All these can be done because you appear at points that the enemy must hasten to defend.

That you may march a thousand li without tiring yourself is because you travel where there is no enemy.

That you are certain to take what you attack is because you attack a place the enemy does not or cannot protect.

That you are certain of success in holding what you defend is because you defend a place the enemy must hasten to attack.

Therefore, against those skillful in attack, the enemy does not know where to defend, and against the experts in defense, the enemy does not know where to attack.

How subtle and insubstantial that the expert leaves no trace. How divinely mysterious that he is inaudible. Thus, he is master of his enemy's fate.

His offensive will be irresistible if he plunges into the enemy's weak points; he cannot be overtaken when he withdraws if he moves swiftly. Hence, if we wish to fight, the enemy will be compelled to an engagement even though he is safe behind high ramparts and deep ditches. This is because we attack a position he must relieve.

If we do not wish to fight, we can prevent him from engaging us even though the lines of our encampment be merely traced out on the ground. This is because we divert him from going where he wishes.

PLAN SURPRISE—MANAGER'S COMMENTARY

Blend subtlety and secrecy to keep the opponent confused so he knows neither where to attack or defend.

Southwest Airlines often waits until the last moment to announce plans to extend its routes to new markets so the competition has little time to prepare.

Secrecy about your own movements can be more threatening to competitors than overt action. Some manufacturers have a corporate policy of no public announcement preceding a new product introduction. Since the unknown often appears more threatening than the known, this secrecy becomes a powerful and threatening ally. Concerning corporate raider Rupert Murdoch, a Wall Street analyst said, "Part of Murdoch's strategy is to play his cards close to his vest. The magic is secrecy."

Secrecy protects your plans, while surprise confuses your opponent. In business, it is not essential that your opponent be taken unaware, but only that he becomes aware too late to react effectively. In that case, your opponent will probably announce that he "misread the market."

Even though your current position may be weak, you can do things to divert the enemy from your position. This kind of bluff is achieved by starting rumors that work to your advantage.

The objective of surprise is to obtain a psychological dominance that denies the initiative to your opponent. Sheridan said the reason for Grant's victories in the Civil War was that, "while his opponents were kept fully employed wondering what he was going to do, Grant was thinking most of what he was going to do himself." When surprise is achieved, the balance of power will often be decisively shifted. As a result, success earned from surprise greatly exceeds the effort expended.

Speed is an essential component of surprise. The longer you take, the more likely your opponent will be aware of your actions. Focus on rapid, hard-hitting thrusts aimed at your opponent's weakness.

GAIN RELATIVE SUPERIORITY—TRANSLATION

Sun Tzu continues:

Accordingly, by exposing the enemy's dispositions and remaining invisible ourselves, we can keep our forces concentrated, while the enemy's must be divided. We can form a single united body at one place, while the enemy must scatters his forces at 10 places. Thus, it is 10 to one when we attack him at one place, which means we are numerically superior. And if we are able to use many to strike few at the selected place, those we deal with will be in dire straits.

The spot where we intend to fight must not be made known. In this way, the enemy must take precautions at many places against the attack. The more places he must guard, the fewer his troops we shall have to face at any given point.

For if he prepares to the front his rear will be weak; and if to the rear, his front will be fragile. If he strengthens his left, his right will be vulnerable; and if his right gets strengthened, there will be few troops on his left. If he sends reinforcements everywhere, he will be weak everywhere.

Numerical weakness comes from having to prepare against possible attacks; numerical strength from compelling the enemy to make these preparations against us.

RELATIVE SUPERIORITY WINS

The concept of relative superiority can be distilled from Sun Tzu's statement: ". . . we can keep our forces concentrated, while the enemy's must be divided."

In the first millennium during the Song dynasty, China had the biggest and strongest army in the world. However, the leaders did not trust their army and ignored Sun Tzu's advice on concentration by splitting their forces between capital and border armies. As a result, they lost to the Mongol invaders, who could concentrate their strength against fractions of the Chinese.

In *On War*, Clausewitz says, "Where absolute superiority is not attainable, you must produce a relative one at the decisive point by making skillful use of what you have."

GAIN RELATIVE SUPERIORITY—MANAGER'S COMMENTARY

Deploy resources to concentrate strengths against weaknesses.

In the 1980s and '90s, the "Killer Bs," Barnes & Noble and Borders, killed off most locally owned bookstores. Their large stores, extensive selections, discounted prices, and ambience provided a shopping experience that the local bookseller could not generally match. Bookstores that continue to thrive found a niche where they could achieve relative superiority. In a megastore built long before the chains came to Portland, Oregon, Powell's main bookstore stocks 200,000 titles of new books plus 300,000 used books. In a unique merchandising set, new and used books are stacked side by side so readers find an awesome selection in every category. Says Michael Powell, "One way to survive is simply to be bigger and offer a more diverse stock than they do."

In the last decade, the dominance of the Killer Bs has been deeply challenged by Amazon. Using the Internet, Amazon built a relative advantage by being an early Internet retailer, achieving a strong position as overall Internet usage grew. Then they built technology for a new personal service—using knowledge of every item their customers purchased, giving them an opportunity to build competitive advantage using that data to the benefit of their customers. Today, Amazon's personal-recommendation software is heavily emulated by other Internet retailers and gave Amazon leverage as they expand beyond books. And their highly successful Kindle software and ebook reader is dismantling the Killer Bs as Barnes & Noble and Borders did to a prior generation of competition.

An inferior force can think strategically about winning if it can tactically achieve relative superiority at each point of contact. This is the way small companies become big companies and competitors in every endeavor become champions. This is the way guerrillas win—they find out where the enemy is weak and overwhelm him at that point.

When you attempt to concentrate everywhere, you have no concentration. The more thoroughly you specialize, the more sure you are to win. Winning strategies mass resources on the main effort and allocate minimal resources to secondary efforts.

Relative superiority is the best strategy for most companies. Although relative superiority is most often thought of as weight of numbers, there is a variety of ways to achieve relative superiority:

- Implementing continuous action—for example, consistent, small ads
- Segmenting by finding a niche or particle market
- Concentrating on your own strengths
- Forming an alliance—for example, joining a franchise
- Achieving superior product or service quality

When you cannot have absolute superiority, you must concentrate your strengths against your opponent's weaknesses to achieve relative superiority. It's a business fundamental that you must focus your resources where you can achieve decisive results profitably.

SEEK KNOWLEDGE—TRANSLATION

Sun Tzu continues:

Therefore, if one knows the place and time of the coming battle, his troops can march a thousand li and fight on the field. But if one knows neither the spot nor the time, then one cannot manage to have the left wing help the right wing or the right wing help the left; the forces in the front will be unable to support the rear, and the rear will be unable to reinforce the front. How much more so if the furthest portions of the troop deployments extend tens of li in breadth, and even the nearest troops are separated by several li!

Although I estimate the troops of Yue as many, of what benefit is this superiority in terms of victory?

Thus, I say that victory can be achieved. For even if the enemy is numerically stronger, we can prevent him from fighting.

Therefore, analyze the enemy's battle plan, so as to have a clear understanding of its strong and weak points. Agitate the enemy so as to ascertain his pattern of movement. Lure him in the open so as to find out his vulnerable spots in disposition. Probe him and learn where his strength is abundant and where deficient.

Now, the ultimate in disposing one's troops is to conceal them without ascertainable shape. In this way, the most penetrating spies cannot pry nor can the wise lay plans against you.

SEEK KNOWLEDGE—MANAGER'S COMMENTARY

Knowledge helps stack the odds in your favor.

When Ford introduced the Taurus, engineers tore apart competitors' cars to find features to adapt. In an extensive research campaign, Ford went to end customers and dealers' sales and service personnel to find out what customers wanted. Eventually, a want list of over 1,400 items was generated. About 50 percent of these "wants" were incorporated in the Taurus, which became one of the hottest selling new cars of its time.

Knowledge of the current situation makes it possible for victory to be created. As Patton said, "Intelligence is like eggs, the fresher, the better."

Here are active ways to produce the kinds of knowledge about your opponent that help determine the correct strategy for winning:

- *Watch what he is doing.* As Yogi Berra said, "You can see a lot by observing."
- *Watch what he is not doing.* This is key to obtaining relative superiority.
- *Probe.* This reveals the opponent's strengths and weaknesses.
- *Benchmark.* This gets people involved in finding out how to develop the best processes.

Centuries ago, Ovid wrote, "It is right to learn, even from the enemy."

Basic to success in business is being close to the customer. That's why executives visit the marketplace; they realize they must not only understand how the customer thinks, they must be able to think like a customer. It is essential to know what your customer wants. The idea of gathering and analyzing information before the battle hasn't been tried and found wanting; it's been found difficult and not tried.

In the timeless classic *The Exceptional Executive,* Harry Levinson says, "A professional is a person who must understand and apply scientific knowledge. Unless he does so, he will be buffeted by forces beyond his control. Given knowledge, the professional can choose courses of action. He is in charge of himself and his work." Absolutely nothing beats using data to make decisions.

BE FLEXIBLE—TRANSLATION

Sun Tzu continues:
Even though we show people the victory gained by using flexible tactics in conformity to the changing situations, they do not comprehend this. People all know the tactics by which we achieved victory, but they do not know how the tactics were applied in the situation to defeat the enemy. Hence no one victory is gained in the same manner as another. The tactics change in an infinite variety of ways to suit changes in the circumstances.

Now, the laws of military operations are like water. The tendency of water is to flow from heights to lowlands. The law of successful operations is to avoid the enemy's strength and strike his weakness. Water changes its course in accordance with the contours of the land. The soldier works out his victory in accordance with the situation of the enemy.

Hence, there are neither fixed postures nor constant tactics in warfare. He who can modify his tactics in accordance with the enemy situation and thereby succeeds in winning may be said to be divine. Of the five elements, none is ever predominant; of the four seasons, none lasts forever; of the days, some are longer and others shorter, and of the moon, it sometimes waxes and sometimes wanes.

BE FLEXIBLE—MANAGER'S COMMENTARY

While strategies remain constant, tactics must be adapted to each new situation.

Recessions provide great opportunities for the nimble to cheaply, opportunistically improve their market position. In 2009, when Sun Microsystems spurned IBM's takeover bid, Oracle quickly swooped in and purchased Sun for just a dime a share more than IBM's final offer. In the same year pharmacy benefits manager Express Scripts significantly improved its market position with the acquisition of a significant rival that, according to one expert, gave Express Scripts 'considerable negotiating clout' versus its rivals.

The opposite side of the coin of flexibility is rigidity. When we are rigid, we are predictable. In competitive battles, predictability can be a weakness. Being predictable can signal your intended actions to your opponent, and the odds of failure increase.

Winning isn't easy; it requires simultaneous planning and action. While preliminary planning is important, too much planning can be deadly. All plans are merely the basis for change. Revise plans in relation to what is happening and make adjustments as you go.

The blitzkrieg (lightning war) used so successfully by the German army in World War II is an adaptation of Sun Tzu's comments about the flow of water around obstacles. The blitz is launched along a wide front with the objective of rapid penetration. When resistance is met, the forces go around until they can get through. This strategy was applied by General Norman Schwarzkopf, commander of the allied forces in Iraq during the First Gulf War.

The blitz in any business operation works the same way. It is a concentrated effort in a short period of time with the objective of going around resistance and focusing resources where results can be attained. The blitz requires a high degree of decentralization. Forget remote approvals; the successful blitz is an empowered front-line offensive with results that can far exceed any ordinary effort. You can find the "lightning war" concept applied throughout organizations in everything from a productivity-oriented kaizen blitz to a volume-oriented sales blitz.

MANEUVERING

Management Rules

- Maneuver to Gain the Advantage
- Achieve the Critical Mass
- Deceive Your Competitor
- Develop Effective Internal Communications
- Gain the Mental Advantage

At the strategic level, maneuvering is a way of thinking about how you are going to act in a manner that puts your opponent at a disadvantage. At the tactical level, maneuvering most frequently involves concentrating or dispersing as you seek the most advantageous route. Without thinking about how to maneuver, the idea of fighting when outnumbered is ludicrous.

The way to avoid what is strong is to attack what is weak. Look for lightly defended positions. Engage in a frontal attack only when you have overwhelming superiority. However, sheer numbers and firepower alone are often not enough to dislodge a competitor in an entrenched position.

Look for situations where real superiority can be attained. In business, as in any battle, the best approach is most often the one that achieves superiority at the decisive point. The marketing maneuver is often an indirect approach to where your customers are and your competitors aren't.

One of the best maneuvers can be to relocate the battle. When an advertising executive arrived at a presentation, he found his client thinking of hiring a new agency. He switched from his prepared presentation to a discussion of what the client needed to do to succeed. Afterward, he commented, "I didn't even talk about the competitive account; I merely changed the battleground."

In all disagreements, including corporate political situations, thinking about maneuvering turns the mind to options. It takes the focus away from confrontation and refocuses on selecting a route that increases the odds of winning. The best win is a maneuver to a win-win.

MANEUVER TO GAIN THE ADVANTAGE—TRANSLATION

Sun Tzu says:
   Normally, in war, the general receives his commands from the sovereign. During the process from assembling the troops and mobilizing the people to deploying the army ready for battle, nothing is

more difficult than the art of maneuvering for seizing favorable positions beforehand. What is difficult about it is to make the devious route the most direct and to turn disadvantage to advantage. Thus, forcing the enemy to deviate and slow down his march by luring him with a bait, you may set out after he does and arrive at the battlefield before him. One able to do this shows the knowledge of artifice of deviation.

Thus, both advantage and danger are inherent in maneuvering for an advantageous position.

Here are military maneuvers adapted for business:

Frontal attack: Head-on attack with overwhelming superiority.

Attack in echelon: Initiate the attack with the strongest products or services; then follow up with weaker ones.

Flanking attack: Attack lightly defended or unoccupied positions.

Blitz: A concentrated effort that keeps on moving as strong points are bypassed.

Encirclement: Launch a variety of competitive products and/or deny key resources to your opponent.

Fabian: Refuse to compete in certain areas, attack in others.

Defense: Maintain position against competitive thrusts.

Relocate the battle: Find a new competitive arena.

Guerrilla: Find a niche and take what you can get when you can get it.

Retreat: Get out of business.

General Pogo's Strategy: He said, "We have met the enemy and they is us." Attack yourself first.

MANEUVER TO GAIN THE ADVANTAGE—MANAGER'S COMMENTARY

The longest way around can be the shortest route to success.

Major victories have been won by doing the impossible through the impassable. By figuring out how to do the impossible of getting a package from one office to another overnight, Federal Express founder Fred Smith maneuvered to a unique position in the market. When competition began encroaching on FedEx's "overnight turf," it redefined overnight to mean "before 10:30 A.M." At the same time, FedEx set up a tracking program so it could rapidly answer questions concerning the en-route location of every package. By innovating this system of early delivery and tracking, FedEx established difficult obstacles for competitors who wanted to achieve parity in service. FedEx has continued its maneuvers to provide services that give it an advantage. Years ago, Smith laid out an overarching strategy for these maneuvers and others since when he said, "The information about the package is as valuable as the package itself."

Since the easiest routes are often the most heavily defended, the longest way around can indeed be the shortest way home. The course of action that appears most advantageous usually contains the seeds of disadvantage. For example, if you take too long to organize you will probably arrive too late; however, if you are not organized your efforts will be too fragmented to win.

The key to success is turning a circuitous route into a straight route for you alone. Move rapidly; the longer you are en route, the more difficult it may be to get your resources to the market before your competitor.

Extended warranties have been a successful maneuver to a position of product or service superiority for many organizations. Although this works only until your competitor establishes parity, it can be a pre-emptive maneuver to win customers.

ACHIEVE THE CRITICAL MASS—TRANSLATION

Sun Tzu continues:

One who sets the entire army in motion with impedimenta to pursue an advantageous position will be too slow to attain it. If he abandons the camp and all the impedimenta to contend for advantage, the baggage and stores will be lost.

It follows that when the army rolls up the armor and sets out speedily, stopping neither day nor night and marching at double speed for 100 li to wrest an advantage, the commander of three divisions will be captured. The vigorous troops will arrive first and the feeble will straggle along behind, so that if this method is used only one-tenth of the army will arrive. In a forced march of 50 li the commander of the first and van division will fall, and using this method but half of the army will arrive. In a forced march of 30 li, but two-thirds will arrive. Hence, the army will be lost without baggage train; and it cannot survive without provisions, nor can it last long without sources of supplies.

One who is not acquainted with the designs of his neighbors should not enter into alliances with them. Those who do not know the conditions of mountains and forests, hazardous defiles, marshes and swamps, cannot conduct the march of an army. Those who do not use local guides are unable to obtain the advantages of the ground.

Strategic initiatives can be either sequential or cumulative:

A *sequential initiative* requires planned consecutive steps to achieve success. A new product launch requiring orderly introduction to the sales force, trade channels, and end customers would most often be a sequential strategy. So would a plan to initiate a new program over time in successive units.

A *cumulative initiative* is the result of a series of random actions piling on top of one another until at some undetermined point the critical mass is reached. The brand manager who uses sponsorship and events to build brand awareness is often using a cumulative strategy, as is the plant manager who initiates a quality campaign in units throughout the plant.

ACHIEVE THE CRITICAL MASS—MANAGER'S COMMENTARY

Apply overwhelming force at the decisive place and time.

Companies that compete sometimes form alliances to achieve sufficient mass in a particular area. In the United States, Google, Yahoo!, and Microsoft are competitors; but as players in international information, they sometimes run into common criticism for their actions in countries that restrict free speech such as China. To give themselves protection from these criticisms in their profitable Western markets, these three companies jointly announced a set of principles on how to do business in nations that restrict free expression and speech. Said Google about these companies' agreement, "Common actions by these diverse groups is more likely to bring about change in government policy than the efforts of any one company or group acting alone." True, but this joint action will also give these businesses the critical mass to achieve greater PR protection in the core countries they draw their profits from.

For years, one of the major buying decisions of gasoline station owners was which brand of gasoline pump to buy. Then as the convenience store component of the gas station emerged, these storeowners found they needed merchandise sales recorded through a software system. The gas pump (hardware) buying decision became secondary to the more important software buying decision that provided a full range of inventory and sales information. Many companies in the computer hardware business have been beaten by companies who understood the importance of being in the software business. Strategic initiatives must focus on the critical factors that give you a competitive advantage. When you have a unique enough advantage, you should be able to get a significant portion of the market.

The critical mass is simply the concentration of energy required to achieve success. What counts is not only the strength of resources but the speed with which it is delivered. That energy concentration can be in any facet of the organization; for example, purchasing, production, marketing, distribution, etc. Nike is one of the world's most recognized brand names, and it sells more than $15 billion of shoes and other sports apparel and equipment each year, yet owns no factories. They have concentrated on design and marketing and achieved the decisive advantage in those areas.

In business as in nuclear fission, a concentration of energy must be attained to achieve the critical mass. The manager must focus her energy on performance of the tasks most critical to success.

DECEIVE YOUR COMPETITOR—TRANSLATION

Sun Tzu continues:

Now, war is based on deception. Move when it is advantageous and change tactics by dispersal and concentration of your troops. When campaigning, be swift as the wind; in leisurely march, be majestic as the forest; in raiding and plundering, be fierce as fire; in standing, be firm as the mountains. When hiding, be as unfathomable as things behind the clouds; when moving, fall like a thunderclap. When you plunder the countryside, divide your forces. When you conquer territory, defend strategic points.

Weigh the situation before you move. He who knows the artifice of deviation will be victorious. Such is the art of maneuvering.

DECEIVE YOUR COMPETITOR—MANAGER'S COMMENTARY

Deception is always targeted at the competitor—never the customer.

In baseball, deception is part of the surprise throw to catch the runner off base; in football, it's the hidden-ball play; in basketball, it's the faked pass. Why should we consider deception unsportsmanlike in business competition?

Contemporary managers may wonder about Sun Tzu's emphasis on the importance of deception; any deceptive action might seem to be immoral. In business, the subtle difference is that deception is practiced to confuse the competitor—never the customer.

A South American company and a competitor agreed to maintain high prices on a new product both were introducing. After a few months, the competitor cut prices in violation of the agreement, causing a loss of business. When questioned, the competitor replied that it reduced prices to increase sales. The victimized company was not aware of the admonition from an ancient strategist who said, "Do not do what your enemy wants, if for no other reason than he wants it."

Much of the success of the invasion of Europe in World War II was the result of deception. This misinformation succeeded so well that when the actual invasion took place, the German officers thought the invaded beaches were the deception. You have often seen deception used as a tactic in negotiations. One side attempts to gain a psychological advantage by appearing to be naive and uninformed when, in fact, it is smart and knowledgeable. Alternatively, one side attempts to gain knowledge that the other doesn't have. Frequently, when getting a company ready for sale, companies raise prices to temporarily grow profitability and sell the business for a higher price. While this can obviously lose customers and damage the business for the long term, it can work in the short run. Savvy investors are aware of this tactic and carefully examine the books of the company they are considering buying, looking at historical as well as recent performance.

Another deceptive approach in negotiation is to appear to be dejected and crestfallen about your opportunity for prevailing. An opponent who thinks she is winning is likely to be overconfident and vulnerable.

Secrecy can also be a means of achieving deception. This forces your opponent to second-guess your next move. The bigger you are, the more psychologically threatening the unknown becomes to your opponent.

The only thing better than having your opponent not know what you are doing is to have him think you are planning to do something entirely different than what you really intend to do. This is deception. Go for it.

DEVELOP EFFECTIVE INTERNAL COMMUNICATIONS—TRANSLATION

> *Sun Tzu continues:*
>
> The book of Army Management says: "As the voice cannot be heard in battle, gongs and drums are used. As troops cannot see each other clearly in battle, flags and banners are used." Hence, in night fighting, usually use drums and gongs; in day fighting, banners and flags. Now, these instruments are used to unify the action of the troops. When the troops can be thus united, the brave cannot advance alone, nor can the cowardly retreat. This is the art of directing large masses of troops.

SIMPLE COMMUNICATIONS WORK BEST

In Sun Tzu's time, the only available communications were quite simple. Today, we have a wide range of communication methods available and use them all. Invariably, people at the bottom complain about lack of communication and people at the top complain about receiving more information than they can process.

With computers, the solution to more communication capacity is to break the problem into segments and look at each segment. With people, the solution is a similar decentralization: You break down the problem and achieve decisions by the people at each level instead of sending it all to the top, where you overload the head person's brain. With decentralization, you lessen the need for communication at every level.

Regardless of the level, simplicity clears the mind. Keep in mind the rule of three: never make more than three points about an issue. The problem is that long lists are confusing and, as a result, nothing is remembered. As an example, here are three facts concerning a nineteenth-century Prussian command system:

1. An army cannot be effectively controlled by direct orders from headquarters.
2. The man on the spot is the best judge of the situation.
3. Intelligent cooperation is of infinitely more value than mechanical obedience.

DEVELOP EFFECTIVE INTERNAL COMMUNICATIONS— MANAGER'S COMMENTARY

Implement ways to get messages received and understood.

Sears tracked the links in the chain of cause and effect running from employee attitude to customer behavior to profit. It modeled how an improvement in employee attitude changed behavior. The better behavior created an improved customer impression that resulted in a measurable increase in revenue.

Awareness of this employee-customer-profit linkage made Sears management determined to give every employee the information needed to develop an enlightened opinion about how to do her job better. Town meetings were held to spread the word and get employees initiating improvements. A corporate university was established. All of the training was focused on changing employee perceptions and attitudes so that attention and behavior would be focused on customers. As operating managers changed their behavior toward employees, front-line employees changed their behavior toward customers.

Note the sequence: The change in behavior at the management level caused the change in behavior at the front line. Behavior is a form of communication; management must walk the talk.

In every industry, we receive and process so much information so fast that it's easy to hear only what we want to hear. It's becoming increasingly difficult to break through the clutter and get our message communicated to our own people.

Effective internal communication happens only as the result of a well-designed plan. This plan is organized around the understanding that all messages are not delivered in the same manner. Good news may need to be delivered only once to be heard. Instructions and changes that disrupt existing paradigms must be communicated in several different ways and often repeated before people will accept the new information. In these instances, a single method of communication is not enough; every message needs to be reinforced by using different methodologies such as one-on-one meetings, department meetings, and interactive forums.

GAIN THE MENTAL ADVANTAGE—TRANSLATION

Sun Tzu continues:

A whole army may be robbed of its spirit, and its commander deprived of his presence of mind. Now, at the beginning of a campaign, the spirit of soldiers is keen; after a certain period of time, it declines; and in the later stage, it may be dwindled to naught. A clever commander, therefore, avoids the enemy when his spirit is keen and attacks him when it is lost. This is the art of attaching importance to moods. In good order, he awaits a disorderly enemy; in serenity, a clamorous one. This is the art of retaining self-possession. Close to the field of battle, he awaits an enemy coming from afar; at rest, he awaits an exhausted enemy; with well-fed troops, he awaits hungry ones. This is the art of husbanding one's strength.

He refrains from intercepting an enemy whose banners are in perfect order, and desists from attacking an army whose formations are in an impressive array. This is the art of assessing circumstances.

Now, the art of employing troops is that when the enemy occupies high ground, do not confront him uphill, and when his back is resting on hills, do not make a frontal attack. When he pretends to flee, do not pursue. Do not attack soldiers whose temper is keen. Do not swallow a bait offered by the enemy. Do not thwart an enemy who is returning homewards. When you surround an army, leave an outlet free. Do not press a desperate enemy too hard. Such is the method of using troops.

GAIN THE MENTAL ADVANTAGE—MANAGER'S COMMENTARY

Understand the psychological factors affecting human resources.

Opportunities for victory are found in the mental capacity of the leader to integrate strategy (planning) and tactics (execution). The ultimate responsibility for victory or defeat lies with the leader, not because he must do everything but because he must have the mental capacity and provide the means to translate sound strategy into successful tactics.

Externally, the mental advantage is achieved through surprise. You must generate a mismatch by getting inside your adversary's observation-orientation-decision-action time cycle. By the time your adversary observes what he thinks you are doing, becomes oriented to it, decides what to do, and takes action, "it" will be too late.

Internally, several key issues are basic to good management psychology:

- *Attitude:* A positive outlook and a cool head are the foundation of a good attitude.
- *Morale:* Napoleon said, "The moral is to the physical as three is to one." The word "moral" refers to a worthwhile cause, a belief that what we are fighting for is just and right. It is the "moral cause" that produces high morale. The moral issues required in business are both the moral courage to make the right decisions and act on them and the leadership style that helps make everyone feel good about herself. The business equivalent of military courage is confidence. However, confidence must be based on knowledge and experience.
- *Physical:* Keep yourself physically fit and nurture a healthy business environment.
- *Adapt to circumstances:* No plan can see beyond the first engagement. Although it is important to follow the plan, it is equally important to know when and how to modify the plan.

- *Rewards:* Internal motivators include profit sharing, gain sharing, glory sharing, and fame sharing. The simple pat on the back can accomplish much.

We often hear that golf and tennis are mental games. So it is in business. The mental advantage begins with the warm confidence of a positive attitude.

VARIATION OF TACTICS

Management Rules

- Consider Tactical Options
- Prepare Adequate Defenses
- Avoid the Faults of Leadership

Strategy determines direction. The actual execution of the plan to achieve objectives is called tactics and it begins with contact. Internally, that contact may be with the development or production process of a product or service. Externally, that contact is usually with a customer. The contact makes personal relationships an important issue in tactics and explains why tactics must vary. At the point of contact, unpredictable personal equations become part of the scenario.

While strategic principles are unchanging for all time, tactics (implementation of the strategy) vary with the times and circumstances and must be tuned to current situations.

The purpose of tactical maneuvering is to relocate the battle to a place where superiority can be obtained. In a study of 300 military campaigns, in only six was a decisive result achieved by a direct frontal approach to the main army of the enemy. Why would the results of a frontal attack be any different in other kinds of campaigns? Although the idea is appealing, the highly touted "head-on attack" has been consistently unsuccessful; the most successful tactics are usually based on some form of maneuver.

Strategies at any level are the tactics of the next lower level in the chain of command. The best tactical school is experience, and the people with prior experience in their industry have the soundest tactical foundation.

As you shape tactical options, focus on the customer. The key to success is what the customer wants, not what you can do. What ConAgra could do tactically in frozen foods was low-cost mass production. What the customer wanted was healthy foods with great taste. To develop the Healthy Choice brand to meet the customers' taste standards, ConAgra sent food technologists to the Culinary Institute. The result: a successful brand that dominates the market.

CONSIDER TACTICAL OPTIONS—TRANSLATION

Sun Tzu says:

Generally, in war, the general receives his commands from the sovereign, assembles troops, and mobilizes the people. When on grounds hard of access, do not encamp. On grounds intersected with highways, join hands with your allies. Do not linger on critical ground. In encircled ground, resort to stratagem. In desperate ground, fight a last-ditch battle.

There are some roads which must not be followed, some troops which must not be attacked, some cities which must not be assaulted, some ground which must not be contested, and some commands of the sovereign which must not be obeyed.

Hence, the general who thoroughly understands the advantages that accompany variation of tactics knows how to employ troops.

The general who does not is unable to use the terrain to his advantage even though he is well acquainted with it. In employing the troops for attack, the general who does not understand the variation of tactics will be unable to use them effectively, even if he is familiar with the Five Advantages.

A wise general in his deliberations must consider both favorable and unfavorable factors. By taking into account the favorable factors, he makes his plan feasible; by taking into account the unfavorable, he may avoid possible disasters.

CONSIDER TACTICAL OPTIONS—MANAGER'S COMMENTARY

Victory depends on our strength, which we control, and the opportunities provided by our opponent, which we cannot control.

At Microsoft, senior managers meet nightly in a triage meeting during the final months of the software development process. Triage is a ruthless assessment that determines priorities for immediate action. In the Microsoft meeting, managers representing all perspectives are engaged in a power interchange. People voice their point of view and the group negotiates a decision. Tradeoffs are made clear by the key question: "Is this the hill we want to die on?" Decisions are immediately communicated so everyone can get on with his work.

Philip Knight, cofounder of Nike, wrote a graduate thesis at Stanford University. The title was: "Can Japanese Sport Shoes Do to German Sport Shoes What Japanese Cameras Did to German Cameras?" A year later he was in the shoe business—the rest is history. He knew where he wanted to go and had a sense of how he could adopt different tactics in the sports shoe business. Because victory is dependent upon both our actions and those of our opponent, maximum effort does not ensure a competitive victory. This situation can be readily seen in every sporting event where maximum effort on the playing field is exerted by every participant. There are winners and losers in every game.

Tactical flexibility is the hallmark of many organizations with a reputation for customer service. That is, within guidelines, associates are empowered to take whatever action is necessary to serve the customer.

In the complexity of the business environment, an organization may be on the offensive with one product or service and on the defensive with another. The same strategies and tactics cannot be used for all circumstances. The question is how much time the manager should spend shoring up weaknesses as opposed to maximizing strengths. The options differ depending upon whether we are attacking or defending. The low-cost competitor and the high-end producer often have different core strengths requiring different tactics. The differences become obvious when you scan the advertising messages in a newspaper or magazine. Regardless of the circumstances, the spirit of the offense must always prevail. At Fort Donelson, when General Grant found his army half-routed, he galloped down the line shouting, "Fill your cartridge boxes quick and get into line; the enemy is escaping and must not be permitted to do so."

PREPARE ADEQUATE DEFENSES—TRANSLATION

Sun Tzu continues:

What can subdue the hostile neighboring rulers is to hit what hurts them most; what can keep them constantly occupied is to make trouble for them; and what can make them rush about is to offer them ostensible allurements.

It is a doctrine of war that we must not rely on the likelihood of the enemy not coming, but on our own readiness to meet him; not on the chance of his not attacking, but on the fact that we have made our position invincible.

STRENGTHENING THE DEFENSE

Strengthening the defense does not mean maintaining the status quo. General John J. (Black Jack) Pershing noted that the arrival of the airplane provided an excellent and efficient means of getting oats to horses! Legendary IBM CEO Thomas Watson is credited with observing, "I think there is a world market for maybe five computers."

Too often, what happens in the implementation of new military and business tools (i.e., quality management) is that the new simply overlays old doctrine and structure. World competition is a powerful new force moving quickly to challenge keepers of the old paradigm. But human nature being what it is, there will always be a struggle to maintain the status quo.

PREPARE ADEQUATE DEFENSES—MANAGER'S COMMENTARY

The best defense is a good offense.

"We will encircle Caterpillar and become the dominant producer in the industry," Komatsu declared as a key tenet of their strategic intent when they began their global expansion. Many observers predicted that Caterpillar would join the long list of American corporations that have fallen to the Japanese.

After surviving Komatsu's attack, Donald Fites, chairman and CEO of Caterpillar, said, "The biggest reason for Caterpillar's success has been our system of distribution and product support and the close customer relationships it fosters." The backbone of that system is a long history of quality relationships Caterpillar has with its world network of independent dealers. So when Komatsu's attack began, the strongest unit of defense, the dealer structure, was in place. Of course, this alone was not enough to overcome Komatsu's cost advantage; Caterpillar also had to make the organization flatter, meaner, and leaner. However, Komatsu could not overcome the marketing strength provided by Caterpillar's network of dealers with strong customer contacts. Understanding the strength of personal relationships has long been a weakness of the Japanese. The strong defense of high-quality dealer relationships and support has brought Caterpillar to the point where its share of the world market for construction and mining equipment is the highest in its history.

Smaller companies or brands have achieved a good defense by owning very strong positions in a niche or particle segment of a product line or business. When they own a position in the customer's mind, they can hold off the big competitors. Witness Maker's Mark in bourbon, Danner in boots, and regional grocers or pizza parlors in your home town.

Even on the defensive, the rule is to seek every opportunity to seize the initiative and achieve results by offensive action. When you are constantly in a defensive posture, you can seldom win. Facebook found themselves in this position when it changed their Terms of Service agreement. These changes to content ownership were likely designed to give Facebook an opportunity to form a more profitable business model, but users quickly became irate, viewing it as a major privacy issue. They banded together in groups to protest this change, and major media quickly began covering the issue. Facebook took back the offensive when it rescinded those changes and concurrently announced that users would have a chance to vote on future modifications to these agreements. Facebook sets both what gets voted and the rules of these votes—it still has control—but it moved off the defensive and recreated the impression of a user-focused group.

Too often, the strategy that strengthens the defense is characterized by finding some way to redesign your existing product instead of getting out in front of the trend or technology. The mistake is to try to serve the old market in a new way instead of going where the market is growing. The defensive is not achieved by building better buggy whips.

AVOID THE FAULTS OF LEADERSHIP—TRANSLATION

Sun Tzu continues:
There are five dangerous faults that may affect a general:

- if reckless, he can be killed;
- if cowardly, captured;
- if quick-tempered, he can be provoked to rage and make a fool of himself;
- if he has too delicate a sense of honor, he is liable to fall into a trap because of an insult;
- if he is of a compassionate nature, he may get bothered and upset.

These are the five serious faults of a general, ruinous to the conduct of war. The ruin of the army and the death of the general are inevitable results of these five dangerous faults. They must be deeply pondered.

AVOID THE FAULTS OF LEADERSHIP—MANAGER'S COMMENTARY

Flaws in the personal character of the commander will cause opportunities to be lost.

"Chainsaw" Al Dunlap got his reputation by staging massive cutbacks in personnel at Scott Paper. When the same approach didn't work at Sunbeam, he tried sales and accounting gimmicks to bolster results. Soon he was asked to exit. Jim McCann, president of 1-800-FLOWERS, tells about the lesson he learned from General Electric CEO Jack Welch. McCann had to fire a senior person that everyone knew wasn't right for the job. The guy was a friend, and the prospect of action was brutal. He met Welch at a dinner party and told him about the situation. Welch's response was, "When was the last time anyone said, 'I wish I had waited six months longer to fire that guy?'"

Peers and subordinates will discover the ineffective manager long before her seniors do. The dysfunctional interactions resulting from the discovery will reduce this person's effectiveness—and the effectiveness of the organization.

Here are business parallels to Sun Tzu's character flaws:

Reckless (meaning no forethought): The reckless manager does not understand how to use data. She shoots from the hip. When a win is achieved, it is simply because she did something rather than because the right thing was done.

Cowardly (self-protective or afraid): The person who is afraid to take risks takes the greatest risk of all. This manager is like McClellan in the Civil War, who was so fearful of losing he could not win.

Quick tempered (too easily angered): Reference has been made to the importance of a cool head. Managers who have a reputation for shooting the messenger don't often get bad information and don't know what is really going on.

Delicate honor (exaggerated sensitivity): The business parallel here is being too easily embarrassed, taking things personally, or letting ego get in the way.

Too compassionate (too concerned): Those who have this fault are so concerned about the reactions of people that short-term decisions are made to keep harmony. The result is these managers end up with a long-term disaster. In their compassion people are often left "twisting slowly in the wind," when the kindest thing that could be done is to make the hard decision.

Chapter 3

Mobility and Flexibility Are Key to Victory

ON THE MARCH

Management Rules

- Occupy Strong Natural Positions
- Always Seek the High Ground
- Make an Estimate of the Situation
- Discipline Can Build Allegiance

Strategically, a secure position establishes a base for the offensive. Tactically, this secure position helps you use your natural strengths. Positions where you can occupy a key strong point are important in every endeavor. There are only a few leaders in each industry; everyone else marches in their shadow.

In order for a position to be secure, we must "own" it. We own a position because of a perceived strength—the perception is the reality. People accept only what is consistent with what they already know as they add to their perceptions about the position of a product or service.

All positions are in the mind, and the entry into the mind is through emotions, not logic. Logic sounds most convincing to the presenter; it is in the emotions of the receiver that positions are changed. In thinking about attacking competitive positions, the first rule is: It's very, very difficult to move into a position occupied by someone else.

To build a strong position, you must first determine what position you want and who you want your customers to be. Then figure out how you are going to meet the needs of those potential customers better than anyone else.

In business, the most secure positions are owned by those who achieve a base of loyal customers. Premier positions are earned by organizations that have systems for really listening to their customers. They then focus resources on meeting or exceeding needs in a manner that delights customers. The idea is to make customers so happy that not only do they not buy anything else, they don't even *think* of buying anything else.

However, the more secure your position seems to be, the greater the danger can be. When you feel most secure, you are most vulnerable to surprise.

OCCUPY STRONG NATURAL POSITIONS—TRANSLATION

Sun Tzu says:

Generally, when an army takes up a position and sizes up the enemy situation, it should pay attention to the following:

When crossing the mountains, be sure to stay in the neighborhood of valleys; when encamping, select high ground facing the sunny side; when high ground is occupied by the enemy, do not ascend to attack. So much for taking up a position in mountains.

After crossing a river, you should get far away from it. When an advancing invader crosses a river, do not meet him in midstream. It is advantageous to allow half his force to get across and then strike. If you wish to fight a battle, you should not go to meet the invader near a river that he has to cross. When encamping in the riverine area, take a position on high ground facing the sun. Do not take a position at the lower reaches of the enemy. This relates to positions near a river.

In crossing salt marshes, your sole concern should be to get over them quickly, without any delay. If you encounter the enemy in a salt marsh, you should take position close to grass and water with trees to your rear. This has to do with taking up a position in salt marshes.

On level ground, take up an accessible position and deploy your main flanks on high grounds with front lower than the back. This is how to take up a position on level ground. These are principles for encamping in the four situations named. By employing them, the Yellow Emperor conquered his four neighboring sovereigns.

OCCUPY STRONG NATURAL POSITIONS— MANAGER'S COMMENTARY

Find the strength of natural positions that cannot easily be occupied by your opponents.

Experienced travelers know that Jet Blue has one of the newest fleets, and because of that has televisions in every seatback of every plane—a nice convenience at no extra charge and an immediate win with customers. Challenging that position is taking competitors years because of the costs and normal replacement time of changing out existing older fleets.

Tesco dominates retailing in England the way no one company does in the United States. It got there with an everyday pricing position similar to what Wal-Mart used in the United States. It stays there by maintaining that position and using loyalty card data better than anyone else to layer on unique services that build further price and value perceptions.

Many companies are gaining strength by going back to their roots. At these core positions, they have the most inherent natural strength. In the recession that started in 2008, many companies found their natural strength to be just right for the quickly changing buying behaviors of financially shocked consumers. After losing money for a decade, Revlon found itself in the right natural position as consumers abandoned expensive department store cosmetics. When these customers arrived at the cosmetics departments of drug stores, supermarkets, and mass merchants, they found a recognizable brand in Revlon and dramatically lower prices than in department stores.

The perception of what we are is based on what we have been. Over time, the perception of what we are matches what we really are. We, ourselves, or our product or service, can't be something else. Everyone who has tried to win by copying has failed, often caused by not understanding the subtleties. To change your position in the customer's mind over time, you must change who you really are.

Efforts focused on reinforcing your natural position make it easier to communicate your position. When you say that you are what you really are, the believable message gets through to your audience.

Going up the positioning ladder to achieve a stronger share of mind requires a well-conceived and executed plan. Coming down is what happens when you are not going up. Ask any former sports star like good old "what's his name."

ALWAYS SEEK THE HIGH GROUND—TRANSLATION

Sun Tzu continues:

Generally, in battle and maneuvering, all armies prefer high ground to low, and sunny places to shady. If an army encamps close to water and grass with adequate supplies, it will be free from countless diseases and this will spell victory. When you come to hills, dikes, or embankments, occupy the sunny side, with your main flank at the back. All these methods are advantageous to the army and can exploit the possibilities the ground offers.

When heavy rain falls in the upper reaches of a river and foaming water descends, do not ford and wait until it subsides. When encountering "Precipitous Torrents," "Heavenly Wells," "Heavenly Prison," "Heavenly Net," "Heavenly Trap," and "Heavenly Cracks," you must march speedily away from them. Do not approach them. While we keep a distance from them we should draw the enemy toward them. We face them and cause the enemy to put his back to them.

If in the neighborhood of your camp there are dangerous defiles or ponds and low-lying ground overgrown with aquatic grass and reeds, or forested mountains with dense tangled undergrowth, they must be thoroughly searched, for these are possible places where ambushes are laid and spies are hidden.

THE HIGH GROUND

The most desirable position in war has always been the high ground controlling the surrounding terrain. Frederick the Great referred to selection of positions as the talent of great men—the ability immediately to conceive all the advantages of the terrain. He said, "The first rule that I give is always to occupy the heights."

ALWAYS SEEK THE HIGH GROUND—MANAGER'S COMMENTARY

The high ground is the strongest position.

The high ground in business today is owned by names with brand strength like Microsoft in software, Coca-Cola in soft drinks, Nike in athletic shoes, and McDonald's in fast foods.

Attaining the high ground is one battle and keeping it is another. In the battle for dominance of internet browsers, Netscape got to the high ground in market share by giving away free product. Then Microsoft entered the market with free software while Netscape started to charge for its browser, and down went Netscape's market share.

Jelly Belly, with 75 percent of the gourmet jelly bean market, increased its total sales even more by selling through major grocery chains. The concern is that this expanded distribution may affect the brand-name cachet.

Each of these brands faces the problem that market share is either increasing or decreasing. There's no such thing as staying exactly where you are; you either get bigger or you get smaller.

In the military, positioning is occupying a key strong point in the terrain. In business, positioning is occupying a key strong point in the mind. You own a position in the mind either because you are the leader or because of significant differentiation. The unique taste of Dr Pepper provides a significant differentiation.

The worst position of all may be not having a position, the problem experienced by people in the struggling brand name you've never heard of. In the final analysis, it is the perceptions of the market that actually position the brand.

In every industry, the action of moving up in market share erodes the competitor's base. This dysfunction forces displaced competitors to compete for lesser positions that offer even smaller profits. As market positions change, the one who captures higher ground gets the larger revenue base and all the accompanying advantages. Similarly, the loser's losses are cumulative—negatively.

MAKE AN ESTIMATE OF THE SITUATION—TRANSLATION

Sun Tzu continues:

When the enemy is close at hand and remains quiet, he is relying on a favorable position. When he challenges battle from afar, he wishes to lure you to advance; when he is on easy ground, he must be in an advantageous position. When the trees are seen to move, it means the enemy is advancing; when many screens have been placed in the undergrowth, it is for the purpose of deception. The rising of birds in their flight is the sign of an ambuscade. Startled beasts indicate that a sudden attack is forthcoming.

Dust spurting upwards in high straight columns indicates the approach of chariots. When it hangs low and is widespread, it betokens that infantry is approaching. When it branches out in different directions, it shows that parties have been sent out to collect firewood. A few clouds of dust moving to and fro signify that the army is camping.

When the enemy's envoys speak in humble terms, but the army continues preparations, that means it will advance. When their language is strong and the enemy pretentiously drives forward, these may be signs that he will retreat. When light chariots first go out and take positions on the wings, it is a sign that the enemy is forming for battle. When the enemy is not in dire straits but asks for a truce, he must be plotting. When his troops march speedily and parade in formations, he is expecting to fight a decisive battle on a fixed date. When half his force advances and half retreats, he is attempting to decoy you.

When his troops lean on their weapons, they are famished. When drawers of water drink before carrying it to camp, his troops are suffering from thirst. When the enemy sees an advantage but does not advance to seize it, he is fatigued.

When birds gather above his campsites, they are unoccupied. When at night the enemy's camp is clamorous, it betokens nervousness. If there is disturbance in the camp, the general's authority is weak.

If the banners and flags are shifted about, sedition is afoot. If the officers are angry, it means that men are weary. When the enemy feeds his horses with grain, kills the beasts of burden for food and packs up the utensils used for drawing water, he shows no intention to return to his tents and is determined to fight to the death.

When the general speaks in meek and subservient tone to his subordinates, he has lost the support of his men. Too frequent rewards indicate that the general is at the end of his resources; too frequent punishments indicate that he is in dire distress. If the officers at first treat the men violently and later are fearful of them, it shows supreme lack of intelligence.

When envoys are sent with compliments in their mouths, it is a sign that the enemy wishes for a truce.

When the enemy's troops march up angrily and remain facing yours for a long time, neither joining battle nor withdrawing, the situation demands great vigilance and thorough investigation.

In war, numbers alone confer no advantage. If one does not advance by force recklessly, and is able to concentrate his military power through a correct assessment of the enemy situation and enjoys full support of his men, that would suffice. He who lacks foresight and underestimates his enemy will surely be captured by him.

Estimate of the Situation as Used by U.S. Army Officers

1. Mission (assigned or deduced)
2. The Situation and Courses of Action
   - *Considerations affecting the Courses of Action (other operations, environment, enemy, friendly, etc.)*
   - *Anticipated Difficulties*
3. Analysis of Courses of Action
4. Comparison of Courses of Action
5. Decision = Commander's Concept or Intent

Questions to Determine Your Position

- What position do we own?
- What position do we want?
- Who do we have to outmaneuver?
- How much resource expenditure and time will it take?
- Can we stick it out?
- Will the results justify the expense?

Questions to Determine Your Opponent's Position

- What position do they own?
- What signals indicate they are changing or strengthening their position?
- What position do they want? (Where are they going?)

- What will the effect on us be if they are successful in their current activities?
- What opportunities will there be for us if they are unsuccessful?

MAKE AN ESTIMATE OF THE SITUATION— MANAGER'S COMMENTARY

Carefully observe the situation and attack only where real superiority can be obtained.

Amazon.com grew out of founder Jeff Bezos's personal mission to be in business for himself. His course of action was determined when he learned that books were an $82 billion market and annual growth on the web was predicted at 2,200 percent. He analyzed the opportunity for innovative computerized marketing and decided that the Seattle area would be a good hi-tech base.

General Paul Cerjan, retired U.S. Army, explains how he uses the steps in conducting the Estimate of the Situation (see "Estimate of the Situation as Used by U.S. Army Officers") as a great tool for the rapid estimate of any contingency. First, you need to determine the mission. Then you start thinking what course of action you are going to take. Then you work that all the way down until you get to the decision, and from that flows the operations order—the specific orders concerning what you want done.

Depending on the circumstances, the Estimate of the Situation can be achieved rapidly or require a more lengthy analysis. We unconsciously make a rapid estimation of the situation in personal interfaces. When issuing written plans, we usually initiate an extended analysis of the situation.

I have observed real differences between the way managers from Western and Eastern civilizations gather information to make an Estimate of the Situation. The Western manager is more likely to do a quick study while the Eastern manager will often do a thorough, lengthy analysis.

There are a variety of readily perceived indicators that can help you estimate the situation. These indicators signal the competitive strategy and vulnerability. The breadth of these signals can be understood from one of Sun Tzu's translators, who identified thirty-three different signs of enemy activity by Sun Tzu in this chapter.

In personal interfaces, these indicators are called body language. Crossed arms indicate opposition. Someone leaning forward and listening indicates intent acceptance. A furrowed brow signals that your proposition is being questioned.

In business situations, the signals are also subtly visible. For example, in publicizing pricing moves, companies are signaling their desire to raise prices to others in the industry—and may reduce prices if competitors reject the signal.

All of these overt signals help the observant manager develop an accurate Estimate of the Situation. While one does not want to overestimate the opponent, it can be disastrous to underestimate.

DISCIPLINE CAN BUILD ALLEGIANCE—TRANSLATION

Sun Tzu continues:

If troops are punished before they have grown attached to you, they will be disobedient. If not obedient, it is difficult to employ them. If troops have become attached to you, but discipline is not enforced, you cannot employ them either. Thus, soldiers must be treated in the first instance with humanity, but kept under control by iron discipline. In this way, the allegiance of soldiers is assured.

If orders are consistently carried out and the troops are strictly supervised, they will be obedient. If orders are never carried out, they will be disobedient. And the smooth implementation of orders reflects harmonious relationship between the commander and his troops.

THE ROLE OF DISCIPLINE

Colonel Ardant du Picq writes:

What makes the soldier capable of obedience and direction in action, is the sense of discipline. This includes: respect for and confidence in his chiefs; confidence in his comrades and fear of their reproaches if he abandons them in danger; his desire to go where others do without trembling more than they; in a word, the whole of esprit de corps. Organizations only can produce these characteristics. Four men equal a lion.

DISCIPLINE CAN BUILD ALLEGIANCE—MANAGER'S COMMENTARY

Apply the same standards to everyone.

When home run king Henry Aaron was asked the difference between a good team and a great team, he replied promptly, "Discipline." With the discipline should come a warm concern for people.

The ideal leader is best described as one who combines excellence as a task specialist with an equal flair for the human aspects of leadership. She understands that it is people rather than techniques that really count. The manager does not have to be liked; however, she does not have to be disliked. Being fair and impartial does not mean being impersonal. At times, hard decisions must be made; when they are not made, the manager abdicates his authority.

What manager does not have his political favorites, perceived with envy by others less favored? Therein lies a complex problem: These politicians are often perceived as delivering bad information to the boss who, in turn, is perceived as delivering bad orders.

When standards for the performance of each process are established and clearly communicated, then managers can issue praise or criticism based on performance against that standard. The general manager of one of the fine hotels of the world explained to me his reason for having standards: "Maintaining known standards keeps me from playing favorites and being criticized for playing favorites." Although we find a system of standards and measures in manufacturing processes, many other office or service processes operate without clearly defined standards. Too often, where there are no standards, criticism and penalties are imposed at the whim of management. The result is confusion and low morale.

As a manager at Burger King, Herman Cain tells how he set a standard for friendly service with the "Happy B.E.E.s." The B stood for "Bad moods stay home." The Es signified, "Eye contact with customers. Every day." This success with motivational discipline earned Cain an increase in business and a promotion up the ladder.

Consistently maintaining high standards creates the environment where discipline is effective and accepted. In these circumstances, morale is high.

Personal discipline is equally important. Until a person learns how to command herself, it is unlikely that command over others will be successful.

TERRAIN

Management Rules

- Know Your Battlefield
- Obey the Laws of Leadership
- Fight Only the Battles You Can Win
- Know Yourself; Know Your Opponent

Terrain is perhaps one of the most overused words in the translations of Sun Tzu. We will define "terrain" as "your area of operations"—either internal or external.

Management by wandering around the terrain is essential to success. Managers wander around not to manage, but so they can manage. By spending time at the scene of action, managers get a feel for what's happening now. Since many decisions are made at gut level, this "feel" helps process information so managers can determine a successful course of action based on real knowledge of the situation. Too often, we find decisions being made by smart people who know nothing about the circumstances.

Our bias for what we know can lead to misconceptions about the world around us. As Ralph E. Gomory, president of the Sloan Foundation, said, "We are all taught what is known, but we rarely learn about what is not known; and we almost never learn the unknowable." The point is there is a lot of information outside our area of operations. Expanding our knowledge base expands our horizon of possibilities.

Formal input systems for information are essential. However, so are informal systems such as when someone talks with his "customer"—the customer being defined as the person who receives your process.

Internally, the person who receives your process is also a customer. Within a company, people are often organized into functional departments, and these departments become competitors. Since we don't talk to competitors, there is no communication. The solution must be to achieve linkage between all processes and align them to deliver value to the ultimate customer. Until we focus all processes on the needs of the customer, the enemy will continue to be "us."

KNOW YOUR BATTLEFIELD—TRANSLATION

Sun Tzu says:

Ground may be classified according to its nature as accessible, entangling, temporizing, constricted, precipitous, and distant.

Ground which both we and the enemy can traverse with equal ease is called accessible. On such ground, he who first takes high sunny positions, and keeps his supply routes unimpeded can fight advantageously. Ground easy to reach but difficult to exit is called entangling. The nature of this ground is such that if the enemy is unprepared and you sally out, you may defeat him. But, if the enemy is prepared for your coming, and you fail to defeat him, then, return being difficult, disadvantages will ensue.

Ground equally disadvantageous for both the enemy and ourselves to enter is called temporizing. This ground is such that even though the enemy offers us an attractive bait, it will be advisable not to go forth but march off. When his force is halfway out because of our maneuvering, we can strike him with advantage. With regard to the constricted ground, if we first occupy it, we must block the narrow passes with strong garrisons and wait for the enemy. If the enemy first occupies such ground, do not attack him if the pass in his hand is fully garrisoned, but only if it is weakly garrisoned.

With regard to the precipitous ground, if we first occupy it, we must take a position on the sunny heights and await the enemy. If he first occupies such ground, we should march off and do not attack him. When the enemy is situated at a great distance from us, and the terrain where the two armies deploy is similar, it is difficult to provoke battle and unprofitable to engage him.

These are the principles relating to six different types of ground. It is the highest responsibility of the general to inquire into them with the utmost care. Conformation of the ground is of great assistance in the military operations. It is necessary for a wise general to make correct assessments of the enemy's situation to create conditions leading to victory and to calculate distances and the degree of difficulty of the terrain. He who knows these things and applies them to fighting will definitely win. He who knows them not, and, therefore, is unable to apply them, will definitely lose.

KNOW YOUR BATTLEFIELD—MANAGER'S COMMENTARY

Thorough knowledge of the scene of action is an absolute requirement.

If you were fishing in the Southwest some years ago, you might have been approached by two people of Asian descent in a pickup truck offering to clean your rod and reel. They would ask questions about your preferences in fishing equipment. Today, the Japanese are major factors in this business category.

Your "market" is those whom you must persuade to buy your product, service, or idea. The admonition to know your market may seem too basic; however, it is the basics we often miss. To know your market, you must listen to your customers. To listen effectively, you must ask questions to probe for information. This is "shut up and listen" time. Avoid defensive responses.

The big question is, "What do we need to know to make the required decision?" If we do not know what we need to know, then everything looks like important information. It becomes impossible to sort the useless from the useful.

Often, we are told what someone thinks we want to hear. Just as often, our bias from prior knowledge keeps us from finding the truth. That is why time must be spent at the scene of action finding out what's going on so we know what questions to ask.

Napoleon used both his regular army intelligence system and a focused intelligence telescope of select senior officers to gather information. Senior officers were given wide latitude to report on "anything that might interest me." Junior officers in his regular intelligence system were sent on more specific missions. He deliberately kept his telescope staff small in order to establish personal contact with these messengers. The personal contact helped him evaluate the information he received.

This focused telescope overcomes the common problem of intelligence bureaucracies. Too often, information that gets to the senior commanders is filtered through the chain of command and becomes less and less specific. The result is overgeneralization of information; consequently, those in command know the least about what is really happening. The manager's solution to learning how to interpret data is always to spend time face to face in the battlefield where the data was collected.

Don't shoot the messenger. The most rapid way to shell-shock a business is to shell proof its managers.

OBEY THE LAWS OF LEADERSHIP—TRANSLATION

Sun Tzu continues:
There are six situations that cause an army to fail. They are: flight, insubordination, fall, collapse, disorganization, and rout. None of these disasters can be attributed to natural and geographical causes, but to the fault of the general.

Terrain conditions being equal, if a force attacks one ten times its size, the result is flight.

When the soldiers are strong and officers weak, the army is insubordinate.

When the officers are valiant and the soldiers ineffective, the army will fall.

When the higher officers are angry and insubordinate, and on encountering the enemy rush to battle on their own account from a feeling of resentment and the commander-in-chief is ignorant of their abilities, the result is collapse.

When the general is incompetent and has little authority, when his troops are mismanaged, when the relationship between the officers and men is strained, and when the troop formations are slovenly, the result is disorganization.

When a general unable to estimate the enemy's strength uses a small force to engage a larger one or weak troops to strike the strong, or fails to select shock troops for the van, the result is riot.

When any of these six situations exists, the army is on the road to defeat. It is the highest responsibility of the general that he examine them carefully.

If a general regards his men as infants, then they will march with him into the deepest valleys. He treats them as his own beloved sons and they will stand by him unto death. If, however, a general is indulgent towards his men but cannot employ them, cherishes them but cannot command them or inflict punishment on them when they violate the regulations, then they may be compared to spoiled children, and are useless for any practical purpose.

OBEY THE LAWS OF LEADERSHIP—MANAGER'S COMMENTARY

Winning is the responsibility of the leader.

The following characteristics define good command systems:

Decentralization: People have the authority needed to achieve objectives except those expressly forbidden. This reduces the need for detailed control and frees the time of leaders at all levels. Every leader commands his own unit; every subordinate knows from where to expect his instructions.

Freedom: To generate independence, freedom must be delegated all the way through the chain of command. The system doesn't work when middle managers become infatuated with their own power and fail to give up power as they are given more power in a decentralized command system.

Information processing: When senior managers give up control, they must also give up some information flow. If not, subordinates will spend too much time reporting to be effective. The task of senior management is not to confirm plans in detail; rather, it is to encourage greater speed.

Stability: People relationships and informal systems give stability to the structure of the command system.

Mutual trust: The interaction of long-standing relationships creates mutual trust. The replacement system that brings in new personnel should be structured to help create the familiarity that is an indispensable prerequisite of both reliability and trust.

A willingness to assume responsibility: To train people to accept responsibility, authority must be delegated. A decentralized command system leaves much to the discretion of individual commanders and puts responsibility squarely on their shoulders.

The right and duty of subordinate commanders to make decisions and carry them out: Freedom is granted to allow managers to make decisions and utilize available resources to find the best way to the objective.

Expect the unpredictable: Expect that plans will break down, that your opponent will behave in an unexpected manner, and that units will not achieve their objectives. Don't try to overcome the confusion by pausing to regroup after each breakdown. Keep everyone marching in the right direction.

Training: Every manager manages the training of his personnel. This does not mean that he conducts all sessions. It does mean that he has the basic responsibility for training.

FIGHT ONLY THE BATTLES YOU CAN WIN—TRANSLATION

Sun Tzu continues:

Hence, if, in the light of the prevailing situation, fighting is sure to result in victory, then you may decide to fight even though the sovereign has issued an order not to engage.

If fighting does not stand a good chance of victory, you need not to fight even though the sovereign has issued an order to engage.

Hence, the general who advances without coveting fame and retreats without fearing disgrace, whose only purpose is to protect his people and promote the best interests of his sovereign, is the precious jewel of the state.

INITIATING THE BATTLE

There are two mental approaches to launching the attack:

1. Plan everything in detail and then start going. The D-Day invasion of Europe was one of the most thoroughly organized in history. With 175,000 troops from four countries involving over 5,000 ships, every detail was planned scientifically. The invasion was practiced for months in various venues around England. During the run up to the invasion, the Allies created various deceptions about where and when the invasion would occur. These were so successful that for the

first hours of June 6, 1944, as troops scrambled across the beaches of Normandy, Hitler refused to believe this was the long-awaited invasion.

2. **Lay down general objectives only and start immediately.** The offensive is launched with the understanding that forward movement will proceed according to local circumstances. The details are filled in as the attack gains momentum. This system is used by the Israeli Defense Force.

It would seem the choice is either to do it now or spend time preparing to do it later. How difficult it is to achieve the careful balance between getting ready and getting going. The best odds for success lie on the side of action. Most often, the person who does something has the best opportunity to become master of the situation.

FIGHT ONLY THE BATTLES YOU CAN WIN—MANAGER'S COMMENTARY

First understand the situation, then determine whether to fight and how.

Every executive encounters the decision of where and how to expend energy in two primary areas: the political arena and performance of her assigned tasks (either internal or external, depending on job function).

The political battles can be the most time consuming and debilitating. The larger the organization, the bigger is the political morass. David Halberstam explains one type of dysfunction in his description of conflict at Ford Motor Company in *The Reckoning:*

The growing power of the finance people made the creative people more vulnerable than ever. For the creative people always, no matter how good they were, made mistakes. No product man was perfect; for every model that was a success, there were others best forgotten. By contrast, the finance men were careful. They were never identified with a particular product. They never had to create anything. In meetings they attacked but never had to defend, while the product people defended and could never attack.

In internal politics, while defending your position, target your battle against processes and systems instead of individuals. The person you attack may someday be your boss.

In determining where to fight external battles, keep your orientation focused on effectiveness. Where can you add value and win? The larger the target the bigger the results. You cannot be strong everywhere; you must determine where you are going to put your main effort and then exercise the discipline that allocates resources, directly and indirectly, to support this main effort.

If we are not effective, we have no need to be efficient. Ask Ford about its Edsel, Gerber about its failed venture into adult foods, Coca-Cola about its disastrous launch of New Coke, or the corner grocer who went out of business.

Market testing determines whether to launch a full-scale offensive. Your first objective in a test is to determine whether the concept works. Consequently, you must apply full resources to the effort. If the test fails when backed with adequate resources, you know you must abandon the effort. If it succeeds, you can adjust to make it profitable. Half-hearted tests tell you nothing.

You need to be efficient, but not at the expense of the resources needed to achieve success. An inefficient victory is bad, but not as bad as losing—which is extremely inefficient.

KNOW YOURSELF; KNOW YOUR OPPONENT—TRANSLATION

Sun Tzu says:

If we know that our troops are capable of striking the enemy, but do not know that he is invulnerable to attack, our chance of victory is but half.

If we know that the enemy is vulnerable to attack but do not know that our troops are incapable of striking him, our chance of victory is again but half.

If we know that the enemy can be attacked and that our troops are capable of attacking him, but do not realize that the conformation of the ground makes fighting impracticable, our chance of victory is once again but half.

Therefore, when those experienced in war move, they are never bewildered; when they act, they are never at a loss. Thus the saying: Know the enemy and know yourself, and your victory will never be endangered; know the weather and know the ground, and your victory will then be complete.

Now, the key to military operations lies in cautiously studying the enemy's designs. Concentrate your forces in the main direction against the enemy and from a distance of a thousand li you can kill his general. This is called the ability to achieve one's aim in an artful and ingenious manner.

VISIBLE AND INVISIBLE NUMBERS

Even when accurate, statistics can never substitute for looking someone in the eye. Dr. W. Edwards Deming, who championed statistical quality control as a key ingredient of a quality methodology, commented that some managers look only at the visible numbers. He said, "But the visible numbers tell them so little. They know nothing of the invisible numbers. Who can put a price on a satisfied customer and who can figure out the cost of a dissatisfied customer?"

The process of stroking ourselves with our own convictions and ignoring the signals can be a spiral that ends in disaster.

KNOW YOURSELF; KNOW YOUR OPPONENT—MANAGER'S COMMENTARY

Know the strengths and weaknesses of your adversary.

When I visited the Philips office in Sao Paulo, Brazil, a senior manager told me that he employed a woman of Japanese descent as a secretary because she could read the Japanese papers ordered from Tokyo.

Communications are making the world smaller and world competitors better informed. The cost of a three-minute call from New York to London has decreased from over $200 in 1930 to about $2 today. An e-mail or Internet phone call to anywhere in the world is often at no additional expense because the contact time is part of the monthly fee. For most companies, market research has expanded from domestic to world markets because we can sell to the world and the world can sell anywhere.

Countless people call on you as well as on your competitor. The editors of trade magazines know what is going on in the industry. The suppliers who call on purchasing agents know who is buying more and who is buying less—and why. Beware of the supplier who tells you everything about your competitor because he is also telling your competition about you.

Business executives who change jobs will bring their preferences in methodologies with them. They will usually clone the style of their previous organization. You can predict what they will do by where they have been. Look at both the issues and personalities. Review the issues in terms of history—who did something like this before, what happened. Look at the personalities in terms of their background of experience.

Knowledge of the personal style of competitors is the easy part; knowledge of one's self is the hard part. The higher your rank, the more difficult it is to get true feedback on your actions. Don't expect it from anyone internally. The self-examination takes place in three spheres: physical, intellectual, and moral. For physical health, see a doctor; for intellectual health, read, listen, and visit your battlefield; for moral health, find an external guru who will hold up a mirror and give you an honest picture.

THE NINE VARIETIES OF GROUND

Management Rules

- Choose a Favorable Battleground
- Shape Your Opponent's Strategy
- Make Victory the Only Option
- Plan Coordinated Efforts
- Press the Attack
- Learn Winning Ways

An ancient proverb says the first blow is as much as two; the attack has the advantage of the initiative. Since it forces action on the opponent, it relegates him to second place. The offensive action also strengthens the morale and confidence of the aggressor.

The offensive must be a continuing process. Only then does it permit you to maintain freedom of action, meet unexpected developments, and determine the future courses of action.

Tactical considerations influence strategic plans. That is, you may need to launch your offensive where it is tactically possible, not where it is strategically desirable. For example, a company with a high-end product strategy might determine that competitive success with a specific product in a mid-priced position is more readily attainable.

Two important components of the successful campaign are to strengthen customer value and know your opponent's strengths and weaknesses. In the attack, a fundamental principle is to avoid that which is strong and attack that which is weak.

While it is important to do things that give you an advantage, give serious consideration to actions that also put your competitor at a disadvantage.

The concepts of niching and segmentation provide excellent opportunities for maximizing strengths in developing offensive thrusts. Segmentation is a way for anyone of any size to secure a position by focusing strengths on a specific, narrow frontage of the market.

CHOOSE A FAVORABLE BATTLEGROUND—TRANSLATION

Sun Tzu says:

In respect to the employment of troops, ground may be classified as dispersive, frontier, key, open, focal, serious, difficult, encircled, and desperate.

When a chieftain is fighting in his own territory, he is in dispersive ground. When he has penetrated into hostile territory, but to no great distance, he is in frontier ground. Ground equally advantageous for us and the enemy to occupy is key ground. Ground equally accessible to both sides is open. Ground contiguous to three other states is focal. He who first gets control of it will gain the support of the majority of neighboring states. When an army has penetrated deep into hostile territory, leaving far behind many enemy cities and towns, it is in serious ground. Mountain forests, rugged steeps, marshes, fens, and all that is hard to traverse fall into the category of difficult ground.

Ground to which access is constricted and from which we can only retire by tortuous paths so that a small number of the enemy would suffice to crush a large body of our men is encircled ground. Ground on which the army can avoid annihilation only through a desperate fight without delay is called a desperate one.

And, therefore, do not fight in dispersive ground; do not stop in the frontier borderlands.

Do not attack an enemy who has occupied key ground; in open ground, do not allow your communication to be blocked.

In focal ground, form alliances with neighboring states; in serious ground, gather in plunder.

In difficult ground, press on; in encircled ground, resort to stratagems; and in desperate ground, fight courageously.

The principle of terrain application is to make the best use of both the high and the low-lying grounds.

CHOOSE A FAVORABLE BATTLEGROUND— MANAGER'S COMMENTARY

Control of the location of the battleground results in control of offensive and defensive actions.

In retail, always be careful about attacking a competitor on its home turf. Safeway, based outside San Francisco, has a dominant market share of Northern California. It can be successfully attacked at some of its far-flung outposts. Safeway has exited major markets over its history, but it is dominant in its home market. Safeway knows its local landscape better than anyone else and has built a strong defense with relationships with local customers. There is an emotional response to defending your home market that partially transcends any ROI calculations. Any competitor looking to enter Safeway's hometown knows its likelihood of winning market share is lower, and it invests in different territories.

To discover new marketing battlefields, Pfizer organized its drug-discovery teams to pursue development of drugs for every major disease. It built speed into the process so that its drug-discovery teams needed less than one-third the industry's average person years to move a compound from conception to clinical trials. When Pfizer researchers found themselves in a race with a Japanese company for an Alzheimer's drug, they opted to drop research and form a more favorable joint venture so they could comarket the drug.

Twenty-five thousand new products are launched every year. The average forecast is that one in several hundred will succeed. Research, targeting, and luck are critical to determining where resources should be invested.

Big Island Candy in Hilo, Hawaii, selected a unique battlefield that avoids retail distribution where its product would compete with the bigger mass-marketed brands. Instead, the focus is on the tour operators who are pleased that the visit to the Big Island Candy store and factory offers an experience and products that are not available in retail stores. This marketing approach is quite immune to the moves of big competitors.

The most favorable battleground is always where you can concentrate your resources profitably with minimal competition. To control the battleground, you must offer a distinctive differentiation and the customer must desire that differentiation. Otherwise, you are another player in a low-margin commodity market.

SHAPE YOUR OPPONENT'S STRATEGY—TRANSLATION

Sun Tzu continues:

In ancient times, those described as skilled in war knew how to make it impossible for the enemy to unite his van and his rear, for his large and small divisions to cooperate, for his officers and men to support each other, and for the higher and lower levels of the enemy to establish contact with each other.

When the enemy's forces were dispersed, they prevented him from assembling them; even when assembled, they managed to throw his forces into disorder. They moved forward when it was advantageous to do so; when not advantageous, they halted.

Should one ask: "How do I cope with a well-ordered enemy host about to attack me?" I reply, "Seize something he cherishes and he will conform to your desires."

Speed is the essence of war. Take advantage of the enemy's unpreparedness, make your way by unexpected routes, and attack him where he has taken no precautions.

SHAPE YOUR OPPONENT'S STRATEGY—MANAGER'S COMMENTARY

**Move swiftly to disrupt your opponent and
place him at the disadvantage.**

Campbell's owns 70 percent of the canned soup business. A company called Play-By-Play dominates the carnival prize market with a 50 percent market share. Salesforce.com overshadows all competitors in the small business CRM market. Each of these companies determines the marketing situations in its industry. They own the market and their opponents must shape their attack around the strategies of these giants of their industry because the gorilla sleeps anywhere he wants.

Whether or not you can shape your opponent's strategy in business situations is a function of your relative strength. Although this relative strength is most often seen in established gorillas, new entrants with a differentiation who move rapidly can become powerful gorillas. Witness the rapid rise of Amazon.com in web marketing, Bloomberg in business information, and Staples in office products. These organizations matched differentiation with speed in order to attain strength.

You can force your opponent to react when you rapidly accumulate a critical mass of power. Napoleon said, "Force must be concentrated at one point and as soon as the breach is made, the equilibrium is broken."

In 1914, Captain Johnstone wrote that full strength is recognized as a key principle in shaping success. He said, "The best thing is to have as much as you can for yourself and as little as you can for the enemy." It is strength at a given point that shapes the opponent's reaction.

In every competitive endeavor, a concentration of energy must be rapidly achieved to attain the breakthrough. The winning manager must give priority to those items that are the most critical to success. The ultimate judge of whether you win is the customer. Her decision to buy is the critical vote. If the customer doesn't vote with a favorable decision, nothing else matters.

MAKE VICTORY THE ONLY OPTION—TRANSLATION

Sun Tzu continues:
    Throw your soldiers into a position whence there is no escape, and they will choose death over desertion. For if prepared to die, how can the officers and men not exert their uttermost strength to fight? In a desperate situation, they fear nothing; when there is no way out, they

stand firm. Deep in a hostile land they are bound together. If there is no help for it, they will fight hard.

Thus, without waiting to be marshaled, the soldiers will be constantly vigilant; without waiting to be asked, they will do your will; without restrictions, they will be faithful; without giving orders, they can be trusted.

Prohibit superstitious practices and do away with rumors, then nobody will flee even facing death. Our soldiers have no surplus of wealth, but it is not because they disdain riches; they have no expectation of long life, but it is not because they dislike longevity.

On the day the army is ordered out to battle, your soldiers may weep, those sitting up wetting their garments, and those lying down letting the tears run down their cheeks. But throw them into a situation where there is no escape and they will display the immortal courage of Zhuan Zhu and Cao Kuei.

He orders his troops for a decisive battle on a fixed date and cuts off their return route, as if he kicks away the ladder behind the soldiers when they have climbed up a height. When he leads his army deep into hostile territory, their momentum is trigger-released in battle. He drives his men now in one direction, then in another, like a shepherd driving a flock of sheep, and no one knows where he is going. To assemble the host of his army and bring it into danger—this may be termed the business of the general.

Set the troops to their tasks without revealing your designs. When the task is dangerous, do not tell them its advantageous aspect. Throw them into a perilous situation and they will survive; put them in desperate ground and they will live. For when the army is placed in such a situation, it can snatch victory from defeat.

MAKE VICTORY THE ONLY OPTION—MANAGER'S COMMENTARY

Lead your forces into situations where they cannot retreat.

Underlying Sun Tzu's comments is the idea that the need to survive can do much to rally everyone to achieve goals. The pressure here is of two types: personal or corporate survival.

Corporate Survival: We have seen dramatic success from a common understanding of the need for corporate survival. This was particularly true during the early days of the quality revolution when higher-quality imports threatened lower-quality domestic products. Then the rallying cry was to improve quality in order to stay in business.

Personal Survival: The threat of getting your job done right or losing it has been used by aggressive management at all levels. At companies like Pepsi, it has historically been common knowledge among managers that you make your numbers or you leave.

Competition for personal survival is also keen at the real-world management schools within corporate America such as Disney. Although renowned as a training ground for leaders, the survival process ranges from tough to brutal. For years, the Disney system pitted strong division managers against a strategic planning group that acted as a check on their power. This created inherent conflict between the groups. The best survival strategy was to fly under the radar for as long as possible.

Each individual must build the kind of career strength that makes him marketable. Says Intel's Andrew Grove, "No matter where you work, you are not an employee. You are in a business with one employer—yourself— in competition with millions of similar businesses worldwide . . . . Nobody owes you a career—you own it as a sole proprietor. And the key to survival is to learn to add more value every day."

With each job change or promotion, you increase your career knowledge and your value to the next employer. If you aren't moving up in your organization, then consider moving on.

In hiring people, I have always been impressed when the background indicates that one of the prior employers had a reputation for thorough screening of new hires. After selection comes training. If your company isn't training you, then you should be sending yourself to training—and that includes training inside and outside your profession.

PLAN COORDINATED EFFORTS—TRANSLATION

Sun Tzu continues:

Troops directed by a skillful general are comparable to the Shuai Ran. The Shuai Ran is a snake found in Mount Heng. Strike at its head, and you will be attacked by its tail; strike at its tail, and you will be attacked by its head; strike at its middle, and you will be attacked by both its head and its tail. Should one ask: "Can troops be made capable of such instantaneous coordination as the Shuai Ran?" I reply, "They can." For the men of Wu and the men of Yue are enemies, yet if they are crossing a river in the same boat and are caught by a storm, they will come to each other's assistance just as the left hand helps the right.

Hence, it is not sufficient to rely upon tethering of the horses and the burying of the chariots. The principle of military administration is to achieve a uniform level of courage.

Thus, a skillful general conducts his army just as if he were leading a single man, willy-nilly, by the hand.

The general principles applicable to an invading force are that the deeper you penetrate into hostile territory, the greater will be the solidarity of your troops, and thus the defenders cannot overcome you.

TEAMWORK WORKS

French military historian Colonel Ardant du Picq crystallized the fundamental principle underlying teamwork: "Four brave men who do not know each other well will not dare attack a lion. Four less brave, but knowing each other well, sure of their reliability and consequently of mutual aid, will attack resolutely. There is the science of organization of armies in a nutshell." There is the science of organization for teamwork in a nutshell, as well!

Colonel du Picq continues, "At any time a new invention may assure victory. Granted. But practicable weapons are not invented every day . . . the determining factor, leaving aside generals of genius, and luck, is the quality of troops, that is, the organization that best assures their esprit, their reliability, their confidence, their unity."

PLAN COORDINATED EFFORTS—MANAGER'S COMMENTARY

A united effort has strength.

There are many different ways to coordinate efforts. Coca-Cola has focused on making its worldwide bottling operations more cohesive by building its strength around its larger, stronger partners.

Acquisition is another approach to obtaining a stronger united effort. The most effective acquisitions are "bolt-ons" to existing core strengths. When Disney bought Marvel Comics for $4 billion, purchasing Marvel's 5,000 comic book characters, the company acquired an asset that could easily add value to its existing business—movies, animation, and theme parks.

Many holding companies have reorganized and decentralized in the past decade to improve shareholder value by increasing the accountability and ownership of key business segments—Sara Lee divested several business units into freestanding companies (Coach, Hanes).

Successful companies spend a lot of time forming small teams with the mobility to maneuver. Illinois Tool Works operates through 365 small, decentralized business units that actively practice teamwork with customers and suppliers. Some may think it is inefficient to break the unit into small groups. So is defeat.

Two-time Baldrige winner Solectron is just one of many who have saved billions of dollars with teams focused on process improvement. To achieve this kind of savings, organizations have invested in training people in quality management and teamwork skills. Trained team facilitators are used to enhance team performance.

Forming effective teams takes time and training. The most successful teams are those with the best training and leadership. Successful strategic decisions are most likely to be made by teams that promote active and broad conflict over issues without sacrificing speed. The key to doing so is to mitigate interpersonal conflict. Too often, the absence of conflict is not harmony, it's apathy.

When people are empowered and trained to work effectively in teams, they take ownership of the task, and the entire management process moves from control to commitment.

The team structure must be cascaded throughout the organization. Teamwork is only successful when it is led from the top. When the senior management staff functions as a team, the stage is set for all other units to operate as teams.

PRESS THE ATTACK—TRANSLATION

Sun Tzu continues:
Plunder fertile country to supply your army with plentiful food. Pay attention to the soldiers' well-being and do not fatigue them. Try to keep them in high spirits and conserve their energy. Keep the army moving and devise unfathomable plans.

It is the business of a general to be quiet and thus ensure depth in deliberation; impartial and upright, and thus keep a good management.

He should be able to mystify his officers and men by false reports and appearances, and thus keep them in total ignorance. He changes his arrangements and alters his plans in order to make others unable to see through his strategies. He shifts his campsites and undertakes marches by devious routes so as to make it impossible for others to anticipate his objective.

The different measures appropriate to the nine varieties of ground and the expediency of advance or withdrawal in accordance with circumstances and the fundamental laws of human nature are matters that must be studied carefully by a general.

Generally, when invading a hostile territory, the deeper the troops penetrate, the more cohesive they will be; penetrating only a short way causes dispersion.

When you leave your own country behind, and take your army across neighboring territory, you find yourself on critical ground.

When there are means of communication on all four sides, it is focal ground.

When you penetrate deeply into a country, it is serious ground.

When you penetrate but a little way, it is frontier ground.

When you have the enemy's strongholds on your rear, and narrow passes in front, it is encircled ground. When there is no place of refuge at all, it is desperate ground.

PRESS THE ATTACK—MANAGER'S COMMENTARY

Keep the pressure on.

The success of organizations like Southwest Airlines and Nordstrom was not achieved with a single thrust; instead, they kept pressing the attack as they invaded each successive market.

Southwest Airlines developed systems for turning around planes faster and having crews perform multiple tasks. It kept costs low and innovated low-priced fare structures. Today, Southwest and its successful imitators (like Jet Blue) are continuing to remake the domestic airline business, driving consolidations at legacy carriers and taking prices down with each new market they enter.

Nordstrom developed a customer service philosophy and high-end brand presentation that has made it the envy of the department store industry. In an industry where it is difficult to find a clerk to take your money, Nordstrom made customer service a hallmark. While new discount stores flourish with low-end products, Nordstrom continues its offensive of high quality and value merchandise.

Several key ingredients are common to all growing organizations:

Customer focus: It matters not whether you are in a high-end business category like Nordstrom or more value oriented like Southwest; both are rated high by customers because they have created systems that deliver perceived value.

Selection: The most important contributor to the success of any organization is the ability to hire good people. I spent hours interviewing Phillip Fulmer, head football coach at the University of Tennessee, as I assisted with his book *Legacy of Winning*. Fulmer had one of the top winning records in college football and as such attracted good people. However, he didn't sit around waiting for them to knock on the door; he had a well-organized, systematic campaign to analyze candidates and encourage the best to sign up on his team.

Training: Hiring good people alone is not enough. Whether coaching a sports team or leading a business venture, you must be able to train the unit to be the very best. Extensive training on an ongoing basis is the hallmark of premier organizations where learning sessions are highly interactive.

The pressure necessary for success is applied by good people working within good systems that empower them to use their skills.

LEARN WINNING WAYS—TRANSLATION

Sun Tzu continues:

Therefore, in dispersive ground, I would unify the determination of the army. In frontier ground, I would keep my forces closely linked. In key ground, I would hasten up my rear elements. In open ground, I would pay close attention to my defense. In focal ground, I would consolidate my alliances. In serious ground, I would ensure a continuous flow of provisions. In difficult ground, I would press on over the road. In encircled ground, I would block the points of access and egress. In desperate ground, I would make it evident that there is no chance of survival. For it is the nature of soldiers to resist when surrounded, to fight hard when there is no alternative, and to follow commands implicitly when they have fallen into danger.

One ignorant of the designs of neighboring states cannot enter into alliance with them; if ignorant of the conditions of mountains, forests, dangerous defiles, swamps, and marshes, he cannot conduct the march of an army; if he fails to make use of native guides, he cannot gain the advantages of the ground.

An army does not deserve the title of the invincible Army of the Hegemonic King if its commander is ignorant of even one of these nine varieties of ground. Now, when such an invincible army attacks a powerful state, it makes it impossible for the enemy to assemble his forces. It overawes the enemy and prevents his allies from joining him. It follows that one does not need to seek alliances with other neighboring states, nor is there any need to foster the power of other states, but only to pursue one's own strategic designs to overawe his enemy. Then one can take the enemy's cities and overthrow the enemy's state.

Bestow rewards irrespective of customary practice and issue orders irrespective of convention and you can command a whole army as though it were but one man.

LEARN WINNING WAYS—MANAGER'S COMMENTARY

Problems are opportunities.

Winning companies are always on the offensive: Dell with new products and new markets overseas, Nucor Steel with the lowest labor cost per ton, and Wal-Mart with its ever-expanding international network of new stores.

Here are a few fundamental characteristics of winners:

Fight the battles that count: While you should not fight political battles you cannot win, when you win political battles and make enemies, you run the risk of becoming weaker. In too many cases, qualified, active people are not promoted because they have made enemies. When you can win and retain good relationships, only then can you become strong.

Avoid the avoidable: The process of avoiding the avoidable is understanding that physical hazards are identifiable obstacles against which specific measures can be taken. In contrast, the human element is completely unpredictable. Take specific actions to reduce the possibility of defeat as a result of physical conditions. This lets you devote full resources to dealing with unpredictable human elements.

Every document you present has both form and substance. You must go for the ultimate quality in the physical element of form so it doesn't detract from the more psychological elements of substance.

Considering the fragility of the human element, leave all possibilities for controllable physical mistakes to your opponent and organize for minimum physical defects in your operation. Do not allow your plan to fail because of the quality of the product or the delivery time or any physical element. The organization for excellence does not require that headquarters assumes control of everything—often decentralization is the best way to avoid physical problems.

Communicate expectations; reward achievements: Everyone must understand performance expectations in terms of specific, identifiable goals and rewards. People respond in relation to the way they are measured and rewarded.

Use a written charter to assign tasks to a team and establish boundaries. The team develops a mission statement and reconciles it with the chartering authority. Hold a celebration when results are achieved.

Set high goals: The way to consistently hit your target is to plan to achieve beyond the target. Then when you fall short, you will probably hit your goal.

ATTACK BY FIRE

Management Rules

- Be Disruptive and Intrusive
- Consolidate Your Gains
- Exercise Restraint

People who concentrate all of their efforts on tactical issues only are working short-term. They will eventually be overwhelmed by those who are doing the right thing today as part of a longer-term strategic plan. We can find the overemphasis on tactics in those who work in the more tactical selling and advertising areas of business. The overly tactical salesperson is characterized by one who concentrates only on the immediate sale and not on the long-term selling and service relationship with the customer. Overly tactical advertising concentrates on low prices without considering the debilitating effects of too much price advertising. There's an admonition: "People don't buy price; they are sold price."

The right long-term strategy can be in conflict with the need for immediate results. While a particular strategic approach may appear conceptually sound, the organization may deplete its resources before the plan yields results.

Battles can be won with tactics; however, long-range business victory comes only with the proper balance of strategy and tactics. Strategic results can be achieved only with the right mix of thinking and doing.

The offensive military commander has always known that breakthroughs are opportunities that must be exploited. Somehow, this simple truth often gets lost in the bureaucracy of organizations.

For organizations to change, the culture must change. One of the most difficult tasks facing managers who want to initiate change is how to overcome the ghosts of past corporate cultures. Even when senior managers let go of control and try to decentralize, they find scores of subordinates patiently waiting for instructions or authority. Leaders who want to reshape organizational culture must continually and actively reinforce the messages they want to deliver.

BE DISRUPTIVE AND INTRUSIVE—TRANSLATION

Sun Tzu says:

There are five ways of attacking with fire. The first is to burn soldiers in their camp; the second, to burn provision and stores; the third, to burn baggage-trains; the fourth, to burn arsenals and magazines; and the fifth, to burn the lines of transportation.

To use fire, some medium must be relied upon. Materials for setting fire must always be at hand. There are suitable seasons to attack with fire, and special days for starting a conflagration. The suitable seasons are when the weather is very dry; the special days are those when the moon is in the constellations of the Sieve, the Wall, the Wing or the Cross-bar; for when the moon is in these positions there are likely to be strong winds all day long.

Now, in attacking with fire, one must respond to the five changing situations: When fire breaks out in the enemy's camp, immediately coordinate your action from without. If there is an outbreak of fire, but the enemy's soldiers remain calm, bide your time and do not attack. When the force of the flames has reached its height, follow it up with an attack, if that is practicable; if not, stay where you are. If fires can be raised from outside the enemy's camps, it is not necessary to wait until they are started inside. Attack with fire only when the moment is suitable. If the fire starts from up-wind, do not launch attack from down-wind. When the wind continues blowing during the day, then it is likely to die down at night.

Now, the army must know the five different fire-attack situations and wait for appropriate times.

Those who use fire to assist their attacks can achieve tangible results; those who use inundations can make their attacks more powerful. Water can intercept and isolate an enemy, but cannot deprive him of the supplies or equipment.

BE DISRUPTIVE AND INTRUSIVE—MANAGER'S COMMENTARY

Disrupt the mind and intrude into that disruption.

The Swatch Watch brand initially launched itself in Germany with a fully functioning 150-yard-long watch on the side of a prominent bank building in Frankfurt. When I wanted to emphasize a profit opportunity in software, I arranged for $1 million in one-dollar bills to be stacked in a giant 20-foot high display at a trade show. When FedEx launched its Saturday delivery service it sent 30,000 coffee cakes to FedEx customers—delivered by FedEx, of course.

Every commander in battle strives to achieve the breakthrough. In business, too often the search is confined to the need for sheer numbers to achieve the breakthrough. As we increase our efforts, so do our opponents. After each failure to achieve the breakthrough, the reaction is to call for a little more effort.

When we wish for just a little more time, more funds, more prospects, or more customers, we fail to realize that "just a little more" is not enough. While one company may be planning for just a little more, a competitor may be focusing on achieving a lot more. Guess who wins? Expect unexpected competition and organize for extraordinary achievements.

When we are successful in the attack, it is because of a carefully planned, extraordinary effort. Military leaders say that in order to achieve a breakthrough, two major events must happen:

1. Dislocation: You cannot hit the enemy unless you have first created the opportunity.
2. Exploitation: You cannot make that effect decisive unless you exploit the opportunity before he can recover.

The business equivalent to dislocation and exploitation is to be "disruptive" and "intrusive." You must disrupt the mind and intrude into that disruption.

Disruptive and intrusive communications have been achieved in a variety of ways. The activity ranges from the unexpected appearance of the boss at an employee event to the publicity stunt that achieves worldwide coverage.

Neither the disruption nor the intrusion that creates attention should be crass or offensive. If the disruption puts people in a negative frame of mind, the strategy backfires. To be effective, the intrusion must be directly related to your message.

CONSOLIDATE YOUR GAINS—TRANSLATION

Sun Tzu continues:

Now, to win battles and capture lands and cities but to fail to consolidate these achievements is ominous and may be described as a waste of resources and time. And, therefore, the enlightened rulers must deliberate upon the plans to go to battle, and good generals carefully execute them.

CONSOLIDATE YOUR GAINS—MANAGER'S COMMENTARY

Develop sustainable loyalty.

Your objective is not just to win; your objective must be to sustain victory. When the values of the organization focus on rewarding and motivating all stakeholders, continued victory is assured.

Make the sale and lose the customer and you lose the war. In any endeavor, the highest cost is the first sale. Earning that sale is only the basis for future relationships.

The sales manager of one of the world's largest container manufacturers told me he could attribute 58 percent of his business to long-term partnering arrangements. In each instance, his company served as the sole or primary supplier to the customer. Business partnerships between customers and suppliers have become an excellent way to convert a series of transactions into a lasting relationship.

Loyalty programs that reward repeat customers are another way to develop continuing relationships. Winning is not achieved in completing one transaction; victory is in the value of multiple purchases over time. Customer loyalty is earned by those organizations that "delight" the customer. That is, these companies do not just make a sale; they satisfy the customer in such an overwhelming manner that a long-term relationship is established. Considerable evidence exists that repeat customers spend more money and are more profitable. The lifelong value of a customer at a gas station accumulates into revenue of tens of thousands of dollars and at an automobile dealership into hundreds of thousands of dollars.

Strong leaders understand that employee loyalty is as important as customer loyalty. At Hewlett-Packard, when Lewis Platt's wife died, he was thrust into the role of a single parent. When Platt reached the chief executive's position, he found that women employees were leaving in droves. Platt developed a new workplace strategy that actively encouraged employees to adjust their workweeks to meet personal responsibilities. In a memo to employees, Platt stated, "Attention to work/life issues strengthens HP's competitive edge and improves teamwork." When Platt moved up to chairman, his replacement became the third woman to head a *Fortune* 500 company.

EXERCISE RESTRAINT—TRANSLATION

Sun Tzu continues:

If not in the interests of the state, do not act. If you are not sure of success, do not use troops. If you are not in danger, do not fight a battle.

A sovereign should not launch a war simply out of anger, nor should a general fight a war simply out of resentment. Take action if it is to your advantage; cancel the action if it is not. An angered man can be happy again, just as a resentful one can feel pleased again, but a state that has perished can never revive, nor can a dead man be brought back to life.

Therefore, with regard to the matter of war, the enlightened ruler is prudent, and the good general is full of caution. Thus, the state is kept secure and the army preserved.

EXERCISE RESTRAINT—MANAGER'S COMMENTARY

Do not fight battles you cannot win—or win those that lose the war.

External Restraint: Manufacturers who want to invade new foreign markets have not been very successful with the head-on attack of heavy advertising investments and massive campaigns. New markets are conquered by deliberate, skillfully executed campaigns focused on methodically outmaneuvering entrenched competitors.

Coke has a large share of the Japanese market for soft drinks because it took the time and made the investment to build a full range of functional strengths. When Coke made its first move into Japan, it found a complex, multilayered distribution system. Using local bottlers, Coke recreated the kind of sales force it uses in the United States. Instead of servicing accounts with independent wholesalers or distributors, in Japan today the Coke van replaces empty bottles with new ones. By investing heavily in resources in the distribution system, Coke redefined the domestic game in Japan. Short-term financial returns were sacrificed to achieve long-term gains. Now, as it establishes itself in China, Coke is adapting this same game plan to another fast-growing market.

A different approach in the invasion of markets is to use existing distributors and/or sales representatives as the delivery system. Only after strength is achieved is the transition made to corporate distribution centers by either purchasing distribution facilities or buying out agreements. The growth of successful distribution in many industries nationally can be traced to the use of outside agents to internally controlled delivery systems.

Internal Restraint: The issue of fighting a battle you cannot win has special applications for corporate politics. Good politicians negotiate; bad politicians fight battles.

Hundreds of years before Christ, a Chinese warlord gave the following advice, which has real application for corporate politics:

One who gains one victory becomes the Emperor;
One who gains two, a King;
One who gains three, Lord Protector;
One who gains four is exhausted;
One who gains five victories suffers calamity.

EMPLOYMENT OF SECRET AGENTS

Management Rules

- Invest in Intelligence Resources
- Establish an Active Intelligence System
- Practice Counterintelligence

In many organizations, a major problem is organizing, synthesizing, and disseminating information. Most organizations are plagued with "islands of information." Many people know many things, but no system exists to put it all together for verification and application to specific objectives. Even in the CIA, most of the information is obtained from overt, not covert, sources. The biggest job for any intelligence unit is organizing and interpreting readily available information.

Uncertainty surrounds many of the issues challenging the manager. The antidote for uncertainty is more relevant information. The more information available, the longer the time needed to process it and the greater the danger of failing to distinguish between the relevant and the irrelevant.

According to General Gordon R. Sullivan, a retired army chief of staff, "The paradox of war in the Information Age is one of managing massive amounts of information and resisting the temptation to over-control it. The competitive advantage is nullified when you try to run decisions up and down the chain of command . . . . Once the commander's intent is understood, decisions must be devolved to the lowest possible level to allow these front line soldiers to exploit the opportunities that develop."

Wegmans Food Markets, headquartered in upstate New York, has been described in the *Wall Street Journal* as a retailer somewhere between Nordstrom and Harrods. Wegmans's store managers regularly hold focus-group sessions with eight to ten customers to discuss their likes and dislikes. Because this front-line research is conducted by store managers with their own customers, suggestions can be immediately implemented. This is just one reason why Wegmans's average store volume is four times greater than the national average.

INVEST IN INTELLIGENCE RESOURCES—TRANSLATION

Sun Tzu says:

Generally, when an army of one hundred thousand is raised and dispatched on a distant war, the expenses borne by the people together with the disbursements made by the treasury will amount to a thousand pieces of gold per day. There will be continuous commotion both at home and abroad; people will be involved with convoys and exhausted from performing transportation services, and seven hundred thousand households will be unable to continue their farmwork.

Hostile armies confront each other for years in order to struggle for victory in a decisive battle; yet if one who begrudges the expenditure of one-hundred pieces of gold in honors and emoluments remains ignorant of his enemy's situation, he is completely devoid of humanity. Such a man is no leader of the troops; no capable assistant to his sovereign; no master of victory.

COLLECT ALL AVAILABLE DATA

The first rule of data collection is stated in the army regulations of the People's Republic of China:

Every commander must organize reconnaissance within his unit's zone of activities. He must not wait for instructions from his superior, nor must he seek his superior's decision as to whether he should organize reconnaissance.

The second rule of data collection is that much of what you need to know is already known. To learn what needs to be done, search your neighborhood or benchmark the world, and you will find someone who is already doing "it" successfully. Theodore Levitt says it this way: "The future doesn't descend on us on some prophetic day . . . it grows out of forces which are now turbulently in motion."

INVEST IN INTELLIGENCE RESOURCES— MANAGER'S COMMENTARY

Information is crucial to winning.

Successful ventures do good intelligence homework so they can target their products.

Accurate intelligence allows for better use of your resources. The information derived reduces risks because you have the data that gives you better odds. Only a gambler with inside information can rationally bet her whole stake on a single race. Good marketing research management puts you in the business of managing risks instead of taking risks.

The key assumption of intelligence is that an impression of what is not known can be pieced together by studying what is known. Good strategy needs good assumptions, and good assumptions are a product of good intelligence.

America's most successful corporations have large cadres of internal and external market research services. They treat marketing research as a corporate asset because it helps them market more effectively and efficiently.

It is easy to do bad market research because we so often want to ask the questions that will tell us what we want to hear. Before determining questions, you must learn everything you can about the area you want to study. That means personal visits to the places where your product or service is consumed.

Too often, we think that knowledge of ourselves and our opponent is a destination we've already reached. Gathering knowledge is an ongoing, dynamic, feedback process.

Improper action from advance signals can exacerbate the problem. An abundance of information incorrectly interpreted can lead to fatally wrong conclusions.

In intelligence failures, the problem is not that the information is unavailable; rather, it is not taken seriously by commanders who, once committed to a course of action based on bureaucratic consensus, refuse to recognize the validity of contrary data and are unwilling to abandon the original operation.

You must know your opponent and understand her strengths and weaknesses. You must understand everything you can about the current and future markets for your product, service, or idea.

ESTABLISH AN ACTIVE INTELLIGENCE SYSTEM—TRANSLATION

Sun Tzu continues:

Now, the reason that the enlightened sovereign and the wise general conquer the enemy whenever they move and their achievements surpass those of ordinary men is that they have foreknowledge. This "foreknowledge" cannot be elicited from spirits, nor from gods, nor by analogy with past events, nor by any deductive calculations. It must be obtained from the men who know the enemy situation.

Hence, the use of spies, of whom there are five sorts: native spies, internal spies, converted spies, doomed spies, and surviving spies.

When all these five sorts of spies are at work and none knows their method of operation, it would be divinely intricate and constitutes the greatest treasure of a sovereign.

Native spies are those we employ from the enemy's country people. Internal spies are enemy officials whom we employ.

Converted spies are enemy spies whom we employ.

Doomed spies are those of our own spies who are deliberately given false information and told to report it.

Surviving spies are those who return from the enemy camp to report information.

Hence, of all those in the army close to the commander, none is more intimate than the spies; of all rewards, none more liberal than those given to spies; of all matters, none is more confidential than those relating to spying operations.

He who is not sage cannot use spies. He who is not humane and generous cannot use spies. And he who is not delicate and subtle cannot get the truth out of them. Delicate indeed! Truly delicate!

ESTABLISH AN ACTIVE INTELLIGENCE SYSTEM— MANAGER'S COMMENTARY

Establish a methodology for processing information.

Organize your information flow. The process of gathering intelligence is one of collecting and filtering. All information is not useful; too much information can make it difficult to separate the useful from the useless. One of the key decisions in processing information is how to be selective in the information flow to each level of management.

The ultimate solution is a combination of:

- Structure, which sizes the organization's decision-making process;
- Good information available at all levels;
- Personal reconnaissance on the part of decision makers at every level.

Make information useful. To make scattered information useful, it has to be pulled together piece by piece and developed to form distinct patterns to enlighten all echelons. This coordinating process is what makes intelligence useful. Confronted with a task and not having enough information to perform the task, an organization will either centralize or decentralize.

Centralizing keeps decision thresholds high and increases the information flow. Centralization also requires more information processing capability, thereby creating a more complex system.

Decentralizing divides the task into parts and establishes focal points to deal with each part. This relocates the decision thresholds to lower levels.

Most often, the best choice will be to decentralize and segment the task into manageable parts. This requires management that is willing to accept less certainty at the top in order to have more certainty at the bottom.

Systems are not solutions. Too often, managers are disappointed because they expected the new information system to provide new solutions. Battles are not won with systems; they are won with that supreme weapon—the personal factor.

Although it would seem the command structure should determine whether the information system should be centralized or decentralized, often the reverse is true. It is the ability of the system to absorb and process information that determines whether a centralized or decentralized command structure can be the most effective way to organize.

PRACTICE COUNTERINTELLIGENCE—TRANSLATION

Sun Tzu continues:

There is no place where espionage is not possible. If plans relating to spying operations are prematurely divulged, the spy and all those to whom he spoke of them should be put to death.

Generally, whether it be armies that you wish to strike, cities that you wish to attack, and individuals that you wish to assassinate, it is necessary to find out the names of the garrison commander, the aides-de-camp, the ushers, gatekeepers, and bodyguards. You must instruct your spies to ascertain these matters in minute detail.

It is essential to seek out enemy spies who have come to conduct espionage against you and bribe them to serve you. Courteously exhort them and give your instructions, then release them back home. Thus, converted spies are recruited and used. It is through the information brought by the converted spies that native and internal spies can be recruited and employed. It is owing to their information, again, that the doomed spies, armed with false information, can be sent to convey it to the enemy. Lastly, it is by their information that the surviving spies can come back and give information as scheduled. The sovereign must have full knowledge of the activities of the five sorts of spies. And to know these depends upon the converted spies. Therefore, it is mandatory that they be treated with the utmost liberality.

In ancient times, the rise of the Shang Dynasty was due to Yi Zhi, who had served under the Xia. Likewise, the rise of the Zhou Dynasty was due to Lu Ya, who had served under the Yin. Therefore, it is only the enlightened sovereign and the wise general who are able to use the most intelligent people as spies and achieve great results. Spying operations are essential in war; upon them the army relies to make its every move.

PRACTICE COUNTERINTELLIGENCE—MANAGER'S COMMENTARY

While you get their secrets, protect your own.

You should take deliberate steps to keep competitors from learning what is going on in your business. For example, at one headquarters, a poster in the company cafeteria reminds employees that, "Loose lips sink ships." The media has run enough stories about corporate espionage to make managers aware of the danger, but constant reminders are needed.

When a smaller entrepreneur visited Japan, he found to his surprise that the practice of gathering competitive information is not confined to big companies. After a few drinks one evening, his host took him to a file cabinet and produced a file containing information about the visitor's company.

The first bastion of counterintelligence is usually a memo that requires all employees to refer outside inquiries for information to the public relations officer. This is a good practice since the stories are legion from managers who tell about making a phone call to a targeted company and learning everything they wanted to know.

At the next level of protection are security measures such as a paper shredder in key offices and numbering systems to control key documents like new product plans. Every manager should be concerned about documents on his desk in view of visitors because too many people have learned how to read upside down. The best way to handle visitors is to meet them in a separate conference room with no visible company information.

Security measures are not limited to the office. Although laptop computers are useful on an airline flight, keep in mind that the information may also be useful to a nearby passenger.

The top level of protection is active measures involving checking for bugs in telephones and making sure that rooms engaged for outside conferences are secure and no material is left behind after the meeting.

PART TWO

Sun Tzu

FOR EXECUTION

Chapter 4

Simplicity

Great business successes are most often based on simple ideas:

- Michael Dell revolutionized computers by making them to order.
- Southwest took costs out of the airline business and offered customers lower fares.
- Whole Foods brought a wide selection of organic foods to customers across the country.

Simple ideas, executed with gusto, have a tendency to work. And they work despite their shortcomings.

- Dell computers started out less reliable than store-bought computers.
- Southwest forced customers to travel to less familiar airports.
- Whole Foods' nickname—"whole paycheck"—is almost as familiar as the brand itself.

Executing with simplicity lets you win versus larger competitors. The airline business is being remade by companies with simple business models. Southwest is not alone in offering a focused low-price model. Jet Blue executes that model well, also. Both companies are doing very well against competitors with a more dizzying array of strategies.

United fights back with an expensive (expensive for them, free for flyers) rewards program, an off-price airline named Ted, and their international Star Alliance. They also copy Southwest innovations like boarding by group instead of by seat number. You pick a strategy, they've got it. Complexity built on complexity.

Which airline would you bet on?

Simple ideas win in the marketplace. They win because they:

Lower cost structures. Complexity is expensive. It is expensive to maintain. It is expensive to teach to your employees. It is expensive to explain to customers. More than anything, the intricacies of complexity require costs that are sometimes hidden. Southwest operates one kind of plane—their competitors offer many. Whole Foods is small versus many of their competitors and overall lacks "scale" in its buying—but among organic food producers, it is the big kahuna (and it aggressively uses its relative importance to those particular producers to buy those foods well).

Build mass on a single idea. People can understand simple ideas. It's not that people are simple—it's that people lead complicated and busy lives. In research study after research study, Whole Foods was found to mean "organics." They can be beat on many other measures, but they own that idea in consumers' brains.

Are simple enough that your employees can execute them. Your employees can execute ideas they understand. Your employees' lives are busy too—and their complicated or challenging personal lives will make it difficult for them to focus on their work sometimes. "Work/life balance" will more frequently tilt to an emphasis on their personal life and issues. If you can make it easy for your employees to understand how to succeed at work, and reward them in a way that encourages that behavior, they are more likely to give you what you want. The simpler the idea, the easier it is to get everyone to understand it and make daily decisions that support it.

Think of the changing of the guards of the world's largest companies—from General Motors to Wal-Mart. For years Wal-Mart executed one simple thing—low prices. They built logistics and IT strengths that allowed them to deliver goods to customers at lower prices than anyone else.

Wal-Mart replaced General Motors as the world's largest company. GM operated many divisions, with confusing product lineups. Many of their brands lost their simple distinctiveness (think of the clarity of "Mercedes" versus "Oldsmobile" or "Buick"). There is little simplicity in the positioning of any GM brand. GM brands that are fuzzy in their meaning—Pontiac and Buick and even Saab—are regularly rumored to be at risk of following Oldsmobile to the brand scrap heap. Today, GM continues to slip in performance.

Advice on simplicity reverberates through history—in the U.S. Army's *Infantry in Battle,* the U.S. Army advises, "In war the simplest way is usually the best way. Direct, simple plans, clear, concise orders, formations that facilitate control, and routes that are unmistakably defined will smooth the way for subordinate elements, minimize the confusion of combat and ordinarily increase the chances of success. In brief, simplicity is the sword with which the capable leader may cut the Gordian knot of many a baffling situation."

IKEA, the chain of mammoth furniture stores, says succinctly, "Simplicity is complexity resolved." IKEA is a mammoth store—but always consistently mammoth. If you have been in one, you know what to expect. You know the layout will be a "racetrack" around the store. You know they sell ready-to-assemble furniture. And you know they sell just furniture and closely related items. IKEA may sell a giant selection of items, but they make that selection very understandable for their shoppers.

IKEA embraces simplicity in their merchandising strategy as well. When IKEA wants you to understand they have chairs for you, they merchandise them—with mass. They put numerous chairs, in a variety of styles and settings, in the front of their stores. Whoever you are, you can't miss that IKEA has a chair for you—and you immediately see how it fits into your lifestyle and your home.

Any merchandising person will tell you simplicity works. In fact, an old merchandising phrase is "Pile it high, and watch them buy." Pile one thing high. A week later, pile up something else and watch that item sell too! Simplicity doesn't limit creativity. It simply channels it.

Committing to a simple idea works.

COMMUNICATE WITH SIMPLICITY

Execution Rules

- Keep it brief.
- Say it over and over again.
- Make it relevant.

> To direct a large army to fight is the same as to direct a
> small one: it is a matter of command signs and signals.
> —Sun Tzu

Great communication—winning communication—starts with simplicity. When you deliver a simple message over and over again, you create great clarity with your customers, your employees, and in the marketplace. Thus, a simple, clear message creates an opportunity for your customers or employees to understand, and take action, on the message you are sending.

In advertising, this is called a positioning statement. In a positioning statement, you outline one benefit.

- Volvos are safe.
- Wal-Mart has low prices.
- Target is fashionable.
- FedEx is on time.
- "Nobody doesn't like Sara Lee."

One idea repeated consistently over time has great impact.

Procter and Gamble for years said that Secret antiperspirant was "Strong enough for a man, but made for a woman." Brand manager after brand manager worked with, and executed, that one simple line in a variety of ways. It worked—the Secret brand has done well in the market for many years. After decades of using that same line, how do you evolve it for a new millennium? "Strong enough for a woman." It's a subtle change and a nice evolution—the simple statement subtly says something about the strength of women. Yet the new line still builds on decades and tens of millions of dollars of investment in the prior line.

It is memorable when an advertising communication works in the marketplace and contains more than a single benefit. The original Miller Lite campaign is one such example. Miller Lite built its business with memorable communications that carried two benefits: "Tastes great, less filling." In the early years, each commercial revolved entirely around those words, with famous athletes arguing over whether the beer was great because it was less filling or it tasted great. The arguments in the commercials told the story of the dual benefits. Repeated over years, with a giant beer industry advertising budget, the campaign worked. And the campaign achieved some fame in the advertising industry precisely because of the multiple benefits of the communication, and the TV ads that effectively delivered that message.

Think of the flip side of simple communications. Companies and brands that change their message annually have no meaning. What's Burger King communicating today? Undoubtedly, something different than they communicated a couple of years ago.

Sometimes, simple communications seem to get lost in corporate gobbledygook. Samsung says, "A better world is our business." NEC is "Empowered by innovation." Fujitsu says, "The possibilities are infinite." Siemens? "Global network of innovation" is their line. Any of these lines could be swapped interchangeably between these companies (and across a variety of additional industries). That's not the simplicity customers look for—good simplicity boils concepts down to their essence. In marketing and branding, taglines that can easily be switched across companies and industries don't reflect that crystallization. Thus, companies need to work even harder and spend more to add relevant meaning to the brand.

Most airlines jump from tagline to tagline. Delta over time has told us "Delta is ready when you are," "You'll love the way we fly," and "We love to fly. And it shows." Each communication may be valid, but failing to execute a *consistent* idea over time deprives your customers of the chance to deeply understand, and identify with, your story.

In politics, the latest term is *framing,* defined by Matt Bai of the *New York Times* in "The Framing Wars" in his July 17, 2005 article as "choosing the language to define a debate and, more importantly, with fitting individual issues into the contexts of broader story lines." In essence, framing is fitting your communication into a relevant context and then telling that story over and over.

Simple Communications to People

When CEO Roger Smith retired from General Motors, he was leaving a company in difficult condition. His time with the organization included a reorganization of questionable merit, an acquisition of EDS that provided questionable benefits, and a product line of questionable quality. Yet, at the time of his retirement, he felt his greatest failure was in communicating a consistent strategy to his people.

Jack Welch and his disciples do the opposite. They repeatedly sell their strategy to their people. With repetition, they believe, the message gets through to, and eventually gets understood by, the employees of a large organization.

The Sam's Club division of Wal-Mart is a big business whose results have, until recently, lagged its largest rival—Costco. Results improved under Sam's Club president Kevin Turner, who consistently talked to the Sam's team about five priorities. He has said to analysts, "I don't have a different five points for you this afternoon than I did this morning. They are the same five points that we'll have next week and that everyone at every level of our organization is working on." At a recent Wal-Mart annual meeting, CEO Lee Scott said the president of the Sam's Club division had "brought a consistent message to the organization."

Storytelling is an old tradition. Consultant Bob Rosenfeld, of Idea Connections, continually urges his clients to "tell stories." By telling a story, you give people a context in which to understand your communications (a "frame of reference" in advertising terminology). In people terms, storytelling frequently can add a level of sincerity and believability.

Telling a story to people can be a personal experience. It can be a way of connecting a strategy with people in human terms. Norm Rich, the CEO of Weis Markets, says, "You can't sell your ideas until you sell yourself." Use personal stories to sell yourself.

CHOOSE YOUR TIMING

Execution Rules

- Pick the time that works for you.
- Be disciplined.
- Move swiftly to consolidate gains.

When torrential water tosses boulders, it is because of its momentum; when the strike of a hawk breaks the body of its prey, it is because of timing. Thus, in battle, a good commander creates a posture releasing an irresistible and overwhelming momentum, and his attack is precisely timed in quick tempo. The energy is similar to a fully drawn crossbow; the timing, the release of the trigger.
—Sun Tzu

You are in control. That is a simple fact many of us minimize in the marketplace. The projects you choose to work on and the timing you select to launch them are all up to you.

Every company is buffeted by the actions of its competitors. Those competitive actions do affect us—we can't ignore our competitors. However, you can't allow those competitive actions to dominate your every action in the marketplace. If you do, the competitor has already won because it is controlling your agenda. Competitive reactions are just part of the process of business.

Taking control of timing lets you dictate your priorities—and your competitors' priorities. You can't control the competitive marketplace, but you can control the timing of your most important initiatives. Choose to be the competitor in charge of the agenda. Keep your competitors working on reacting to *you*. Remember:

Where your competitor is weak, choose to strike there. A weak store location, a weak line of goods, or a poorly priced set of products all represent opportunities. That weakness may not last forever. When a retailer expands its geography unsuccessfully, look for competitors to move in next to the vulnerable stores. When a company has a narrow line of goods and is successful, look for larger competitors to introduce "flanker" products that compete directly with the smaller competitor. A supplier of mine recently said in a meeting that he was introducing a new line of goods in the coming year specifically to take the sales of a smaller niche player and drive it out of business.

When your competitor stumbles, move in. Look at the airline industry. Southwest's move into the East Coast a few years back created additional troubles for an already struggling US Air. Southwest did not wait for someone else to come in and take US Air's business—it took it itself.

Where you have a temporary advantage, exploit it, and see if you can build long-term advantage from it. Some meat companies own their own livestock (or birds). Some buy on the open market. When the markets are in your favor, your profits are higher than your competitors'. And companies with a cost advantage use some of their additional profits to pick up business at accounts they believe they can keep for the long term.

You can only do a few things well. So execute your most important priorities on the timing that is best for you. Disrupt the marketplace, and your competitors' plans, by being disciplined about bringing your best products and services to market at a timing (and place) of your choice. Bring your best ideas to market just before a key seasonality or with your best customer or with a large customer you would like to pick up.

Good companies make plans and work to execute them. Great companies will also be opportunistic and quickly take advantage of opportunities when they arise—fitting these opportunities into *their* plans as they choose to.

Many well-run retailers alter their growth plans when real estate becomes available. When Kmart sold off significant chunks of real estate, Home Depot moved in and snatched up some new locations. When pressure from Wal-Mart put Northeastern retailers Bradley's and Ames out of business, regional supermarket retailers added many new locations to their portfolios. None of these new locations were in their annual business plans, but plans need to change. And all these real estate acquisitions likely fit a broader framework—the timing simply changed as the opportunities arose.

Move Swiftly

In many Internet businesses, acquiring customers is relatively easy compared to retaining them. A fast-growing, Internet-based deliverer of fresh foods in New York City is FreshDirect. After they acquire a new customer, the hard work begins, and that work needs to be done quickly. Why? Because the speed with which someone makes their first *several* purchases dictates their loyalty. If FreshDirect gets them to make several purchases fast, that customer has changed his or her habit. If the customer makes that switch slowly, he or she may not make that switch at all.

Many businesses find that building loyalty is about moving swiftly. When you acquire new customers, keep them buying from you. "Continuity" programs are designed to do this. Coffee clubs at your local coffee shop are an example of these—buy five cups and your sixth one is free. A strong trial promotion ("first cup of coffee free") combined with a continuity promotion ("buy five cups of coffee, the sixth one is free") is a good way to move customers swiftly into the habit of buying your product.

Keep your programs and timing simple. Complicated plans with complex timing rarely work.

CLARITY

Execution Rules

- Synchronize your actions to get clarity.
- Set expectations.
- Reinforce behavior you want to see again.

> Hence, in night fighting, usually use drums and gongs;
> in day fighting, banners and flags. Now, these instruments are used to unify action of the troops.
> —Sun Tzu

For customers, a strong brand has great clarity in its meaning. Consistent execution, repeated over years, brings clarity to a brand. Some examples:

- Hertz has executed a high-service strategy for years. Hertz Gold service levels and ad campaigns like "Not Exactly" (if it's another rental company, it's not exactly Hertz, not quite as good as Hertz) have given the brand clear service leadership. Maybe not whom you call first for the best price, but the place you know will give you the best service.

- Apple has consistently innovated in computers and electronics. Their brand isn't always the sales leader, but it is the perceived innovator. This strength allowed the brand to jump into digital music, and the company to shift its sales mix significantly into this new business.
- Godiva sells upscale chocolates. With premium packaging and premium prices, it has resisted cheaper offerings. Godiva remains a vogue choice for gift giving. Have you ever seen Godiva displayed in a low-end retailer? In general, you will find Godiva in higher-rent districts, in settings that reinforce the fashion mystique of the brand. New York's new Time-Warner Center has very pricey real estate— and you will find a Godiva chocolate shop there. When Godiva seeks distribution outside of its own stores, it is very selective. Godiva is found in department stores, a few specialty shops, and a few upscale food retailers.

Clarity of distribution reinforces clarity of a brand. Manufacturers who proactively manage their distribution generally end up with retailers who add value to their brand. Godiva is found in settings that reinforce the brand's fashion imagery. The premium settings for Godiva strengthen the meaning of the brand.

Years ago, Coors had a mystique fueled by its distribution. For most of its history, Coors's distribution was restricted to eleven states near its Colorado home. Travelers coming home from business trips to that geography would bring home a six-pack of Coors. Stories grew up (some false, but still complimentary to the brand) about why Coors was available only in a limited geography. Sometimes the story was that Coors could travel only so far because of the way it was made or because of the refrigerated trucks Coors had to be transported on. Or Coors was just so popular in its home geography that there wasn't enough for the whole country. The 1977 movie *Smokey and the Bandit* centered on a shipment of Coors from Texas to Georgia. In fact, the product was not pasteurized and so needed to be kept cold, increasing the complexity and cost of distribution.

When they expanded nationally, that mystique was lost. Two breweries were opened outside of the West. And a tagline of fifty years, "Brewed with pure Rocky Mountain spring water," had to change. The product itself was forced to stand on its own merits—taste. While Coors is good, it is not necessarily better than any other beer. Today, the Coors mystique has been so diminished that it now lags its Coors Light "flanker" in sales. Regional "craft" beers (Kona Brewing in Hawaii, Brooklyn Beer in New York, and many others) now own the mystique of the regionally available beer.

Clarity Through People

Plans need to be executed by an organization's people. Guiding your people to good execution requires clarity in how you communicate to them. Bring clarity of your company's vision, or your company's desired meaning, to customers by:

Building Core Values. Building a consistent set of expectations can drive desired performance across levels of management. At Costco, the culture encourages getting ever more value for its "members." Stories are told about products, like salmon, where the company was able to get even greater value for its members—lowering prices and increasing quality over many years as Costco grew. Building value for members drives actions of employees across the organization. Anyone at Costco knows that adding value to members is what that company is about.

Making "heroes" of employees. Make heroes of employees who bring your values to life. Skillful communicators are constantly involving their audience. Skillful leaders constantly involve their own people as examples of behaviors they want repeated. Employee-of-the-month-style programs can build this—particularly when simple criteria for selection are communicated. These programs celebrate behaviors that you want replicated throughout the organization.

Celebrating successes. The successes you choose to celebrate will build an expectation of the behavior that gets rewarded. If you want to build a culture of customer service, build some customer service measures—and publicly celebrate when those measures are reached. Then go set some more. Try to set measures that can be accomplished but still reflect sincere progress.

Trader Joe's president Doug Rauch said of managing his workforce (a relatively high-turnover retail workforce) at a January 2006 food conference, "There's no magic to it other than keeping it simple and continuing to execute."

INSPIRATION

Execution Rules

- Choose where to be strong.
- Utilize unconventional tactics.
- Build strong beliefs.

> In war, numbers alone confer no advantage.
> —Sun Tzu

Throughout history, smashing victories have been won by people with fewer resources. Look at examples from military history such as Horatio Nelson's victory at Trafalgar against a more numerous French and Spanish fleet, by an American Revolutionary army that was poorly trained by the standards of the day, and by successful guerilla movements across the globe that, when started, were significantly undermanned in comparison to their more organized opponents—whom they eventually beat.

The winners in these examples all had some intangible advantages on their side:

Trust in a leader. Nelson was clearly the most brilliant naval mind of his day. With a track record of significant victories, his unconventional plan at Trafalgar was faithfully executed by ships full of people who believed in his leadership.

New tactics or technology. Faster, better adoption of new tactics or technology can bring significant advantage. The longbow allowed a smaller British force to defeat a much larger French force in the 1300s. Outnumbered four to one at the battle of Crecy, the British, armed with the longbow, won handily. Today, adoption of Internet solutions is allowing many smaller companies to achieve market success against much larger and better-financed rivals.

Belief in a cause. Successful revolutionary movements generally articulate a belief in an alternative vision, a cause to rally around—a set of words or beliefs that come to have meaning.

Help your employees find the inherent value of their work. Most work serves people—it serves your customers. Products and services get used by people who find value in them. Profitable enterprises provide good livings for the families these companies support. Helping your employees feel the inherent value, or the "higher calling," in their work builds loyalty to your company and a willingness to sacrifice a little to make your company successful. There are many organizations that people do not join for pay or status or advancement—religious, teaching, and charitable professions are examples. These companies are filled with highly loyal people whose motivation and allegiance to the organization, or the principles of the organization, have greater depth. Why can't some portion of that motivation be harnessed to your company?

Helping your employees find the greater good in their work is also inherently motivating. CEO Ian Lazarus writes about a job he had with a health-care call center: "I arrived at work one morning to learn that one of our nurses, upon taking a call from a diabetic patient, recognized the risk of shock and persuaded family members to take him to the hospital. The ER doctor confirmed the patient was approaching diabetic shock and would have died without timely treatment."

Teddy Roosevelt said, "Far and away the best prize that life has to offer is the chance to work hard at worthwhile work." Help your employees feel their work is worthwhile.

Find inspiration in:

Customer satisfaction with the work. Remind your employees of how their work is valued by their customers. Use customer testimonials to connect people's work with the value your customers find in that work.

Being of service to others. When I got into retailing, a mentor of mine advised me, "Retailing isn't a job, it's a lifestyle" (because retail stores are open seven days a week, and in some cases twenty-four hours a day). Over the years, my kids have asked me, "Why do you have to go to work tomorrow?" (or "tonight" or "this weekend"). The stock answer I have become comfortable giving is, "Because people are counting on me." I am comfortable with that answer because it is true, and it reflects the meaning of work I want my kids, and employees, to embrace.

What it means to your family. Some people I have worked with have expressed their loyalty to a company by talking about how a company, and the paycheck that comes from that company, "puts bread on our table." With the right sincerity, it's an expression that puts a positive, loyalty-oriented meaning on the need to work for a living.

Communicate a Common Inspiration

Building consistent execution across a company can be tough. We all want every individual to be using his or her knowledge to build a company in a common direction. We want people's commitment, so we want some amount of their personal creativity in the company. That personal creativity, that ability to do their job their way, is what makes them psychologically invested, or "bought in," to your company and its goals. But you need that creativity to be channeled in a specific direction. It must be focused on a consistent vision for the company. Otherwise, costs can get out of control and the actions of your employees will be random and uncoordinated with larger strategic objectives. A little common inspiration can drive common focus to people's execution.

Managing is an inexact science. Much of the communication that goes out to an organization's employees is never even understood. Many companies have a mission, a vision, values, *and* objectives—whew! The CEO and executive managers read these—but few, if any, companies can get that volume of corporate word-ology understood by their employees. It just becomes noise that distracts them from their day-to-day work. Corporate strategies that can be understood at an emotional level are much more likely to be understood and followed.

Stylish Wegmans food markets take their inspiration from Europe. Their food is European-inspired—with French patisserie shops and European brick ovens in-store. Their newer stores have a façade like a European village; some even have a clock tower. European inspiration drives a consistency of execution and supports an internal language about food and the shopping experience.

The president of Haggen's Supermarkets in the Northwest states simply, "Food is the fashion business." This simple statement gives their merchandising and marketing departments permission to change and innovate. Would an employee of this company expect to be on the leading edge of food trends—of course!

IKEA defines its inspiration as "people's lives at home." Simple and clear—it tells everyone in the IKEA organization where the company's forces will be concentrated.

Inspiration like this is shareable. It doesn't tell you exactly what to do, but it does give a group of people common notions about what to build toward.

LEAD

Execution Rules

- Set your own agenda.
- Be focused.
- Stay in touch through constant listening.

> When the general is incompetent and has little author-
> ity, when his troops are mismanaged, when the relation-
> ship between the officers and men is strained, and when the
> troop formations are slovenly, the result is disorganization.
> —Sun Tzu

When Wal-Mart, the world's biggest (and perhaps most feared—by its competitors) retailer, entered the UK retailing market with the purchase of Asda, many thought they knew what the outcome would be: Wal-Mart would dominate the market. After all, Wal-Mart has great buying clout, well-developed systems, and a very good track record. Tesco, one of the United Kingdom's largest retailers, had other ideas. "We decided that instead of waiting to see what they would do and respond, we at Tesco would set the agenda for Wal-Mart," said Sir Terry Leahy.

Tesco set the agenda for Wal-Mart based on price. In its 1992 Annual Report, it stated simply, "We sell for less." An unlikely strategy against the world's largest company, but one that Tesco thought it had the cost structure to support. It also had service, as Tesco is the world's largest Internet-ordering service for grocery delivery. They also place a high value on in-store service. Tesco thought it had a winning hand.

And Tesco achieved strong success—the number-one market share in the UK food business. In 2005 Wal-Mart's international president said, "Our biggest challenge is Asda in the UK. Total market growth in the

UK has been declining this year. If you follow the UK market, you know that profit warnings are everywhere. There's been one winner so far and that's Tesco."

David always has a chance against Goliath, if he can execute his plan.

GM used to be the world's largest company. But GM continues to slide and lose market share and cut jobs. A culture that lacked leadership was partly to blame during GM's slide in the 1970s, '80s, and '90s.

John DeLorean, the GM executive who left to start his own car company, told of a meeting where a minor point of compensation was being discussed. Suddenly, then-chairman Richard C. Gersternberg says, "'We can't make a decision on this now . . . I think we ought to form a task force to look into this and come back with a report in 90 to 120 days. Then we can make a decision.' He then rattled off members of the task force he was appointing. The whole room was bewildered but no one had the courage to say why. Finally Harold G. Warner, the snow-white-haired, kindly executive vice president, who was soon to retire, broke the silence. 'Dick, this presentation is the result of the task force you appointed some time ago. Most of the people you just appointed to the new task force are on the old one.'"

Leaders accept risk. They work to understand the risks they are taking, to manage those risks, and to reduce them.

Lead by Listening

Procter and Gamble's CEO, A. G. Laffley, came up through the P&G ranks. Like many successful leaders, listening takes an important role in his leadership. Laffley's listening is often targeted toward customers. Focus groups, one-on-ones, and various forms of research are one of P&G's most basic stocks in trade. A. G. Laffley, like many at (or trained by) P&G, makes listening to customers a foundation of its management. In a recent article, he said, "The simple principle is find out what she [the customer] wants and give it to her."

Leading companies do this repeatedly—they find out what their customers want, and they give it to them. Leaders listen:

Formally. They have structured feedback loops that regularly give customer, employee, or market feedback. These provide highly organized feedback like monthly tracking surveys that ask the same set of questions of customers month after month. Changes in response to these surveys can frequently be tied back to organizational, or competitive, changes. This kind of feedback is very easy to share with peers and subordinates. Accordingly, it can frequently be used to drive actions and improvements.

To knowledgeable industry experts. It helps to have a network of people you can rely on for advice. The best resources are people who know some aspect of your business deeply that is different from your personal experience or knowledge. If your specialization is classic brand marketing—seek out and learn from people who know direct marketing.

To the man on the street. Talking with people who use your business, or a competitor's, also provides informal feedback. This feedback may be anecdotal but it adds to a leader's breadth of knowledge about his or her business. You shouldn't take anecdotal information at face value, but it does provide helpful clues for further investigation and formalized research.

To employees. A customer's products or services need to be executed through employees. If the employees feel they are being listened to, they will have a greater buy-in and a greater mental/emotional stake in the business. They frequently are among your company's strongest backers and are out talking to their friends and neighbors about your company. Use their ideas.

Chapter 5

Create Alignment

> When aligned around shared values and united in a common
> vision . . . ordinary people accomplish extraordinary things.
> —Ken Blanchard

Good people, working toward a common goal, can accomplish virtually anything they set their mind to. The ancient Greeks were a fearsome fighting force because they arranged themselves in a formation called a phalanx. This fighting structure allowed each Greek to support his neighbor in battle. Centuries later, the Scots won many battles against the English with their tight formations and coordinated tactics. In business, alignment builds strength.

Much alignment can be built through the basics of:

- Setting objectives
- Measuring performance against those objectives

Setting objectives communicates to your employees what is important and what should be prioritized in your organization. When this is done well, your people will unite their individual objectives for personal performance and recognition to larger company objectives.

BUILD ALIGNMENT, AND EMPOWER INDIVIDUALS

Few employees get up each morning intending to do a bad job at work. Most every employee gets up wanting to do what is right for the organization. They come to work looking to do their job—and looking to do it well.

As a former senior leader of a company once rated number one on *Fortune*'s 100 Best Companies to Work For list, I know that hourly employees are much like those in management roles. No manager wants to be told exactly what to do and how to do it. We all want to be able to bring a little bit of ourselves to the job. We want to be able to figure out how to solve a problem, and to utilize our own creativity and judgment in doing so.

Everybody wants to feel good about the work he or she does. But few organizations empower hourly workers or lower-level employees to make decisions. To a large extent, most companies don't know how to give workers the right amount of latitude. Empowering employees means that management must take a different role, and that teams must change the way they work together.

EVALUATE QUALITY OF THOUGHT, NOT QUALITY OF THE RESULT

If people are going to have the freedom to bring a little bit of themselves to a job, then they are going to execute the job differently than you might. How do you evaluate that work when it is done differently than you would do it? You have to look at what people were thinking when they made their decisions.

When I worked in brick-and-mortar retailing, I would travel to different stores and evaluate the quality of their in-store displays. I could visit each store only infrequently, and I wanted to ensure that good decisions would be made by the in-store staff on the many days I was not able to be there.

When I saw something that was wrong, I focused not on changing it, but instead on changing the thinking that had created it. By asking questions, rather than making statements, I gained information. I asked questions such as, "What are you thinking here?" "Why did you decide to do it this way?" Sometimes the employee's thinking was exactly right (though the result was off), and I would understand how he or she got to where he or she was—and learn something new in the process. At other times I would find out where his or her thinking or assumptions had gone astray and correct it for the future. If the thinking behind the decisions is right, then the right things will have a tendency to happen even when you are not around to manage them directly.

GUIDELINES ARE NOT RULES

Guidelines provide principles for decision making. They provide the framework for making the right decisions in changing circumstances. Building guidelines into your businesses lets your people make the right daily or hourly decisions in alignment with broader goals.

Wegmans Food Markets published key guidelines for operating their in-store sub shops. The guidelines gave employees at the store level the latitude to make good decisions. They also set limits on where employees shouldn't have decision-making authority (like which breads to use) and inherently gave permission to make decisions in other areas (like the hours of each sub shop). These guidelines maintained the consistency of the service experience and of the brand. The guidelines enabled the corporate-level managers to maintain control over key aspects of the product and service experience, ensuring a consistent product and experience. Those guidelines also gave employees at the store level the opportunity to make decisions that best serve the day-to-day running of the store.

GAIN BUY-IN FOR OBJECTIVES

Setting objectives then measuring against them is more effective if the people accountable for the objectives truly buy into or support them. Discern where your goals and objectives match those of people around you. This is known as "safe ground." From these common objectives, you can start negotiating or discussing the issues at hand. Create wins here, at the intersection of everyone's objectives. You will find that creating wins on safe ground creates new safe ground. The next set of objectives you set will also be readily attainable—and then the next, and then the next, as you continue to build buy-in. As you progress, you will find ideas that previously might not have been supported are now safe ground.

A friend of mine describes this as "supporting someone else's objective." Find someone whose objectives mirror your own and lend them your support. You have discretion over what you decide to support and how much of your time you choose to give. However, since you are supporting an objective that someone else is already invested in, the buy-in will already be in place. Few important accomplishments can be done by ourselves. Aligning people to our goals allows each of us to achieve larger accomplishments.

MASS

Execution Rules

- It's not how much you spend—it is when you spend it.
- Identify critical points.
- Don't just win at the critical point—win decisively.

> We can form a single united body at one place, while
> the enemy must scatter his forces at ten places.
> —Sun Tzu

Before World War II, the U.S. Army gave infantrymen the following instruction: "Generalship consists of being stronger at the decisive point—of having three men to attack one. If we attempt to spread out so as to be uniformly strong everywhere, we shall end by being weak everywhere. To have a real main effort—and every attack and every attacking

Chapter 5: Create Alignment

unit should have one—we must be prepared to risk extreme weakness elsewhere."

The end result of successfully building alignment is to get as much mass at the critical point as possible. You do not want to place mass (be it in troops, supplies) randomly. You want mass where it will do you, and your organization, the most good. History has taught us that the battle doesn't always go to the side with the biggest army. You want to be "bigger" at the decisive point—not at points that don't matter very much.

For example, Wal-Mart wins every time on price—it has made that its decisive point. It has built an organization that wins on low-cost delivery of goods to a store. That is a *consumer-relevant* point—customers care about price. Wal-Mart has utilized its mass where it counts for the customer.

Disney's theme parks beat its competitors every time on service. Spend half a day at Universal Studios in Orlando, Florida, and half a day at Disney World, also in Orlando. The service difference is clear. Disney runs on time and its employees are better trained. You may have to wait in lines, of course, but Disney executes the people processes around those lines well. Disney's people know how to answer your questions. Disney's staff seems to be well organized. Even Disney's internal bus system has a high on-time rate. Universal, by comparison, just doesn't execute with the same dependability. Waiting times at Universal's lines are unpredictable. Hourly service personnel lack the attention to customer service you feel at Disney. Universal has some faster rides and bigger thrills (for Universal, this may be a decisive point *they* win on for teens)—but the dependability of the experience at Disney is demonstrably more consistent and better. For many families, that's a decisive point. Particularly when backed up by the obvious creativity and storytelling Disney brings to the experience.

Having mass at the decisive point doesn't excuse extreme weakness elsewhere. The Yugo automobile won on price, but that low price was delivered at the expense of reasonable quality. Webvan won on service with many customers during its brief existence, but it never had a solid economic model.

In a competent organization, with a reasonable business plan, creating mass at a decisive point:

- Wins over customers—because they know *something* to love about you.
- Builds good profitability—because customers who choose to shop with you will be willing to pay fairly for the advantages you deliver.

Inherently, where you build mass must matter to enough customers that they are motivated to buy more of your products and services or to recommend your products to other potential customers.

A few years ago, a food product that featured low carbs mattered. That was, briefly, a very decisive point to win on. But that has faded significantly. Laptop computers used to compete aggressively on size and weight. But as more and more reasonably priced lightweight laptops have become available, manufacturers shifted to compete on other features (like quality of the flat-screen picture). Over time, make sure the decisive point you compete on is decisive with your customers.

Coordinate and Communicate

Consumer marketers use repetition in their communications. One metric they look for is frequency. They want each target customer to see the same message several times. They know repetition motivates action. It takes a while for any message to make enough impact to motivate customers to action, that is, buying a product or service.

When introducing a new product, consumer packaged goods companies spend extensively on marketing and promotions in the first few months of the life of that product. This is the critical point. Lots of money is spent getting a new product into distribution. The marketing and promotion creates product movement that drives sales and maintains distribution. Expenditures against other products/brands from that company may suffer in that year to ensure there is sufficient spending to make the new product a success.

When Gillette introduced its six-blade razor, it even bought a Super Bowl advertisement *before* the new product was fully available. This is similar to how movies are advertised in advance of their distribution, to ensure people show up at the movie when it premieres, because there are always plenty of movies that can fill up a theater and knock out an underperformer.

Marketers build mass across all of their communications by executing a single, tactical idea well. UPS is "brown"—in its planes, trucks, and the dress of its people. Target's bull's-eye logo is used in all forms of its advertising and in its store designs. For many years, gifts from Tiffany's have come in a soft blue box. It's now become a distinctive part of Tiffany's branding, and the receiver knows what retailer the gift is from before they even open the gift.

As you go to market, overwhelm your customers. Pick the points where you will have greater mass, greater focus, than your competitors. That could be a point in time—like when you introduce a new product. It could be a particular feature of your product or service—like price. After you pick where you will create advantage, work hard to win at that decisive point.

FIGHT YOUR MOST IMPORTANT FIGHT

Execution Rules

- Put your resources where they will have greatest leverage.
- Use Pareto thinking to build focus.
- Just say no. Frequently.

In encircled ground, I would block the points of access and egress.
—Sun Tzu

Limiting a competitor's ability to compete with you is a common practice in business. It forces your competitors to compete with businesses other than your own. Limiting a competitor's access is commonly practiced in the real estate industry by using a couple of different methods:

Restricted-use agreements. When a supermarket exits a popular strip mall, it commonly signs an agreement that prohibits the re-leasing of that spot to another supermarket. Those agreements are not free. However, when you consider the fact that most supermarkets vacate their current location because they are relocating nearby, preventing the opening of a new competitor in their own backyard is worth the investment.

Keeping open a poorly performing location. Retailers frequently allow a poorly performing location to remain open in order to keep a competitor from coming in. The company feels that the risk of losing customers to a competitor that might take over that location outweighs the cost of keeping open the underperforming location.

Secondary branding. Some retail chains operate secondary brands that keep competitors out of strip mall locations. These secondary brands don't carry the company's flagship brand but instead compete under another, less well known and less advertised brand name in the same category. These secondary brands are not as strong as the flagship brands—sales per location are lower. But the secondary brands lock up a certain amount of locations away from their competitors. Better to run a secondary brand, which doesn't cannibalize your primary brand, at breakeven than to allow the growth of a strong competitor in those locations and disrupt your flagship brand.

Buying up land. In some developed, populous real estate markets, there is only so much land available that is zoned for particular uses. Buying up land that is available can effectively lock a competitor out of a geographic region. This is a strategy a variety of retailers have used against retailing giant Wal-Mart. In many communities, local supermarkets have bought land near their locations. They may or may not develop that land someday—but in the meantime, it ensures that Wal-Mart, or other competing retailers, can't open a new superstore next door to them. This tactic keeps their competition farther away from their own profitable operations.

All of these techniques involve spending money to avoid a fight with a competitor. Obviously, these companies believe that the money spent to avoid a fight is less money than the cost of the fight itself. Or as Sun Tzu says, "Neither is it the acme of excellence if you win a victory through fierce fighting."

The Pareto Mentality

A Pareto chart ranks a problem from its most frequent instance to its least frequent instance. A common use for a Pareto chart is to rank defects in a manufacturing operation. Generally constructed as a bar chart, it gives a visual picture of a problem. The most frequent defects stand out—they will be the highest bars on the bar chart. Conversations, and work, then go toward fixing the problems that occur most frequently, now that they have been identified. Pareto charts help focus an organization on it most important work. Since some defects can be more expensive to fix than others, Pareto charts also build a common framework for decision making.

As an example, say you want to look at reducing the amount of defects in manufacturing operations. A series of Pareto charts can define the problem—and make sure your work is organized to address it. What are the most frequent defects? What are the defects customers complain about the most? What are the problems that cost the most to fix? A couple of Pareto charts that address those questions can help define where problems reside in your organization and its processes.

Pareto charts help create alignment because they bring facts to a situation in both an impartial and an actionable way. Complaints are one example of this. Frequently complaints have an emotional aspect to them. Perhaps a particular complaint goes directly to the president, or a particularly angry customer's complaint is circulated. Those may not be the most important problems to focus on fixing. They may instead be issues that have gotten unusual visibility. Pareto charts take the emotion out of addressing a problem because the issues are arranged in a factual and unbiased way. Using Pareto charts helps you get past emotions and tread-worn conversations and can enable you to achieve a clearer focus on important, granular pieces of a particular issue. A Pareto chart is a tool that can help you focus on what the real issues are and where you should marshal your resources. Organizations that use this tool frequently are said to have a "Pareto mentality"—they are organizations focused on improving their most important problems. They know they are working on the most important problems because they are continually rank ordering their issues—continually doing Pareto charts.

Be Finicky

For most companies and brands, what you *don't* do best defines your efforts. Coach doesn't sell cheap handbags. Celestial Seasonings tea doesn't contain artificial ingredients. The products and customers they *don't* pursue say as much about who they are as the products and markets they *do* cater to.

In essence, companies that are focused are finicky. They are finicky about what they do and how it is executed.

Be finicky about costs. No company can afford to do everything. Really good companies are particular about the costs they add. Any airline is eager to get new customers into its frequent-flyer program—it builds loyalty and frequency of higher-margin business travelers. Thus, airlines will work hard to get you signed up.

Not JetBlue. Want to register for the JetBlue frequent-flyer program? Register online. At the airport, waiting to get on a flight? Register online. Why would JetBlue take a chance on losing the enrollment, and future revenue, of potential high-volume frequent fliers by turning them away at a point of contact to do business online? Because they know that a discount carrier needs a disciplined approach to costs—and the Internet is a frugal way to manage such a program because there is little employee training involved, and your customers enter and manage their own information.

Be finicky about your brand. Whole Foods is known for organic and natural foods. The company's CEO, John Mackey, talks about being a socially responsible company. In 2005, Whole Foods announced it was not going to sell live lobsters unless a more humane way to hold and transport live lobsters was developed (it would, however, continue to sell frozen dead ones). This move seemed a bit quirky to industry insiders. But it also underscored the core beliefs of the company and the meaning of their brand.

Mid-quality retailer Trader Joe's exhibits a similar finickiness. Trader Joe's is known for its interesting assortment of packaged goods—almost all sold under its own brand name at very good prices. In fact, if the product can't be packaged under its own brand name, you might not find it there at all. Want Coke or Pepsi? Go somewhere else. Both Whole Foods and Trader Joe's do an outstanding job with their particular niches—and they are demonstrating that niches can be big businesses.

Be finicky about your business model: Increasingly, companies are just focusing on what they do best. Remember the conglomerates of the 1980s, with disparate companies linked only by a common holding company? Some examples: AMF made both bowling equipment and Harley-Davidson motorcycles; Sara Lee Corporation made pound cake, Hanes underwear, and Coach leather bags. These holding companies are generally gone or broken up. Harley-Davidson and Coach leather are now their own independent companies. Frequently, the dismembered companies are doing much better on their own. What you refuse to do allows you to focus your resources on your most important fights. And win.

COORDINATE RESOURCES

Execution Rules

- Choose to champion others' ideas.
- Support ideas that build toward your vision.
- Give others the opportunity to make decisions.

> Generally, management of a large force is the same in principle
> as the management of a few men: it is a matter of organization.
> And to direct a large army to fight is the same as to direct a
> small one: it is a matter of command signs and signals.
> —Sun Tzu

Toyota president Fujio Cho once remarked that, "Detroit people are far more talented than people at Toyota. But we take averagely talented people and make them work as spectacular teams." Is there a science to teamwork? How do you create the alignment that leads to spectacular teamwork?

Bottom Up Versus Top Down

Teamwork comes, in part, from team members who know their opinion counts. Organizations that have a strong team culture often give decision-making power to those people who are closest to the decision. This is often referred to as "delegating to the lowest possible level in an organization." If someone underneath you can make a capable decision, then that is who should make it.

Be proactive. If you, instead of your boss, can make a decision in your organization, make it. If you are a manager, empower your people to do so.

Maurice of Saxony, the sixteenth-century German military and political leader, writes, "Few orders are best, but they should be followed up with care." More orders don't bring clarity, they bring confusion. Or, as Maurice also writes, "Many generals believe that they have done everything as soon as they have issued orders, and they issue a great deal because they find many abuses." Identify problems when you find them, of course. But keep focused—issuing a few important instructions is much preferable to many orders. People who work with you will better understand their priorities—and your instructions will be treated with a greater importance—if you issue few of them.

Additionally, work to keep decision making at the lowest possible level as you issue instructions. If subordinates will identify the areas to be worked on, and issue orders accordingly, that is preferable to the next-level-higher supervisor's issuing the exact same instructions. The buy-in to performing the work will be greater. The same is true for your peers—the more you can help them identify and prioritize the issues in their organizations on their own initiative, and issue their own instructions to fix those issues, the better, and faster, those issues will be fixed.

Customer Centricity

Let the customer be your lightning rod. Decisions made without the customer in mind have a tendency to not stand the test of time. What costs do you add to your organization? What innovations do you bring to market? Are these innovations and the costs associated with them adding value for the customer? Are you spending money where your *customers* would choose for you to spend that money? For example, your organization may think that new fancy packaging is appealing, but does it serve customers who have gotten familiar with your brand and don't want to hunt for it on the store shelf?

Customer-driven organizations ask customers what they are looking for. And make decisions accordingly. We all have ideas on what our customers want us to do. But organizations that add costs and features that customers don't want, or don't understand, aren't investing for the long-term health of their business.

There are two factors that have to come together for true customer centricity:

- Customers have to want your offering. Your product or service has to fill a need.
- Customers have to understand your offering. They won't connect with something they don't understand.

I recently had a presentation from a food company that wanted me to carry its premium-priced products. It told me its food products were:

- All natural
- Made with a proprietary process
- Made from raw materials whose genetics it controlled
- Personally endorsed by the leading expert in that field
- Produced in small quantities so it could control the quality

Whew! No wonder its product was premium priced—and it was struggling to get the premium for it in the marketplace. It had more stories to tell about its product than any one customer could understand. You won't be surprised to know that the company goes from crisis to crisis because of high prices and low volume. This company just couldn't pick the idea it wanted to get behind—and, thus, neither could its customers.

Know Your Position

A great basketball team doesn't send out three centers and two guards to play a game. No football team plays three quarterbacks at the same time on offense. The roles are defined, and people know what role they are supposed to play in the game. That works for the team. In business, make sure each member of your team knows what his or her role is. What does success in each person's position look like? The better each is able to describe it, the more each is able to achieve it.

Steve Jobs and Steve Wozniak made a natural team inventing the first ready-made personal computer. They had different skills. Wozniak's talents were in engineering; Jobs had great creative and marketing instincts. Together their combined skills turned Apple into a billion-dollar company.

Share Common Sacrifices

Most every company or industry has some work the business requires that is out of the norm. If you have a business in a summer resort area, extra hours will be required in the summer. If you are a seller of garments, then you may work 100 hours during "fashion week" so you can spend as much time as you can with your buyers. Sharing these sacrifices around the organization—and getting the entire organization in tune with these important business needs—builds a culture of teamwork.

One HR executive I knew joined a fashion retailer and created alignment in the organization around the seasonal needs of the business. It is common among fashion retailers to "go black" from Thanksgiving to Christmas—meaning no one in store operations gets to take any vacation days over that time. The nature of the business just doesn't allow for it—seasonal sales increases are huge and even require the hiring of significant short-term seasonal labor. This new head of HR immediately built a strong bond between HR and store operations by having HR "go black" over this period of time as well—even though it wasn't necessary for the daily needs of the business. That particular move let store operations know they had a committed partner—the action drove that understanding better than any words could.

Build Common Goals

Work first on the ideas where you can build a consensus. I have championed many different ideas in my career. The ones that were easiest to accomplish were those that I was able to get others to champion.

The reality is that you will never have time to champion *every* good idea you have. Even the most successful and dynamic organizations do not have enough staff or money to work on everything they choose to. They constantly have to prioritize. And prioritizing is not perfect—there is always a certain "fog of war" around it.

So you can always *choose* to work on ideas someone else wants to work on. Champion someone else's idea or agenda. You, as a manager or leader, have the opportunity to invest your time, your "weight," behind those ideas you think make sense for the organization. Find the ideas that someone else has that align with your priorities. If you do, you will have inherent support.

When you come into a new position or organization, take inventory of the ideas around you. Ask questions. Learn what people are working on—and what they wish they were really working on. Find the ideas other people want to work on that match your vision of where you want the organization to go. You will find plenty to work on—and it will all match where you want to take the organization! You will start with people willing to commit resources to your vision, because it is their vision as well.

CREATE LINKAGES IN YOUR MANAGEMENT TEAM

Execution Rules

- Build linkage with balanced scorecard reporting.
- Decide where to lead and where to follow.
- Experienced teams will have the advantage of informal alignment.

> In frontier ground, I would keep my forces closely linked.
> —Sun Tzu

Napoleon said, "One bad general is preferable to two good ones." Why? Because two good leaders create different visions, ideas, and directions that people try to execute. Conflicting direction creates confusion, which never helps in executing results—no matter how good each direction may be. Do you know any great companies with co-CEOs? Schwab, Kraft, and SAP have tried this. These arrangements never last and rarely produce good results. Kraft disbanded this setup and demoted one of its co-CEOs after just two years, announcing declines in sales. Do you know of a great football team that rotates quarterbacks within a game? Almost every year some major college football team decides they have equally talented quarterbacks and rotates them. However, by and large, these are not teams you see in the big bowl games at the end of the year.

Rotating quarterbacks fails because the receivers and the quarterback never develop intuitive linkage with each other—they don't anticipate each other's moves as experienced quarterback/receiver combinations do. The same holds true with co-CEO arrangements. The organization doesn't know whose vision they are supposed to follow. When the CEOs disagree, who does the organization listen to? It creates a situation ripe for dissension and turf wars.

Many companies use a balanced-scorecard approach to drive some level of linkage and success in a variety of important areas. A balanced scorecard measures multiple factors of an organization's success together. Frequently, a balanced scorecard pulls together some combination of financial, customer satisfaction, and employee satisfaction measures. The thinking behind a balanced scorecard is that such diverse measures are frequently in conflict. Lower costs can yield higher profits in the short term, but cost-reduction moves can sometimes reduce customer satisfaction. A balanced scorecard tries to encourage a balancing of these diverse measures. In effect, when practiced at higher levels of an organization, this also balances short-term and long-term performance, as short-term financial performance can sometimes be "bought" at the expense of long-term customer or employee satisfaction.

In buying functions, many retailers use a balanced scorecard to evaluate their vendors. A balanced scorecard ensures vendors are being evaluated on their total effectiveness with the organization. Issues that don't normally factor into a buyer's decision can be taken into account. As an example, on-time truck arrival at a warehouse isn't normally a factor buying organizations take strongly into account. But backups at a warehouse increase labor costs, reduce service levels, and reduce sales. In the normal course of business, a buyer might not see the extra costs at the warehouse—buyers have a tendency to focus on the delivered price of the product. The balanced scorecard encourages taking the warehouse's service needs into account. Thus, buying functions and warehouse functions become linked.

In manufacturing, a balanced scorecard can take into account the different standards of a well-run plant. Costs are an obvious factor. But what about quality? Employee safety? Consumer safety? A balanced scorecard of plant performance keeps perspective on performance against a broad number of measures. No one measure is allowed to dominate at the expense of the others.

Build Common Knowledge

Every organization has its own methods and processes. Most of these are not written down. This common knowledge of an organization is important to daily execution. It is one reason why high-turnover organizations never quite become efficient. Shared common knowledge is the informal glue that helps experienced teams perform expertly.

Webvan was a company that built too much too fast. Webvan was an Internet retailer of the late 1990s that promised fast delivery of groceries, DVDs, and other frequently purchased items. Their business model had many problems—they made "promises" to their customers that were difficult to keep, such as thirty-minute delivery windows in crowded urban environments. But a core problem was that Webvan built out before they knew how to operate and execute their business. So, instead of operating one large money-losing warehouse and delivery system, they built several locations too quickly and ended up operating eight different money-losing warehouses and delivery systems. The business eventually folded.

During the Internet bubble, first-mover advantage—being the first to bring a new idea to market—had a lot of credibility. The thinking was that the first company to bring out a new idea would quickly capture most of the available demand, and subsequent entrants would have to take the business away from the "first mover." When the Internet bubble burst, we were reminded that businesses have to have a business plan that eventually makes money. Building common knowledge is expensive. Building an Internet-based business today capitalizes on the knowledge gained, and mistakes made, by others. Business processes that had been unique are not common knowledge in the industry.

Many Internet businesses now outsource their direct-marketing systems—they let others build the customer relationship management systems they use. With rich customer profiles, these databases are a key asset of many Internet-based businesses. But it is the knowledge owned *behind* the system that builds uniqueness, not the system itself. The longer a company operates that system, the more knowledge that company builds and owns. Putting that knowledge to work, in alignment with the core business proposition of the company, builds the value of the enterprise.

Building on someone else's knowledge is cheaper than building your own. Where possible, consider building on lessons that cost *someone else* the money to learn.

Pick your learning opportunities—and tie them closely to your business strategy. You can learn to do some things well. And that can competitively insulate your company. Dell has become a world leader in just-in-time production of computers. Their latest plant in North Carolina is supposed to be state-of-the-art in many ways. There is also a lot of stuff you don't see Dell doing. Their marketing is solid but certainly not spectacular. They ship through UPS. But they build the computers themselves.

Proactively make "buy," not "build," decisions. "Build" decisions have a strong tendency to be decisions where you are creating some new knowledge. If you buy, you are capitalizing on someone else's learnings. This obviously relates to new technology. But it also applies to something as simple as servicing your own trucks or outsourcing that service to someone that only does that. Many high-tech companies buy their customer service call center software off the shelf. That service aspect of technology has been well developed by plenty of call centers that operated for years before us. It is part of that industry's common knowledge.

When making buy-versus-build decisions with technology, consider if you are a technology company or not. If you aren't, then your competitive advantage likely doesn't lie in the technology itself—it likely lies in how you apply the technology. Carefully consider undertaking the cost, and risk, of building significant technology applications yourself. That money may be better invested in operating that technology well and building it into your business operation in unique ways.

Decide to be a slow follower. Innovation feels good, right, and strategic. It is what we are "supposed" to do. But in some aspects of your business, it is okay to be a slow follower. It is how you keep your costs under control.

Many companies do this by limiting the investment of resources outside of the areas "core" to their business. Vitamin retailers like GNC are up on all the current trends in vitamins and supplements. Want to see what's new? Look at the displays at a GNC. They invest in the human talent that is knowledgeable in these areas, attend the appropriate trade shows, and subscribe to the periodicals to know what is happening next.

By contrast, visit your local mass merchant and see what vitamins and supplements are stocked there. They won't carry most of the newest ones. Instead, they will probably occasionally visit a GNC-like retailer, see what is new and what seems to be selling, talk to vendors, and try to add just the best sellers to their own selections.

Common knowledge is an important commodity within the operation of any company. In a younger company, building common knowledge is particularly important—the corporate understanding of how things work together is simply less mature. Young companies will be building common knowledge as they manage through their normal annual business cycles. Younger companies therefore have greater opportunities to get more efficient year to year. You can capture this efficiency by:

Reducing turnover. By reducing turnover, the same people see the problems and opportunity year to year. They will work to get better each time, improving the errors they remember from the prior year.

Documenting opportunities for immediate improvement. In food retailing, you traditionally write down your notes on Thanksgiving the week after Thanksgiving, while the insights and successes are fresh in your mind.

Building simple standardized processes. A simple common form, a "job aid," can help maintain institutional learnings.

USE ADVERSITY TO UNITE YOUR TEAM

Execution Rules

- Use competitive actions to unify your company.
- Involve key team members in determining responses.
- Use adversity to create needed change.

> The deeper you penetrate into hostile territory, the greater will be the solidarity of your troops, and, thus, the defenders cannot overcome you.
> —Sun Tzu

Challenging situations give you the opportunity to build new strengths. Sun Tzu writes about "solidarity." Groups of people who have been through difficult times together can develop that solidarity, or feeling of mutual trust. That psychology, the result of having borne difficult situations together, can linger from these experiences. In Sun Tzu's world, that solidarity was generated by overcoming military enemies. In business, these challenges can be the result of competition in the marketplace, shifts in your industry, or internal shifts in your organization—such as a change in management or staff.

An example in the business world is in the growing online DVD rental business. This is a segment Netflix pioneered. For years, it essentially had market share domination in this business. When Blockbuster decided to enter this business, Netflix responded aggressively. Blockbuster is the number one and dominant national brick-and-mortar store renter of DVDs. Blockbuster spent significantly on advertising and promotions to gain share in the direct-to-consumer DVD business. Netflix responded with aggressive promotions and marketing of its own. These expenditures mounted, but Netflix continued to invest. Said Reed Hastings, chief executive of Netflix, "Online rental is the only thing we do, and (our) advantage is focus and desperation. So we have nowhere to go, right? It was win or die, and that's very focusing." And that's an example of how diversity can build strong belief in a particular objective. Blockbuster had thousands of retail stores and a chance to get into a new business—online DVD retailing. Netflix had only the business Blockbuster wanted to get into. Very focusing for Netflix.

Sometimes the Best You Can Do Is All That You Can Do

During the 2005 Christmas season, the New York mass transit system went on strike. It was its first strike in twenty-five years. And the 5,000 buses of the New York Metropolitan Transit Authority (MTA) stopped, and the 230 miles of subway track lay idle. Seven million people had to find a new way to work, and a new way home.

For online grocery retailer FreshDirect, the MTA was the lifeline for employees to get to work. Eight hundred employees a day rode the subway. With a mass transit strike, other provisions needed to be made, or the plant was going to have to close for the duration of the strike. FreshDirect's new lifeline became four rented motor coaches and two vans. These were dispatched on three pick-up runs to major employee population centers—to try and get most employees to work.

You can imagine the relief when the first bus pickup from the Bronx returned with forty people on it. The next few buses were similarly full. And the production facility operated each night during this strike with these transportation arrangements.

Customers were amazed that FreshDirect delivery trucks made it through the traffic and congestion of a transit strike. One e-mail from a grateful customer ended with "Kudos to FreshDirect." And for FreshDirect employees, doing business in these difficult conditions was a source of pride and accomplishment. It was also a unifying event, because all managers shared the risk and uncertainty of not knowing whether employees would be able to find a way to work and if there would be enough employees to operate a department.

Lessons from CEOs

Businesses frequently use adverse situations to build and unify a team. Xerox is a company that has bounced back from some very difficult times. So difficult, in fact, that the *Wall Street Journal* called Xerox's financial shape in the early 2000s a "near death experience." These difficult times were particularly challenging for the employees of Xerox who grew up in a company that for years held patent protections on key aspects of their business and had traditionally been a benevolent company with a high level of employee security.

Newly promoted CEO Ann Mulcahy used Xerox's challenging financial condition to build commitment to certain objectives and unify her team. Ann talks about having "town meetings" in her early days as CEO, where she could talk about where the company was going and build some confidence that it was going to get through its difficult times. And working with the senior management team in 2000, she says, "We wrote a story that described how various constituencies would talk about us—investors, analysts, reporters—and we dated it December 2005. We took it from the perspective of what the customers would see in terms of what had happened to the product portfolio, keeping it very tangible about what was possible." And she says much of what they put down as their December 2005 goals happened.

Using difficult experiences like this to unify a team and build commitment to a new goal is a common theme among CEOs who have managed through adversity. After Coke had a series of management turnovers and failed products, they tapped a retired Coke veteran to return as the CEO, Neville Isdell. Isdell refused public comment on the company during his first 100 days in this role. He says about this time, "We were working with the top 150 [executives] in terms of building the strategy of what we wanted to do going forward. . . . It probably could have been written in six to eight weeks by six people, but then it wouldn't have been something that people were able to sign on to easily because it would have been what I call the edict from the mount." Leaders use adversity to build a vision, or a plan, that is shared by their key leaders. That vision or plan does not come from the most senior person—like the CEO in the cases of Xerox and Coke. That shared vision comes from making the effort to get other people to contribute to, and buy into, a plan. The adversity these companies were going through added a sense of urgency in building a plan.

In listening to CEOs who have managed through difficult times, you hear a couple of consistent themes:

Seek support. It may be tempting in difficult times to issue mandates. But business leaders who have successfully come through challenging times consistently talk about building support and buy-in for their initiatives.

Create a picture of the future. This gives people something to work for. And something that also lasts when the unifying pressure of outside adversity passes.

Work with all stakeholders. Work with employees, customers, and perhaps vendors and shareholders. Build support for your vision among key stakeholders.

Adversity then becomes an accelerator that lets change occur faster than it would normally occur in less challenging times. Adversity makes you focus on solving the largest problems. Quickly. While we never seek out this level of adversity—like the Xerox corporate "near death experience"—these experiences can be used to solidify commitment to a course of action that in more peaceful, calmer times would seem less necessary. So adversity—when used with skill—can be used to accelerate a company's progress toward needed and long-lasting change.

People Always

孫子

The Marine Corps uses the phrase "Mission First, Marines Always." It means that while the primary objective is to accomplish the mission, you are going to be able to do so only if you take care of, and utilize, the people you have. Every investment banker, when he talks about the latest company he has invested in, will extol the virtues of its "great management team." Almost any CEO will tell you about the quality of his or her employees. Building great companies depends on great people.

Attracting and retaining great people requires some combination of superior performance in five areas:

COMPENSATION

While salary and benefits are never enough in and of themselves to create loyalty, compensation that is below industry levels or doesn't reward and incentivize performance can cause you to lose good people your organization can't afford to lose. People have a tendency to find the pay level that they can make. At its most simplistic, if you pay $7 per hour, you will have a tendency to attract $7 per hour people. In general, people rise or fall to a certain level of compensation in terms of performance, morale, and initiative. People have a level of pay that they think they are worth. Maybe it is what they have been paid before, or maybe it is what they think they can make, but if you pay more for a given job, you will tend to attract people who think they are worth more.

TRAINING

Good people have a tendency to want to get better. They want to learn new skills. Companies that don't have training programs may lose good people who want to progress in their industry. Conversely, they will keep those employees who are not motivated. That's a recipe for disaster.

Unless your organization continues to train and challenge its people, it will experience a "brain drain" of its best and brightest employees. If your employees decide to change jobs within the same industry, your competitor is going to reap the rewards in terms of inside information about your plans and practices.

PERCEIVED OPPORTUNITY

People want an opportunity to advance professionally and financially and to contribute a little bit of themselves to the jobs they hold. Employees will stay where they see an opportunity to acquire credibility or a reputation that can serve them later in their career. For years, Procter & Gamble has acquired a stable of superior talent in its brand-management ranks, in part because each candidate understood the occasionally used line "If you get into P&G, you can go wherever you want next." Being "selected" by P&G traditionally has given brand-management job candidates credibility with other marketing-oriented companies. A few years at P&G often allows candidates to write their own ticket at other companies when and if they decide to move on. It also benefited Procter & Gamble—by giving people "portable equity," they had more leverage than their competitors to recruit the most talented people.

TREATMENT

Caring about people is a significant factor in employee retention. If you can do it with sincerity and some measure of consistency, it can even become part of your company's culture—something that employees feel throughout the organization. Research shows that employees' opinion of an organization is largely based on how they feel about their immediate supervisor. Thus, treating people well needs to become an expected behavior at all levels of management.

VALUES

For years, the Container Store has been named one of the top companies to work for in America. They give a lot of the credit for this achievement to their adherence to their six foundation principles. Simple principles about what they believe about how they do their business—how they treat customers and their own people. As an example, one of the Container Store's foundation principles is, "Fill the other guy's basket to the brim. Making money then becomes an easy proposition." The "other guy" is employees, and customers. In other words, you make money by growing your base of loyal, satisfied customers—and having satisfied employees who can deliver the level of service that makes customers loyal. If you have a lot of satisfied customers, you can build your sales and profits—financial success follows the customer-satisfaction success. That makes sense—and that also sounds like a company many people would want to work for. If they live values like those—if those values are transferred down through the management ranks—that would be considered a special company by many current or prospective employees because principles like this put an emphasis on how you treat others. That's the kind of value that resonates with employees.

Companies that have high employee turnover have great difficulty executing results and great difficulty succeeding. Companies that retain, train, and motivate their employees better than their competitors do win at execution.

HIRE SKILLED COMMANDERS

Execution Rules

- Help your employees build new skills.
- Give your people peak experiences.
- Look for peak experiences for yourself.

> [A skilled commander] is able to select the right men and exploits the situation. He who takes advantage of the situation uses his men in fighting as rolling logs or rocks. It is the nature of logs and rocks to stay stationary on the flat ground and to roll forward on a slope.
> —Sun Tzu

Throughout military and business history, small outnumbered armies have succeeded against much bigger foes. The American Civil War is full of such stories. During the early years of the war, the Southern generals—Robert E. Lee, Stonewall Jackson, Jeb Stuart—won victories against the more numerous and better-equipped Northern troops. They won because of their greater skills—daring tactics, skilled maneuvering, and a sense of when to take a risk.

Skilled commanders, and managers, seem to be few and far between. Why is this so? Businesses are very complex, requiring the application of a large set of skills. One military historian writes "in any organization the opportunities for misplacement of personnel (or anything else) go up as the square of the complexity." The square of complexity simply means as we add complexity to any situation, the likelihood of error goes up. And business has gotten more complex. Managing a business of most any size now requires management of complex IT decisions, negotiating increased government regulation, and making changes with great speed. Fitting the right people into the right jobs is more challenging because the *content* of many business challenges is growing. Managing in large companies, in particular, requires a lot of judgment on what areas of the company to involve in solving a problem. Many issues can require an assessment of PR, legal, or employee (union?) implications.

Also, the strength of the status quo frequently outweighs the need to take measured risks. Wall Street values predictability of results. They do not like surprises in how a company performs. Success is measured by meeting Wall Street's prescribed benchmark—whether that benchmark is realistic and informed or not. Accordingly, in many industries, privately held companies outperform publicly held companies. Privately held companies can choose to take risks that might cause a few poorer quarters but result in the long-term health of their business. Publicly held companies have great difficulty doing these things—they must make each quarter's results.

Or politically able leaders fall into roles they are less qualified for. As one commentator said, "Quite naturally, the least gifted commanders are usually the most political."

Develop Your Leaders

The greater complexity of business decisions—and the greater breadth of knowledge required of business leaders—makes developing employees increasingly important. We count on key people not just to solve problems, but to identify when to bring in additional resources. Managers need to assess and fix problems and know when they need help. In part because competitive situations can change very quickly, and in part because businesses are under greater scrutiny.

One example of this greater scrutiny is the media. Media outlets covering business have multiplied—we have business-only cable stations and radio stations and Internet sites covering many specific business topics. As media has segmented to serve different customer groups, the absolute amount of business reporting has greatly increased. As new media have grown up, new forms of reporting on businesses have come with these new media. Satellite radio spawned new business programming. The Internet allowed the growth of blogs—Web logs written by individuals. Blogs can increase dramatically the amount that is written about a company, an individual, or a specific issue. With radio, TV, and the Internet, much writing and reporting happens in real time. So business responses have to be quicker.

Business managers need to apply a lot of judgments to their work. They need to bring business experience, and add to that an ability to handle new situations that are outside of their direct business experience. For business leaders with the right training, these new challenges can be exciting and rewarding. Without the right training, companies, annual budgets, or promising careers can be put at risk.

For many managers, developing people who can handle new challenges is one of the highlights of their jobs. They may work for companies that put a premium on training and growing employees. Or they may value employee development based on some experiences from their own working careers. But either way, there is probably some combination of the following techniques that they use to develop employees.

Stretch Jobs

Research shows that peak learning experiences happen in jobs where people are challenged to work outside their comfort level and learn new things. During these times, employees will invariably experience stress. They are working extra hours because they are in unfamiliar territory. Their morale may be lower than normal because they are not sure they can handle the extra responsibilities. They may fear failing.

When taken to an extreme, or for too long, this is obviously counterproductive. But the right amount of stretch creates a positive stress— the stress of successfully negotiating your way through some unfamiliar territory. If you give your leaders enough room to succeed, and support them through these experiences, these can be great ways for new leaders to develop. It can also be a tremendous bonding experience for your organization.

New Roles

Some companies proactively switch managers between roles. This can happen as part of a learning experience—some companies recruit new managers into programs where they get to work in many different parts of the organization as part of their training and orientation. Many retailers, when they hire people for their headquarters organizations, first put new hires to work for several months in store operations. They do this because companies find this is a great way for new employees to learn the guts of their retailing operation. If you are a stable organization with seasoned employees, allowing people to switch roles temporarily can be a low-risk way to teach people new things—and to improve communications within your organization. You will also be cultivating employees who have a more holistic view of your organization and bring out-of-the-box thinking to different areas of your organization.

For your own career, look for jobs that give you some new experience. Many good careers involve some lateral moves that provide new learnings. Don't always look for the next promotion—promotions likely take you further up the same functional silo you are already in. In addition to promotions, look for jobs that will give you a chance to add a new skill to your background. If you are in marketing, consider a job in sales. If you are in IT, consider a job in operations. Any new skills you learn are your portable equity. The more skills you have, the more choices you will have in the future. And the more valuable you will be to your employer. Take these skill-building career moves yourself—and help your employees into positions where they get to add to their skills as well.

Mentoring

Most of us have learned our craft from a few select people. It's not that we haven't worked with a lot of different people, read to keep abreast of our industry, and attended different seminars. But most people learn most of their knowledge from a relatively small number of people in their career. Sometimes we find a boss or a colleague who is willing to teach or coach us—those people are invaluable.

Training and mentoring experiences can provide needed learning. Feedback and insight are best delivered at the time employees can use it—don't train in advance of the need. Training and mentoring are most effective when done by fellow employees or experienced teachers who understand the organization and can make the training immediately relevant.

If you are looking to develop yourself, take advantage of opportunities like these. Make a list—which of these are available to you? How could you create opportunities, or relationships, that would increase your own development? As you grow your company's business, don't forget to invest in your own skills development. Remember some skills are technical, like writing a sales plan or running a particular piece of equipment. Other skills are more broadly applicable, like being able to speak in front of a group. Over time, try to develop some of both.

Make the Most of Your Team

Don't ever assume you will have exactly the team you want. Any team you manage will always have some shortcomings. A manager I once worked with would say "Never trade the eight of diamonds for the nine of clubs." He meant that you fire someone only if you believe that you are going to be able to get a much stronger performer in that person's place. It is not a win if you lose someone and trade up only a little bit. The costs of firing someone, having a job vacant, and having to train a new hire are not inexpensive. Constantly replacing people in an attempt to end up with the "perfect" team is ineffective. That can lead to high turnover, and people you want to keep may come to distrust their future in the organization.

The skillful manager gets the right people in the key positions and makes all of the people around him or her better through setting clear objectives and providing training and development. By doing this, the team builds competence *and* trust. Two assets necessary for executing results.

Prior to World War I, the Prussian army regularly played a practice war game called *Kriegspiel* to train its officers. It was played with wooden blocks on a map. Unlike other war games, the participants could not see what their opponents were doing. Nonplayer umpires oversaw the game and implemented orders from the two sides. One military historian writes about Kriegspiel, "The victor was usually the player who anticipated the short-comings of both his subordinate units and bad information." Assuming imperfection, and managing skillfully, is a leader's job. It is also one of the most critical aspects of being a skilled commander. It is one reason why experienced leaders frequently outmanage inexperienced ones. Experienced leaders have failed frequently—both on their own and with a team of people. Because of those experiences, those leaders are better able to anticipate where failure is likely to come from, and minimize the effects of that failure.

Great companies are built on great people. And building great people starts with great commanders. When you find them, hold on to them.

TAKE CARE OF YOUR PEOPLE

Execution Rules

- Your people represent your company.
- Provide the right working environment.
- Build employee programs that help you structure a more profitable business.

> If an army encamps close to water and grass with adequate supplies,
> it will be free from countless diseases and this will spell victory.
> — Sun Tzu

Perennially one of the top 100 companies to work for in America is Wegmans Food Markets. A regional purveyor of premium fresh and prepared foods, Wegmans adds value to its products with the services customers receive at store level. President Danny Wegman teaches the spirit of "caring about one person at a time."

Caring about one person at a time is not as easy as it sounds. It is never convenient—people don't schedule their problems around your convenience. And it requires action—timely action. But it may be the best way to build a culture of caring for people. Stories spread—stories that start from the top.

This is an attitude that is shared among great retailers. Great retailing, brick-and-mortar retailing in particular, is driven by great execution. It doesn't matter how good the products were, if the checkout lines were five people deep. You won't go back. The greatest retailing strategies can easily be defeated by the high school checkout clerk who is the last person you meet at almost any store.

Caring about people helps them work together—and that shows up at the bottom line.

Mike Bingham, who has headed large production operations for companies like Safeway, Rich's, and Del Monte, tells the story of taking over a Frito-Lay production plant that was "broken" in its relationship between managers and employees. They weren't working together effectively. So the plant wasn't working effectively. Mike fixed the plant by learning the names of all 700 hourly employees. That took him four months. And within six months he had the plant's management and employees working together, and plant productivity was back to meeting expectations.

Many successful leaders work hard to have employees feel good about the work they do. Looking employees in the eye and saying words like

"That is an important job" and "Thanks for being here with us today" can make people feel the work they are doing is valuable. Employees who feel their work is valuable will stay with a company longer.

Build the Right Work Environment

The work environment isn't just physical—it is the spirit of the company as well. Many companies today employ a large number of first-generation immigrants. Production facilities that have high employee-retention rates generally provide a language-friendly plant environment for these employees. Examples include bilingual supervisors and managers and promoting workers into management ranks— stories about managers who started as hourly workers and worked their way into plant management can be powerful for attracting and keeping other employees wanting to travel that same path.

Building the right work environment can translate into innovative policies too. FreshDirect has found over time that first-generation employees generally go home and visit their families for an extended time period each year. Airfare is not cheap, and their home countries are not close by. Thus, these trips can last several weeks. FreshDirect has always found ways to accommodate this so that the best employees will stay. However, people were taking their leaves at times that were not convenient to the business. FreshDirect's business has seasonal spikes, and losing good people at the wrong time can be painful. Inspiration hit when a chef told a story about working on a cruise line. When an employee completed a "tour" on a cruise ship, went home, and came back, the cruise line would reimburse his or her airfare. However, the airfare would be reimbursed only after the employee came back.

FreshDirect put a similar program in place for hourly employees— "Summer Leave." The Summer Leave program matched up a seasonal trough in business with an incentive to take a long break from work. This incentive is open to any employee who leaves work for four to eight weeks in July or August—the slowest time of the year. Summer Leave applicants have their job guaranteed if they returned to work by mid-September. Upon return and completion of a few weeks worth of work, they receive a check—essentially enough money to pay for airfare home.

To date, over 95 percent of the people who leave for the Summer Leave program come back and claim their extra paycheck. A win for employees, and help for balancing a workforce across the year.

SHARE REWARDS

Execution Rules

- Pay what you need to pay.
- Rewards should conform to your workforce.
- Communicate to employees as effectively as you communicate to your customers.

> Now, in order to kill the enemy, our men must be roused to anger; to gain the enemy's property, our men must be rewarded with war trophies.
> —Sun Tzu

Most business leaders accept the thought that great companies are built by great employees. A company's creative ideas, and winning execution, come from the work of its employees. Retention of great employees is determined by how you treat them, how you train them, and how you pay them.

Good people have a tendency to know their value and what they contribute to an organization. So if you want to retain good people, you need to pay them what they are worth. If your work environment is demanding or the hours are unusual, you will need to compensate accordingly.

Companies that try to keep good people without investing in them often end up being the loser in the war for talent. An employee who doesn't get training but wants to better himself will seek out an employer that will develop his skills. Employees who know they are doing a good job will want to be paid accordingly for that work.

Jim Siregal of Costco is repeatedly asked questions about why he pays his people so well. Jim says simply, "We pay much better than Wal-Mart. That's not altruism. That's good business." Costco's CFO expounds on this thought more specifically: "From day one we've run the company with the philosophy that if we pay better than average, provide a salary people can live on, have a positive environment and good benefits, we'll be able to hire better people, and they'll stay longer and be more efficient." Senegal's strategy of taking care of his employees above and beyond the call of duty has not gone without criticism. One analyst famously said of Costco, "It's better to be an employee or a customer than a shareholder. He's right that a happy employee is a productive long-term employee, but he could force employees to pick up a little more of the burden."

However, Costco's stock continues to do very well, trading at a price/ earnings multiple higher than most of its competitors'. Costco's head of HR says, "When Jim talks to us about setting wages and benefits, he doesn't want us to be better than everyone else, he wants us to be demonstrably better." Siregal has unapologetically stuck to his guns, saying in one interview, "We want to build a company that will still be here in 50 and 60 years." And he believes maintaining a highly stable workforce is part of how he ensures that future.

Successfully retaining people requires many things:

Rewards that are relevant to the employees. Different employees want different rewards. An older workforce will place more value on good health-care benefits than a younger, single workforce will. Your reward structure should conform to the needs of your workforce, or the workforce you are trying to attract.

Consistently communicating the value of what you offer. Beyond a weekly paycheck, benefits or rewards you offer will not tend to register with your employees. A pay raise (or bonus) is easy to understand—employees see that in their weekly paycheck. Paying more of an employee's health-care benefits, for example, is more difficult for an employee to understand the value of. It's not money they can spend as they wish. Thus, most employees don't understand the significant expense it entails for your company—and the commitment to the employees that it represents.

The only way for your employee to understand the reward you offer it to communicate it to them—directly and consistently. You need your employees to understand the value *they* get from the money you are spending. If not, these are not good expenditures—or good rewards.

Managers and supervisors must understand the rewards. Can you, your managers, and even senior managers recount the benefits offered by the company? The fact is that most managers have gaps in their understanding of their company's benefits and nonpay rewards. Many employees will talk with their direct supervisors regarding their company's benefits and nonwage pay policies. Make sure your managers and supervisors have adequate knowledge to answer those questions accurately, on the spot.

Your employees need to understand what they are receiving—and how it reflects the company's commitment to their talent. Constantly communicate the value of your benefits to your employees. This is particularly important with nonpaycheck rewards such as flextime, casual dress policies, and so forth. If your employees don't know how what you are offering differentiates you from the competitors that want to hire them, they can't find value in that reward. The details are important here. Do you have a diverse staff? How many languages do you need to communicate in? Are certain benefits more valuable to certain employees (e.g., flextime for working parents)? Don't rely on one single communication—too many people will fail to understand what you are trying to say.

A former regional manager of McDonald's tells how he retained employees with attendance contests. The McDonald's workforce is young and highly mobile. A minimum-wage job at McDonald's isn't that different, or better, than a minimum-wage job somewhere else. So one strategy to retain young workers was contests. When the store reached a certain goal, the entire store won a bus trip to the local water park (a crew from a neighboring store would be brought in to run that location for the day). For that particular workforce, that was a relevant reward—and one that differentiated that employer from other minimum-wage choices.

MOTIVATE

Execution Rules

- Define expectations.
- Make the decisions that need to be made.
- Be fair to individuals.

Hence, the general who advances without coveting fame and retreats without fearing disgrace, whose only purpose is to protect his people and promote the best interests of his sovereign, is the precious jewel of the state.
—Sun Tzu

Many different companies in the retail and restaurant industry employ "secret shopper" programs. Commonly, employees of a third-party company pretend to be average customers so they can "shop" the store incognito and observe how the store is run, how employees interact with each other, and the level of service customers receive. Some retailers use the program to reward quality work from their employees, whereas other companies use these programs to identify behavior that they don't want. Time after time, David Rich of ICC Decision Services finds that the companies who use these programs to reward good behavior make more money than those companies who use them to catch employees unawares. Reward, rather than fear of being chastised, is a bigger motivator for employees.

In secret shopping as in life, a positive attitude wins over a negative one. To build effectiveness, leaders need to inspire. They need to get the most out of those around them.

How you set up a situation will determine how your people will react. The French military commander the Marquis de Saxe explains it the following way: "Thus when you have stationed your troops behind a parapet, they hope, by their fire, to prevent the enemy from passing the ditch and mounting it. If this happens, in spite of the fire, they give themselves up for lost, lose their heads, and fly. It would be much better to post a single rank there, armed with pikes, whose business will be to push the assailant back as fast as they attempt to mount. And certainly they will execute this duty because it is what they expect and will be prepared for." Don't set up people into a situation they are likely to fail. Their reactions when faced with failure may not be what you want. Set up situations with positive, realistic expectations.

Sun Tzu expresses this aspect of motivating people as well, similar to the Marquis de Saxe's experiences: "Now, at the beginning of a campaign, the spirit of soldiers is keen; after a certain period of time, it declines; and in the later stage, it may be dwindled to naught." The Marquis de Saxe did his writings in the 1700s while Sun Tzu wrote in 500 B.C. However, the underlying principles of getting the most out of a group of people don't change. How you build the expectations of your team will determine how they react. And that will affect their motivation, and your ability to retain their commitment to your goals.

One organization that is a great example of maintaining the motivation of its employees is the New Seasons market in Oregon. At this small retail chain, employees are given "get out of jail free" cards and permission to do what the customer wants. Printed on the back of the card it says:

> *Dear Supervisor: The holder of this card was, in their best judgment, doing whatever was necessary to make a happy customer. If you think they have gone overboard, please take the following steps:*
>
> 1. *Thank them for giving great customer service.*
> 2. *Listen to the story about the events.*
> 3. *Offer feedback on how they might do it differently next time.*
> 4. *Thank them for giving great customer service.*

This system gives employees permission to take a risk, and supervisors an open and comfortable way to correct behavior and provide training.

One of the roles of a business leader is to get other organizational leaders behind you. These may be peers or subordinates. Getting peers and subordinates to commit to your direction is a great step. As you do this, make sure you are leading people down a path they can succeed on. As a leader, your role is to clear obstacles in their way. Anticipate where internal opposition may come from, and work to manage that opposition. Successful leaders

1. Know who their allies are and win as many senior-level allies as possible to their "cause" early,
2. Know what objections they will hear, and set up early tests to assuage those objections, and
3. Find a way to attach their goals and project to the broader goals a company is already pursuing and committing resources to.

Build High-Quality Management

Research shows that employees will judge a company based on their opinion of their direct supervisor. That relationship defines your company's "brand" to your employees. Thus, your organization needs to make its managers and supervisors as good as they can be. Hiring practices and training practices will dictate how this is done for your particular organization.

Gerald Michaelson, used to say, "It's not the people you fire that cause you stress, it's the ones you don't." In all these decisions, balancing your responsibility to the company, the individual manager, and the people underneath that manager is challenging. How you make these decisions is important—these decisions impact the culture and the trust employees have in the company. And they impact the trust people have in you.

Create trust by:

Maintaining high performance standards. During the course of my management career, I have been hired by several poorly performing organizations to improve their processes and performance. In these situations, you will often find people that by objective standards are not performing well. And frequently "the bar" has been allowed to slip. Performance that is not acceptable had been judged acceptable—otherwise the poorly performing employees would have left on their own accord when they realized they didn't pass muster, or they would have been replaced. I start in these situations by setting—in effect "re-setting"—the performance standard. It could be a process, a measurable result, or a style of interacting. Reset these standards with firmness and also with empathy—failing to meet them immediately doesn't mean the employee will be fired, but he or she will be made aware if he or she doesn't meet the standard. Frequently, you will find many employees, with a little help, rise to the new expectations. People want to succeed.

Use metrics. Emotion is sometimes a useful business tool—but more often than not, it isn't. Most emotional conversations lose some logic and rationality—and can harm business relationships. Setting some simple metrics gives a "grounding" to conversations and keeps things focused on business performance. For example, don't allow your employees to rant and rave about how a particular employee or policy upsets them. Instead, have them focus on how it impacts their ability to do their job. Is the problem at hand diminishing their productivity? Costing the company customers or profits? What are the metrics of the situation? Setting the right metrics lets you focus your conversations on the most leverageable points for your business.

Always respect the individual. Why? You will be more effective. People listening to you will actually hear you better, and they will take your feedback less defensively. They will be more likely to change their performance based on your feedback.

If this approach sounds too soft, don't forget people are watching you as a manager. How you handle these situations will define how people think of you. And these situations will significantly impact how your people believe they will be treated if they were placed in a similar situation with you. Put in place practices that support your motivating, your getting the most out of, the people that you have.

EXECUTION IS DRIVEN BY PEOPLE

Execution Rules

- Hire quality.
- Look for a winning track record.
- Look for leaders who make people around them better.

> When the officers are valiant and the soldiers
> ineffective, the army will fall.
> —Sun Tzu

Start with the best people you can hire. The vice president of operations for the Container Store, one of the best companies to work for in America, according to Fortune magazine, says, "One of our foundation principles is that one great person equals three good people. If one great person equals three good people, one good person equals three average people, and one average person equals three lousy people." With that math, it is clear why the Container Store is so adamant about taking their time in hiring people.

Experienced companies offer some thoughts on what to look for in great people:

Look for "unteachable" strengths. In football, there is an expression: "You can't coach speed"—either you have it or you don't. In business, the same principle holds true. Depending on the job, a certain level of creativity might be needed. In sales jobs, an outgoing personality may be a requirement. These are traits that not all people possess and can't be taught. You just have to hire for them.

Look for a winning track record. Winners will have an appropriate track record. People who have built a business, successfully introduced a new product, or fixed problems know what that success feels like. They likely have the confidence to overcome obstacles.

Look for fire in the belly. Call it character. Call it desire. Jimmy the Greek might call this "the intangibles." Someone who will have the determination or resilience to make the right things happen. At Procter & Gamble, "fire in the belly" is one of the traits they recruit to.

Look for passion. Someone on a mission can accomplish change where others would struggle. This is one of the characteristics top employer Yahoo looks for in its employees. Says one Yahoo! senior vice president, "We want people who are passionate about their subject areas." They even put it on their Web site: "We are looking for people who believe passionately in our mission."

Though talent and track record are critical, you also want to hire people who have a mistake or two along the way. Perhaps a bad career move?

Perhaps a business decision that turned out to be wrong? Someone who has made a mistake—and can fess up to it—has gained maturity. They may also have gained some learning on someone else's dime, so they're less likely to blunder in *your* organization.

Make Plans Your People Can Execute

When the U.S. space program put a man on the moon, our spaceships were relatively simple in overall design. Essentially they were rockets with a capsule on the top. If you look at the earliest footage of rockets, you can see the clear lineage to the Saturn V rockets of the Apollo program. Over time, that program was replaced with the more complicated design of the space shuttle. Designed for a tougher list of requirements—and no longer fully disposable—the main capsule, now a plane, was reusable. The payload was increased significantly, and technology was added to accomplish more tasks in space. This complexity provided a variety of problems: temperature-sensitive O-rings, falling insulation, and damaged tiles. The space shuttle had two massive failures and rarely flew on time after those problems.

NASA has announced that in a few years, the shuttle is slated to be replaced with a much simpler design, likely a rocket with a capsule of some design on top, in concept very similar to the old Apollo design. Simplicity wins out over complexity. Why? Because it is easier for fallible humans to execute. That leads to better results.

Make your plans realistic for the people involved. Set stretch goals, of course. But fit plans into the skills and experiences of the people who will carry them out. As you do this, make the ideas you work on the ideas your people (including peers and others) are excited to execute.

As you work to influence people, you need to be skillful in setting up how people view the ideas you expect them to contribute to. Consider:

Timing. An operation I managed had to cancel almost two days of production at the height of our busy season due to a huge snowstorm.

People worked hard getting the production done, they worked hard getting to and from work, and they were tired. But we needed to crank up production to get out more orders. I waited a day to ask about raising production later in the week—it was the soonest we could take more orders—and I didn't lose anything. The one day of rest helped calm frayed nerves, and people willingly agreed to take more orders. They knew it was what the company needed to do, and they were now in a mind-set to make it their idea. As you would expect, they executed the incremental production very well.

Championing someone else's idea. If you know what your objective is, you can use more than one path to get there. Let someone else choose the path. You will still get to where you are going. But you will have someone else committed to the objective. Focus simply on moving the business forward—let someone else guide the tactics.

Managing what people are thinking about. Set the tone. Ask the right questions. If you are asking questions, and getting other people to help answer those questions, you are setting an agenda. The organization will concentrate on the things you want them to. Don't micromanage and don't be controlling. Instead, keep working on asking the right questions that will lead to fewer problems, new products, and better opportunities for your organization. Thought will lead to action. You will just have to guide the enthusiasm.

The best leaders make the people around them even better. They have the ability to help their people to be successful. Some do this by setting a very clear direction—everyone knows where they are going and what the organization's mission is. Some do it because they have a great grasp for the business and years of experience under their belt, and they have the ability to share that with those around them. Size up your strengths, and work to get the best out of the people around you.

Chapter 7

Flexibility

In business, many companies fear their more successful rivals—those competitors that exceed them in profitability, product design, and market share. However, the competitors to fear are not the ones who try and succeed but rather those that try and fail—and then dust themselves off and try again. Those are the competitors who will, over the long term, excel in their industry and with their customers.

In the early 1980s, Cadillac brought out a small luxury car to compete with BMW and similar competitors. This seemed like a natural offering for the Cadillac brand, which had been associated with luxury but in recent years had acquired a staid perception among consumers. Cadillac's Cimarron offering was an upgrade of a Chevy Cavalier. Unfortunately, the Cadillac was an obvious cousin of the Chevy—not a good thing in the luxury market. The Cimarron flopped. First-year sales were just one-third of Cadillac's expectations, and several years later, the car was discontinued.

In the late 1990s, Cadillac went after this market segment again. Their Catera was again built off of a standard General Motors platform, but this time from a European division. This offering also had a little more differentiation from the core General Motors line. Unfortunately, the car got ho-hum reviews and its "Caddy that zigs" advertising was widely derided. The car sold poorly and was discontinued after four model years.

A few years later, Cadillac tried again with another small luxury car—the CTS. This time their CTS was a sales hit—it was nominated for several Car of the Year awards when it was introduced. It revitalized the Cadillac brand and overall sales for the company. It was a testament to Cadillac's try-and-try-again attitude.

Fast-changing markets illustrate the importance of bouncing back from failures:

- Apple, struggling but never quite completely down for the count in the competitive home computer market, made a significant relaunch with the iPod. Apple's iPods became a cult hit and grew to outsell its computers by more than 10 to 1 and was followed by their category-changing iPad. Not what you would have necessarily expected from Apple fifteen years ago when Michael Dell suggested the company should be closed down and any cash returned to shareholders.

- Las Vegas is one of the most dynamic hotel markets in the country. Steve Wynn's new hotel in Las Vegas, The Wynn, at the site of the old Desert Inn, is one of Las Vegas's most popular and talked-about hotels. Undeterred by critics, Steve just keeps on building. He started by buying Las Vegas's downtown Golden Nugget Hotel and renovating it; later, he built a Golden Nugget Hotel in Atlantic City. Then he sold the Atlantic City property and bought a piece of land on the strip in Las Vegas and built the Mirage Hotel. He followed that up with the Treasure Island and the Bellagio. After selling those properties, Steve opened The Wynn on the site of the former Desert Inn. By many people's measure, Steve Wynn has never really failed. But he does keep on trying and trying—and successfully beating his own personal best each time.

MANAGE YOUR RISK

Trying and failing can be scary. In some organizations, it can even be career threatening. But, if managed well, failing can actually lead you to greater success down the road. The key is to manage failure strategically:

Keep losses small. Testing is part of any business. Testing in small ways lets you learn at a rate the organization can afford. Picking a specific geography, group of customers, or a small set of locations can give an opportunity to learn—without losing everything. Picking a spot that you can monitor closely, and be involved in, can help you maximize your learning. A series of small tests can let you steadily improve a concept and make improvements as you go.

Involve high-level management. Involving top management gives you buy-in and support. It also attaches visibility to your project and can help your test efforts succeed.

Acknowledge the possibility of failure. Expectations can help a team of people support an effort that may not succeed. Do this by building an understanding of the importance of the test itself—how it can yield important information that could possibly build a more successful product or service.

There is an expression from World War II, "The first wave dies on the beach," which refers to the staggering 80 percent loss of the first wave of troops that went ashore on D-Day. If your initiative is that "first wave," it might not work the first time. Manage expectations and build support for the next wave or the follow-up initiative.

Celebrate the win in the loss. This is failing forward. If your test leads to another test, claim victory! Do whatever you can to maintain organizational excitement for the effort.

Manage risk well so that you can tackle bigger risks over time. Successful leaders look to shoulder, and manage, more and more risk. Not unwisely. But in the spirit of creating opportunity, building profits, and growing a business. Managers who can manage risk with success are invaluable to the companies they work for.

SPEED HAS VALUE

Execution Rules

- Move quickly when opportunity arises.
- Prepare for opportunities to enable speed.
- Deliberate preparation enables speedy action.

> Thus, while we have heard of stupid haste in war, we have not yet seen a clever operation that was prolonged. There has never been a case in which a prolonged war has benefited a country.
> —Sun Tzu

Speed pays off. When Hurricane Katrina hit New Orleans, many governmental and business organizations were caught badly off guard. Initially, Wal-Mart was one of them. However, Wal-Mart quickly recovered and got huge positive PR for its speedy response. Days after the hurricane hit, Wal-Mart chairman Lee Scott was at a press conference with former presidents Bill Clinton and George Bush Sr. He quickly offered all displaced former New Orleans employees an immediate job at any Wal-Mart in the country—and got huge positive press. Almost before FEMA figured out that there were people stranded at the New Orleans Convention Center, Wal-Mart had a public relations coup.

Slowness rarely wins the game. In World War II the German blitzkrieg was moving rapidly across Western Europe—so rapidly in fact that many German commanders were surprised by their own success. Instead of continuing to move quickly against the surrounded British army at the French port of Dunkirk, the German army stopped because commanders were worried about stretching their forces too thin. "Dunkirk was to be had for the asking," writes military historian Kenneth Macksey. And hundreds of thousands of Allied troops lived to fight another day—and eventually defeat German forces.

Moving quickly allows competitive advantage. Auto companies try to speed up their product-development cycle to get new products to market faster. Political candidates try to convert polling data into TV ads and election tactics quickly. Retailers move quickly to sell what is in fashion at the moment.

Moving with deliberate speed is more important in the age of the Internet. Blogs can build a rumor into a reality—and if not addressed quickly, unsubstantiated and false claims can take on an aura of truth. Or blogs can be used to build the mystique of a product.

In today's competitive marketplace, speed is an offensive weapon. Use it to reach your market. Regional food retailer FreshDirect was the first to market with a new packaging technology that steamed meals. Fresh-Direct got incredible coverage in the *Wall Street Journal* and *New York Times*, as well as in regional media. A big coup for a small company! Being first to market with this product created a lot of positive buzz for the company and reached many potential new customers.

To organize decision making. One friend of mine says, "Push decision making to the lowest level possible." That's a scary concept for many companies. What if "they" make a mistake? The thing is that "they" will fix it most times before any senior leader ever learns about the particular mistake. Decisions made by the lowest level are decisions made in real time. The empowered hotel clerk who gives a customer a room upgrade and the customer-service representative who satisfies a complaint are examples of people at the lower rungs of an organization intercepting a problem or an issue quickly. Customers like this, and handling customer complaints with speed and fairness frequently can turn a bad customer service encounter into a loyalty builder.

To gain actionable intelligence quickly. Larry Weiss of the research company Linescale uses online consumer testing to give his clients the advantage of speed. Answers to online questions come back in days, and results are instantly tabulated. This approach to research is much faster than phone or mall research, where results take several weeks to be processed. Faster knowledge can lead to faster action.

Create a Sense of Urgency

A sense of urgency drives results. This is obvious in times of a national emergency such as the 9/11 terrorist attacks, the 2004 Indonesian tsunami, or Hurricane Katrina's devastation of New Orleans. In each case, corporations, government, and private citizens responded to support relief. In the business world, we rarely have such obviously galvanizing events. But there are still many ways to create a sense of urgency:

A competitive threat. You can use the growth and success of a competitor as a call to action for your employees and to build a sense of urgency for creating change in the workplace.

Customer data and stories. If you don't have customers, you won't have a business. Trend data on customer satisfaction, or even anecdotes from customers, can build urgency for creating change in your products or services that the customers will see. Most employees know that customers are important—without them, the employees wouldn't have a job to come to every morning. Use your customers to communicate to your employees—be it directly or indirectly, through surveys and research—it will have more impact than if you say those things yourself.

Seasonality. For many consumer companies, the fourth quarter is a huge quarter—the Christmas holiday drives an obvious increase in sales. You can use that as leverage for getting projects completed "before the big surge." You can also make an appropriate call for extra help and work during a busy time.

Sun Tzu was a big fan of speed—provided it was used opportunistically. He writes, *By "situation," I mean he should act expediently in accordance with what is advantageous in the field and so meet any exigency.* Speed, when exercised with good judgment, is a practice that leads to success.

USE A VARIETY OF ATTACKS

Execution Rules

- Be agile.
- Get many opinions in forming your plans.
- Keep your mind open.

In battle, there are not more than two kinds of postures—operation
of the extraordinary force and operation of the normal force, but their
combinations give rise to an endless series of maneuvers. For these two
forces are mutually reproductive. It is like moving in a circle, never coming
to an end. Who can exhaust the possibilities of their combinations?
—Sun Tzu

Business is rarely predictable. We all make plans. However, those plans must change as the business develops. In the military operations, plans change when contact with the enemy is made. Only an unskilled or foolish commander insists on rigidly sticking to advance plans if a battle requires alternative measures.

Says Clayton Jones, chief executive of defense contractor Rockwell Collins in the January 9, 2006, issue of Forbes, "We compete in the land of the giants. What we lack in size we make up for with focus and agility." Jones believes he manages this agility by listening to his customers, who give him new insights as the business battle unfolds.

Netflix invented the online rental of DVDs. In 2005 Blockbuster decided to take its shot at owning that business. Netflix responded by spending aggressively to grow its business, add new subscribers, and maintain its lead in this business. Netflix significantly changed its plans—and watched its stock price plunge from $39 to $9.

However, the strategy proved effective. At the end of that year, Blockbuster crowed about its success at achieving over 1 million subscribers. Netflix, however, remained the dominant industry leader. Its decision to spend aggressively had grown its subscriber base to *over 4 million subscribers*. And by the end of the year, Netflix's stock had rebounded considerably based on its success in growing and maintaining its market dominance.

Netflix changed course and responded well to changes in the marketplace. It deviated from its original plan. A mid-2004 financial release stated, "The Company said it expects to increase profitability through 2006." That clearly didn't happen—though it might have been a reasonable expectation at the time. The situation changes the plan. And Netflix continues to be particularly nimble in changing situations.

Bring a New Perspective

At the World Economic Forum in Davos, Switzerland, consultant Tim Brown advised, "We learn our way to solutions." He advised finding a problem you have never worked on before. That will allow you to bring a fresh perspective. In other words, he advised, approach problems with a beginner's mind.

A new view of a problem is valuable—in meetings and deliberations, strive to get a variety of opinions heard. This simply leads to better decisions. Do this through:

Inviting someone who will likely hold the minority view. Perhaps that is someone from outside your department. Or someone who comes from a different set of experiences (either from outside of the company or someone who came up through a different functional silo within your company).

Encouraging dissenters to speak up. Hear opposing viewpoints. Seek out different opinions. Conduct meetings in a way that makes people feel comfortable and rewarded for speaking up.

Asking open-ended questions. To encourage alternative viewpoints, direct your open-ended questions to people who (1) are likely to disagree with you or (2) have not been major contributors to the conversation.

Research has shown that the IQ of a group is higher than the individual IQ of any one member of the group. This makes sense because the group can use all the talents and experiences of all people in the group. Use this math to your advantage in building your business. But the math adds up only if the contributions of each and every team member are sought. If the team is led by a bully or someone who listens to a chosen few, the IQ of the team may never exceed the IQ of that person.

Sometimes, it is simply a matter of style in hearing new perspectives and allowing you to consider a broader range of choices. An open, collegial style can encourage more open debate and sharing—but only when practiced consistently and with sincerity.

Sun Tzu recognizes this in his management of armies. He advises, *It is the business of a general to be quiet and thus ensure depth in deliberation; impartial and upright and, thus, keep a good management.*

TAKE ADVANTAGE OF OPPORTUNITY

Execution Rules

- Manage opportunities as a good negotiator: Don't overpay.
- Keep customers at the forefront of your decision making.
- Find metrics that disseminate customer-driven thinking.

> The commander must create a helpful situation over and beyond the ordinary rules. By "situation," I mean he should act expediently in accordance with what is advantageous in the field and so meet any exigency.
> —Sun Tzu

Cagey negotiators leave their options open so they can take advantage of the best opportunity. When Michael Dell is interviewed about his company's relationship with Intel (until their acquisition of gaming-computer maker Alienware, Dell used only Intel chips), he says, "We don't have an exclusive arrangement with Intel." That statement leaves the door open for Dell to have relationships with other microprocessor manufacturers and inherently works to keep Intel on its toes—and its price offerings to Dell competitive.

Every publicly held company needs to make its quarterly results. When negotiating for high-ticket items such as software, you can frequently improve the pricing you receive if you negotiate with a vendor who is having a subpar quarter. They will be much more amenable to giving you a price break to secure the sale. Accordingly, if you have flexibility in your timing or are talking to multiple vendors, probe and exploit the weaknesses that let you get the best price.

Sun Tzu was opportunistic in his operations. He advised, *If the enemy leaves a door open, you must rush in. Seize the place the enemy values without making an appointment for battle with him.* Sun Tzu took advantage of opportunities aggressively.

Taking advantage of opportunities means not overpaying in money, time, or the opportunity cost for your organization. You can avoid overpaying by constantly staying ahead of the curve on the areas you are looking at for opportunities. A current knowledge base helps detect and assess opportunities. Gut feelings and hunches play a part in business, but they must be backed up by research and knowledge of the marketplace. You can become a very good negotiator by doing a few things. Great buyers consistently follow a few guidelines:

They are always out testing the market. They meet with vendors they may not even want to do business with. This keeps their knowledge base constantly up to date. They know pricing—because they are always probing for a better price. They know about quality—because any good pricing conversation involves some quality discussion. They know trends, from multiple viewpoints, because they are always asking about what is new. This practice keeps great buyers constantly current on new developments in the marketplace.

They try to never get beholden to a vendor. Granted, that sometimes isn't possible. (No drugstore can avoid selling Crest toothpaste.) But very frequently you can exert leverage by saying no to certain vendors or giving better placement to their competitors. Great buyers keep as much of their business "in play" with as many vendors as possible.

They are loyal to people who have been loyal to them. Test the market and maintain your flexibility, but don't change vendors and relationships on a whim. If you find more competitive pricing and service, give your preferred vendor an opportunity to meet it. Also, look at the benefits of doing business with someone who already knows your business and expectations. Loyalty can translate into real dollars in terms of vendors who will go the extra mile for you on service.

Keep Customers as Your North Star

We all make money by serving customers. Taking advantage of opportunities in a customer-driven way best ensures a long-term payout from decisions made opportunistically. Being customer driven means that the customers' needs and desires are always taken into account in decision making.

Ancient mariners successfully traveled incredible distances using the North Star for navigation. If blown off course, they could get back on track using the North Star. The North Star didn't tell them where to go, but it did give them an unchanging reference point that kept them on course.

Customer-centered organizations use the customer as their North Star. Competitive jostling and changing markets may temporarily knock you off course. But you can always refocus by listening to your customers and what they want. At the end of the day, the customer—not your competitors, Wall Street, or industry pundits—determines who wins.

Customer-centered organizations share several characteristics:

Fact-based decision making. Facts can be market research or sales results. Fact-based decision making keeps emotion and opinions at a proper level. If used well, it will help keep your organization focused on the most important opportunities available.

Listening to the customer. There are different ways to listen to customers. Some companies have formal research programs or conduct regular focus groups. Some companies listen informally to customers—customer complaints can be an example. In retailing, some companies have a culture of listening to customers at the point of contact. This is easy and inexpensive to do as customers are available in the store at any time. Other companies dive deeply into customer complaints—and broadly circulate those (as well as customer testimonials) in their organizations.

Having a customer-comes-first culture. When decisions are made, are the customers' needs taken into account? This is a matter of organizational culture and style. In customer-driven cultures, talking about the customer is commonplace. And customers' needs are taken into account when major decisions are made. This is done through understanding the effect on the customer of a particular decision—how it impacts a customer negatively, how it impacts a customer positively. Many decisions do both.

Investing only where customers will pay for that investment. Great customer-centric organizations have a knack for putting their money where customers would want that money placed. They may invest in better-trained staff because the improvement in service is the most relevant—and immediate—improvement for the customer.

Some companies make profits solely on how they manage their money. Watching costs, maintaining margins, and keeping within budgets are their top priority. In customer-centered organizations, a different view of the world prevails—companies make money by serving their customers better than their competitors do. These companies understand that as long as they are favored by their customers, their financial future is solid. Making money in these cultures is the logical outcome of serving customers.

These companies still watch costs, margins, and budgets. Managing those aspects competently is part of managing any company. But these companies believe that financial metrics will fall into place over the long term when customers are well served. Customer-centered companies find a good balance between short-term financial success and long-term financial success.

Customer-centered organizations talk about customers at all levels, and take actions based on their perceptions of customer needs. At Procter & Gamble, employees are inculcated in a customer-driven culture. P&G believes that two different actions can grow their brands. First, better product—a consumer-relevant product advantage. Second, better communication of that advantage—a better connection with the customer. Those actions are viewed as the two ways long-term value is added to the organization. Other actions may add value, but not in the same long-term sustainable way.

Jeff Bezos of Amazon.com sums it up in the following way: "If you give customers what they want, the rest will take care of itself."

USE SURPRISE

Execution Rules

- Surprise is disruptive to your competitors.
- Capitalize aggressively on successful innovations.
- Look inside for ideas.

> Thus, one who is adept at keeping the enemy on the move maintains deceitful appearances, according to which the enemy will act. He lures with something that the enemy is sure to take. By so doing he keeps the enemy on the move and then waits for the right moment to make a sudden ambush with picked troops.
> —Sun Tzu

In business and in military operations, doing the unexpected can yield a significant advantage. The U.S. Army's pre–World War II advice in

Infantry in Battle was, "Surprise is usually decisive; therefore, much may be sacrificed to achieve it. It should be striven for by all units, regardless of size, and in all engagements, regardless of importance." Because surprise is decisive, it is a significant asset in the business world.

Marketers talk about differentiating. Investment bankers go one step further and talk about being disruptive. That is how you destabilize a market and make a superior return, by disrupting the status quo. Surprise disrupts the status quo.

Surprise can take several forms. A new marketing strategy can surprise the competition—perhaps an unexpected lowering of prices, or a sudden increase in promotion. A particularly pointed advertising campaign can be a surprise—like a "Pepsi Challenge" comparison, where Pepsi is tasted side by side with Coke and wins because most people actually prefer the sweeter taste of Pepsi. An advertising execution like that can make your competitor rethink their core strategy. In the case of the Pepsi Challenge, it prompted Coke to introduce an ultimately unsuccessful reformulation of Coke that tasted more like Pepsi. Coca-Cola subsequently withdrew that product from the market.

Surprise forces your competitors to think in ways they hadn't previously. Hiring a key person away from a competitor can cause surprise and upset preexisting plans. That's why you will frequently see lawsuits when a company hires talent from a direct competitor. A new acquisition can upset a delicate competitive balance and cause an industry shake-up. And new products can recast market shares and force competitors to react, or retrench.

Innovate

Innovation is a form of surprise. It catches competitors off guard. And it gives smaller companies an opportunity to compete against more entrenched competitors. Few innovative ideas are completely and truly new. Most new ideas are a repurposing of an idea that started some-where else. Wal-Mart borrowed the idea of a supercenter (a combina-tion mass merchant and supermarket under one roof) from a Midwestern competitor. Ray Kroc bought McDonald's and simply had the vision to build more. Both of these innovations were young ideas that companies capitalized on aggressively.

How do you develop new innovation?

Talk to customers. Customer-driven organizations generally outper-form organizations that don't listen to their customers. Many companies pay lip service to the idea of listening to customers. Listening to custom-ers requires a willingness to take action on what they have to say—partic-ularly when you don't like what the customer says or when taking action on the feedback costs you money.

Paco Underhill is a popular retailing consultant. In his study of shop-ping, he identifies a shopping difference between men and women. He says, "In one study we found that 65% of male shoppers who tried something on bought it, as opposed to 25% of female shoppers." That's an insight that can affect a store's layout, merchandising, and training programs.

Look at industries next to yours. Innovation frequently comes from outside of an industry. The founder of Amazon.com didn't come from the book business or retailing. Wal-Mart, the largest seller of food in the country, didn't come out of the food industry. Look at industries around you for ideas to apply back to your own.

Talk to industry watchers. Sometimes they are the press; sometimes they are consultants. These are people who talk to industry leaders and travel to see the latest innovations. These are people who will have a broad-based perspective on the industry.

Benchmark best practices. This is particularly helpful when looking at the "extremes." Who has lowest costs? Best service? Highest-quality products? What parts of these best performances can be brought back to your own company?

Listen to your own people. Within every organization is plenty of creativity. And plenty of ideas. Frequently from people who are close to your business—who have been thinking about how to solve problems on their own time.

In developing new products or services, one thing to look for is a "chord of familiarity"—a way a new idea is familiar to people who haven't seen that particular product before. A chord of familiarity gives people a way to understand a new product. For example, a battery-operated razor like Gillette's M3 Power or their Fusion is just a battery-operated version of a familiar, basic razor. Though it is new, it is still an understandable innovation, helping it to have a broad appeal.

Successful new ideas build unexpected value for a company and allow new innovations that build from the initial innovation. These can surprise competitors and dramatically increase the value of an enterprise.

LEAD BASED ON THE SITUATION

Execution Rules

- Manage to optimize performance of individuals.
- Keep flexibility in your management systems.
- Informality is a competitive advantage.

Even though we show people the victory gained by using flexible tactics in conformity to the changing situations, they do not comprehend this. People all know the tactics by which we achieved victory, but they do not know how the tactics were applied in the situation to defeat the enemy. Hence, no one victory is gained in the same manner as another. The tactics change in an infinite variety of ways to suit changes in the circumstances.

—Sun Tzu

When asked why his management style varies from individual to individual, natural foods executive Jeff Tripician says, "Because I want to optimize their performance. Since people are different, I get better performance from them if I manage different people differently."

There's a benefit—"to optimize their performance." We don't manage different people and different situations differently because its easier—frequently it isn't. We manage different people differently because if we optimize their performance, we optimize the performance of our team.

An example in the film industry is managing high-profile actors. Says the *Wall Street Journal* in writing about the success of leading directors, "Fine actors bring their own performances; they may require little more than the director's trust." Because of skill in that area, "That's why actors have been so eager to work with filmmakers like Robert Altman, Woody Allen, Sidney Lumet or Martin Scorsese." These directors understand how to get great performances from great actors.

As a business manager, you have lots of tactics at your disposal to optimize performance:

Annual goals. Most companies tie pay and bonuses to sales, profit, and productivity goals. Use these goals to incentivize performance.

Weekly project reviews. You can use this tactic to keep employees on target with goals and expectations. As a manager, weekly project reviews can be helpful if you are new to the company, department, or trying to come up to speed on a particular project. Use this tool as the situation warrants it—for new team members or if a project has slipped off track.

Informal chats. Spend your time where you can make a difference— both informally and formally. While meetings are a necessary part of organizational life, you will often learn more taking time to have informal talks with your staff. The relaxed atmosphere will yield more candor than the feedback you get in a meeting. Meetings often have agendas. Informal chats are about gaining information.

Personnel reviews. Done well, these can be very helpful in setting future priorities. These should not be forums to cast blame or punish past actions; these are opportunities to direct future actions.

Build Processes Judiciously

Different companies succeed with different processes and management systems. In general, big companies have more processes than smaller companies do. That is often because the dollar risks are greater at big companies, thus driving more processes. You can build your processes to fit your company's unique size and needs by looking at the following factors:

Turnover. In high-turnover organizations, build well-defined processes to pass on company knowledge from one "generation" of employees to the next. This can be important in managing IT departments, or other departments where a booming job market can cause sudden turnover.

Experience of people. The more inexperienced people involved in your organization, the more processes you need. Well-defined processes define the steps in decision making so new people can step into a role and have guidance in making the right decisions. When new college graduates enter brand management at Procter & Gamble, they are given responsibility for managing the budget of several P&G brands. That's generally several million dollars worth of responsibility. But the processes and reporting are clear: every month, the new individual sits down with an accounting manager, and then subsequently a brand manager, to explain the current budget spending and any variances. No new, inexperienced employee would have been able to make too many mistakes without someone finding out fairly quickly. The well-set-up processes for these fresh-out-of-school hires ensures that.

The number of people involved. The more people that need to be involved in a decision, the clearer the process needs to be. Otherwise, decision making slows down or gets muddled. In particular, if decision making goes across multiple departments, simple processes can help make hand-off and project transitions run smoothly.

As you manage through fast-changing situations, some simple rules can keep you on track. These rules can vary with the situation.

An example is the nuclear incident at Three Mile Island. Harold Denton was then-President Carter's representative at Three Mile Island while the accident was occurring. He was in the difficult situation of determining risks and handling the press. And events were moving quickly. He needed to make a lot of decisions in a short period of time. Harold offers this set of rules for managing any crisis:

- Tell it like it is.
- Admit uncertainties exist.
- Don't make statements you will have to retract later.
- Act on the best estimate of a situation.
- Refrain from "value judgments."

President Carter said after the incident, "I went into the control room with Harold, and from then on I saw on television every night his calm, professional, reassuring voice letting the American people know that they need have no fear." Harold Denton's rules gave the foundation for better, quicker, action. They helped handle the situation with both flexibility and decisiveness.

The more flexibility you keep in your management systems, the faster and more flexible your company will be. Build your processes to the specific needs of your company. Build guidelines and rules to help delegate decision making and ensure common criteria for those decisions.

DO YOUR HOMEWORK

Execution Rules

- Make learning part of your daily work.
- Study your business.
- Learn related areas.

> Generally, he who occupies the field of battle first and awaits his enemy
> is at ease; he who arrives later and joins the battle in haste is weary.
> —Sun Tzu

Quarterback Tom Brady is one of the NFL's best players. Brady does his homework before each game by watching films of the opposing team to learn their playing style and strategies. In an interview with *60 Minutes* in November 2005, Brady said, "A lot of time is spent . . . on the film and . . . trying to get as many pictures in your head before the game as you can. So when you do walk on the field, you can just verify what's going on. And it's not just to go back there and wing it. You try that, you are going to wake up Monday morning with headaches." In any business you do your homework, make your plan, and you go out and execute.

One of the world's most famous advocates of doing your homework is Warren Buffett. His philosophy is to buy into only those businesses that you can understand. Buffett has never been a big investor in high-tech companies; he claims not to understand them as well as he does other businesses. But he has done well investing in businesses that he does fully understand. He says, "When you are convinced of a strong business's prospects, be aggressive and add to your position rather than buying the 15th or 20th stock on your list of possible investments." That's the confidence that comes from doing your homework. Like Warren Buffett, when you strongly believe you have a winner, go with it.

Homework in the business world takes a lot of forms:

Practice best practices. Tom Brady isn't the only NFL quarterback who watches game films as part of his preparation. Many of the NFL's best quarterbacks are particularly noted for being game-film junkies. Know the best practice in your industry, and make that part of your routine.

Get into the field. Every job has a version of this. If you work in a corporate office, go on sales calls with your salespeople or account managers. A common part of any job, particularly if you are in the corporate office or executive suite, should be to get out to talk to your customers. Go to where your products are sold and talk with the people that sell them. This is where you learn the effects of the decisions that you and your peers make. Great organizations listen and respond to what they learn about in the field.

Do as much of this as you can with your competitors' products as well. In retailing, a common part of management positions is to visit your competitors' stores and see what they are doing. Every industry has a version of this—get out and get as close to your customers, *and* your competitors' customers, as you can.

Study your business. Digging in and understanding your business will always take some work. Make time to understand how your business is doing. Use your internal reports, use industry data, and use people who know about your business.

Learn related aspects of your business. As you progress through your career, you will frequently work in areas that are unfamiliar to you. However, a new product, acquisition, or strategic direction can create an opportunity to work in a part of the business unfamiliar to you. Use these opportunities to learn—it's good for the business and good for your career. The more you learn about the business around you, the more you can make your part of the business (1) respond to the needs of those around you and (2) fit into the corporate needs.

Learn in different ways. We all have preferred ways of learning. This is good up to a point. But to broaden your base of knowledge, you need to learn in different ways. Many people spend most of their learning time with reports. However, you can also learn from:

- Customers
- Vendors
- Peers
- Your supervisor
- Subordinates
- Industry experts
- Conferences and industry gatherings
- The competition

The best learning comes from your devoted customers. Because of their frequency of interaction, they likely know what needs to be fixed or improved about your company. And since they are your best customers, they already like your product, service, or company and want to see it succeed.

Make Preparations

In Sun Tzu's writings, there is no theme on execution that comes out more clearly than preparation. Sun Tzu writes, *Materials for setting fire must always be at hand.* And he says, *Know the weather and know the ground, and your victory will then be complete.*

Sun Tzu's preparation was thorough. He writes, "If in the neighborhood of your camp there are dangerous defiles or ponds and low-lying ground overgrown with aquatic grass and reeds or forested mountains with dense tangled undergrowth, they must be thoroughly searched, for these are possible places where ambushes are laid and spies are hidden." In Sun Tzu's world, these are the "basics." Take pride in getting the basics done well.

In the business world, preparation takes many forms. Training programs are preparation. An annual marketing plan is preparation. Doing your homework for a big sales call is preparation (as is arriving in town the night before a morning meeting—instead of taking the first flight out that same day). A business continuity plan (a disaster plan) is a form of preparation.

Preparation is about looking at the big picture, but it is also about managing the details. Writer William Feather once said, "Beware of the man who won't be bothered with details." In business you need to know the metrics of your business—what percentage of market share you (and your competitor) has, how much your revenue increased each year over the last five years. Every business has a different set of details that need to be managed well.

Preparation goes hand in hand with flexibility. Good preparation gives you the skills and materials and the opportunity to be flexible on the battlefield. As a situation changes, you can take advantage of it. This holds true in the business world. Being prepared and flexible is a good formula for winning.

GET THE MESSAGE THROUGH

Execution Rules

- Communication takes time: Plan accordingly.
- Go to whatever lengths you need to in order to communicate effectively.
- Vary your communication style with situation and the group.

> Do not allow your communication to be blocked.
> —Sun Tzu

Throughout history, people have gone to extraordinary lengths to make sure their message—and its meaning—gets understood. In ancient Greece and Persia, a technique for sending communications was to shave a messenger's head, write a message on his scalp, and wait for the hair to grow back before sending the messenger off. Only upon shaving the hair off of the messenger's head would the message then be visible. That way, if the messenger was captured, the message would be hidden under a head of hair and not discovered. With the advent of electronic communications, the importance of cryptography—ensuring that a message couldn't be read if the message itself fell into the wrong hands—increased. Stories about Allied code breakers who could break the German Enigma code and the Japanese military code have become a great part of our World War II understanding in recent decades.

In business, many things can affect our ability to get a message through. As a "sender" we may not be an effective communicator. Because we are human and thus experience messages through our perceptions and experiences, communication is more an art than a science.

If you want to create change, you need to communicate. There are different techniques to use to be an effective communicator:

Influence. Teddy Roosevelt described being president of the United States as a "bully pulpit." It was a place he could influence "the people." One of the key strengths of the office for Roosevelt was how it helped him influence and communicate with everyday people.

Influence is more important than commanding people who report directly to you. Being able to broadly influence those people around you is an outstanding way to *support* people who work for you. Consider the human resources department in many organizations. HR is an area that has contact with a lot of different departments and with the public via recruiting new employees. But in many organizations, its clout is generally low—it leads without a lot of direct reports. It doesn't set budgets or create new products or accounts. However, it does have a role as an influencer or mediator in many internal company issues. It dispenses advice to employees at all levels of the organization. In many organizations, a strong HR department gets its strength from its ability to form bonds with people, to develop trust, and to guide outcomes. It may not hold strong positional power, but it holds power in its ability to influence.

Find networks. Networks of people disseminate information among the group. Says one Buffalo, New York, native about the arts community there, "People in the arts, for example, all have connections to one another. This arts community may be small compared to some others, but it is one of the least compartmentalized I've ever seen." Networks like this can spread *relevant* information quickly.

Look for allies. Who can help you spread your message? Most likely, someone who believes that message as well. Look for fellow believers. In any organization, there are people who share your point of view. Maybe you are new to a company and there are other new people who have the same perspective. Perhaps there are people faced with similar business challenges. People who share your opinion without any convincing can be valuable allies.

If a project or initiative is important to you, have a communication plan. You probably already have a project plan or a timetable. That's a good start. But make sure you know how

1. To get informal feedback on your project (that's where you find out how things are *really* going),
2. To continue building organization support for your initiative, and
3. To report results.

When it comes to reporting results, don't naively assume you can report good information in the same manner you would bad information. Bad information needs to be managed. That doesn't mean you should hide it—that's a practice that can endanger your project and your reputation. However, reporting good information, good results, requires less information. Bad information needs to be reported in person; good information can be more formally disseminated.

It's About the Style, Too

How often have you heard this: "I sent out an e-mail and I didn't hear anything back"? E-mail is a very efficient form of communication. The sender can immediately communicate with a broad group of people. Respondents can respond at a time that works for them. However, in part because of its efficiency, it is frequently abused through overuse. Be personally effective in how you communicate. It is important because it affects people's perception of you.

Use e-mail appropriately. If something is really important to you, visit or call the appropriate person. In a world of excessive e-mail communications, a visit or call emphasizes the matter in a positive way.

And don't forget old-fashioned communications. Because they are more infrequently practiced, they may make even more impact now than they did years ago. A handwritten note stands out for the recipient. A senior leader going out of his or her way with a handshake and a thank-you is even more memorable.

Managing in Difficult Times Is Even More Challenging

Managing in a company that is experiencing a difficult time requires a greater emphasis on communications. That's because fewer of your company's communications will be in your control. If your company is big enough, quarterly results or major announcements (a downsizing?) will be posted in the paper.

Managing in good times is straightforward. In difficult times, take control of the flow of information:

- Let your employees hear news from you or your company before they hear it elsewhere.
- Let people know what is next.
- Communicate bad news as aggressively as you communicate good news. Stop the rumor mill before it starts.

Chapter 8

Have Towering Strengths

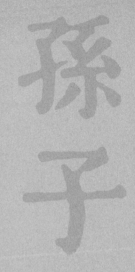

Companies who execute well work at it. If that execution is consistently focused on building competitive advantage, a company can develop towering strengths—strengths that propel the business to a high level of competitive advantage. These strengths come from building one strength on top of another. These strengths can eventually add up to a compelling long-term advantage. These strengths accrue to companies that have invested, and continued to invest, in getting good at a particular aspect or benefit of their business.

Target used to be just another mass merchant. But its lineage descended from a department store—Target's parent company owned Marshall Field's, among other department store brands. Over time, Target brought style and fashion to a mainstream market better than anyone else did. This wasn't an overnight transformation. Target started with designer Michael Graves in 1998 and has added additional designers since then, spreading "design" across its stores and throughout its various departments and products. Now Target designers encompass everyone from Sean Conway for gardening to Sonia Kashuk for makeup.

Intel didn't always make microprocessors. It started by making random access memory circuits. But in the 1980s, the memory chip market was becoming crowded and commoditized. Intel's shift into microprocessors allowed it to take a leadership position in a (at the time) younger market. Now Intel is the microprocessor gold standard—even causing Apple to abandon its G5 microprocessor and move over to the Intel camp.

Japanese car companies' first cars in the U.S. market were cheap—and not of very good quality. Forbes.com nominated the 1978 Honda Accord hatchback as one of the worst cars of all time. But the low prices were enough to achieve sales success and a toehold in the marketplace. Using modern quality-control approaches, the Japanese managed to rapidly improve quality while U.S. companies slipped behind. Now the Japanese have Detroit car companies on the run with their combination of quality and value. Toyota, in particular, has established leadership in the mid-range price segment with various vehicles and a strong presence in the upscale segment with their Lexus brand.

All of these companies are now demonstrable leaders in their fields. They have in one way or another superseded the competition. Maybe in costs, maybe in how they do business, maybe in the image they hold in the customer's mind. Each of their towering strengths allows them to build their business at a faster rate than their competitors can.

Thinking about building towering strengths is a different exercise than most business conversations. A lot of our daily efforts in business are focused on improving things that went wrong. Maybe selling costs were too high for a month, maybe a sales projection was missed, perhaps receivables were too high.

Creating towering strengths requires:

Investing in areas you want to get better at. If you aren't willing to invest a little, you (or your company) doesn't want to excel in that area. In bigger organizations, align yourself with trends or business directions the company is already interested in. Alternatively, find a mentor and low-cost ways to demonstrate a payout for your ideas. Keep the customer as your lightning rod, and your chances of succeeding increase.

Picking areas you can beat your competitors at. Attacking a competitor head-on doesn't work as well as attacking at a vulnerable point. Southwest, JetBlue, and other discount airlines won by building a cost structure that was different than the larger airlines'. They started by winning over the leisure traveler, who was less influenced by the larger airlines' more convenient airports or frequent-flyer programs, which had won over the business traveler.

Knowing what your company can be good at. Wal-Mart's business is based on hiring lower-skilled, lower-wage employees at their stores. This allows Wal-Mart to do a lot of things for low cost. But being able to perform complicated or skilled tasks at the individual store level is not something that Wal-Mart is currently strong at.

Know what your customers want. For a company selling to Wal-Mart, thinking this way can make you a success too—align your thinking and your strengths with the strengths of companies you are looking to sell to. If you sell flowers, package them to move through Wal-Mart's logistics and to the individual stores with minimal handling.

Defining a new standard across your company. Few of us accomplish anything important by ourselves. Spreading the understanding of what a company's competitive advantage will be is as important as defining that advantage. Market research can be a tool to define the competitive, or customer-defined, opportunity that you want to fill.

Towering strengths give you an outsized advantage over your competitors. This can cause your customers to forgive an occasional mistake because what you offer can be difficult to find somewhere else. "Forgiveness" from loyal customers—forgiveness when the company makes a mistake—is one quality of a strong brand.

CREATE YOUR OWN STRENGTHS

Execution Rules

- Execute consistently over time.
- What you don't do also defines your strength.
- Defend your position.

During the process from assembling the troops and mobilizing the people
to deploying the army ready for battle, nothing is more difficult than
the art of maneuvering for seizing favorable positions beforehand.
—Sun Tzu

Sun Tzu's "seizing favorable positions beforehand" is the military version of a business building its own unique strength. For Sun Tzu, a favorable position gave control over the battlefield. He dictated the terms of engagement—or the enemy attacked and Sun Tzu was in an advantageous position. Building unique strengths provides similar advantages to the businessman. Unique strengths can come in a variety of forms:

- A position in a customer's mind
- A business model
- A series of capabilities no one else has developed
- A low-cost structure that is difficult to emulate

If you don't build a towering strength, you are vulnerable. Any traditional retailer competing with Wal-Mart knows this—"The move to value and premium will accelerate and the middle will become even lonelier," says John Lovering, chairman of British retailer Debenhams. The world of retailing is crowded. Creating a towering strength is challenging. What's more challenging is that you have to make money as well.

Low-priced retailer Costco is different from other retailers—and more successful. How does it manage success with low prices and low margins? Costco's is a unique formula:

Make sure each sale is large. You won't find $1 or $2 items at Costco. For example, there are no individual candy bars in the checkout lane. Soup is available only in a six-pack, and beer is available only by the case. By keeping virtually all sales above $5 a package, Costco can make its low-price and low-margin model work. Costco makes sure it makes enough money on each sale. Costco customers just have to buy more at a time to get the savings.

Carry a limited assortment. Each Costco carries no more than 4,000 items. The average supermarket, as one benchmark, carries over 30,000. At Costco you will not find three or four brands of canned green beans— you might not even find canned green beans. At mass merchants, you will find several microwaves to choose from; at Costco, you will generally find two or three—a big one, a small one, and sometimes a medium-sized one.

But Costco members have come to trust Costco's selection—Costco is a trusted buying agent.

Only carry the highest-volume items. With only 4,000 items in a store, you have to be selective. And Costco is known for carrying only items that move quickly. It is also known among its vendors for quickly discontinuing items that move slowly.

These guidelines are carried out consistently by Costco. Over time, its model is understood and makes sense to its customers. No Costco customer expects to find a large selection. But customers also know what to depend on Costco for—and what they can depend on Costco for better than almost any other retailer is value on quality items. In a playing field crowded by mass merchants, supermarkets, and home improvement stores, Costco has built a towering strength on value. It may lose on variety. It may lose on convenience (the lines are almost always long at a Costco). But its customers know that what Costco does, it does well.

Without a unique strength, you are at risk to be in a vulnerable middle-market position. In the "hourglass economy," customers are saving money on basics where they can—at places like Costco—and using the savings to trade up in other areas. Middle-market brands like Kraft and Ford lose because they are neither the staples we buy at good prices nor the brands we trade up to. Kraft loses to Costco's or Wal-Mart's private label at the low end and imported European or artisanal cheeses at the high end. Ford loses to less expensive or more expensive imports.

Starbucks has redefined the coffee market in the last few years. Coffee used to be dominated by Folgers, Hills Brothers, and Maxwell House. It used to all come in cans. Remember Mrs. Olson? What could be more contrary to the current trendy image of coffee? (Mrs. Olson was an older female character in Folgers commercials for twenty-one years—back when mass-market brands ruled.) Today, coffee is more expensive, more hip, and can be fairly complicated, depending on what you are ordering at your local espresso bar.

Folgers used to be "good to the last drop." Folgers had a taste-oriented strength that years ago could have given the brand leverage to transition to an up-market brand before Starbucks established that positioning. But that opportunity has passed as Starbucks clearly owns the upscale coffee market—and "legacy" brands like Folgers either fight it out in the middle or look for opportunities as cut-rate basics.

Despite missing the chance to go up-market in coffee, in many categories, Procter & Gamble has achieved years of growth through a focus on the customer. In more traditionally stable categories than food, where P&G's research and development strength can be leveraged, P&G has created new markets and new standards by harnessing its research and development to a focus on unmet customer needs. This core strength has let P&G innovate trade-up products like the Swiffer dust mop in recent years.

Look at the staying power of P&G's brands in disposable diapers. Pampers was introduced forty years ago! Towering strengths, once created, can provide sales and revenues for a long time.

INVEST FOR LONG-TERM ADVANTAGE

Execution Rules

- Build one rock-solid strength.
- Anyone can pick the low-hanging fruit.
- Leverage your strengths in new ways.

Ground that both we and the enemy can traverse with equal ease is called accessible. On such ground, he who first takes high sunny positions and keeps his supply routes unimpeded can fight advantageously.
—Sun Tzu

Building long-term advantage requires some investment. True long-term advantages are sustainable—there is an aspect of them that makes them difficult for a competitor to exactly replicate, and difficult for a competitor to compete with. But once you have it, you can stay miles ahead of the pack. Or, as Sun Tzu says, you "can fight advantageously."

There are a variety of ways to build long-term advantage.

In retailing, some companies build long-term advantage by their real estate strategies. Some companies buy the best real estate and use that as their advertising—a timeless sort of advertising. These companies follow a real estate strategy called "Main and Main." This refers to rural small towns that invariably have a Main Street that is their busiest street. A location at the corner of Main and Main would be a very busy location! So these companies look for real estate at very busy intersections—the hypothetical "Main and Main"—real estate that is very expensive because of the high volume of traffic that goes by it. This strategy trades the higher cost of premium real estate for a long-term competitive advantage.

In consumer packaged goods, some companies build a long-term advantage through their patents. However, this also can be very expensive. For every product that becomes a successful patent, many products are developed that never get that far. An expensive winnowing out takes place.

In a variety of industries, like credit cards, companies build long-term advantage through their customer databases. These databases take a large amount of technology and experience to operate well. Yet, they are an important tool for retaining customers and building sales significantly.

Consistently, companies that build a long-term advantage invest in one aspect of their business at the expense of other areas. Singapore Airlines is known for its gracious service and dependable on-time performance. Perennially, it is one of the favorite business airlines in the world. It got there through its strong focus on serving the customer. Says one analyst,

"On everything facing the customer, they do not scrimp. On everything else, they keep costs low." An example of scrimping where their customer is not affected is Singapore Airlines' modest offices—they are on the top floor of one of their hangars.

Your Long-Term Advantage Is Not Always Obvious

For years Sears has invested in brands like Craftsman and Kenmore. As Sears sunk over the years, these brands remained solid. Even in Sears's worst year, advertising for Craftsman tools still appeared on TV.

When Sears and Kmart merged, there was much speculation about rebranding Kmart stores as Sears stores. But the tarnished Sears brand wasn't much stronger than the tarnished Kmart brand, and those changes have had uneven results. However, Craftsman and Kenmore appliances sell well at Kmart. The strength of the Sears brand isn't the retail stores or the in-store experience tied to that brand. Actually, the strength isn't the Sears brand itself at all. The towering brand strength at Sears is the in-house, "own brands" that Sears built over the years.

Build a Unique Capability

Achieving a long-term advantage takes some work and planning. To build a long-term advantage, you need to be better at something than your competitors are. And ideally, make your strength, your advantage, something that is difficult to copy. As Gerry Hodes, formerly of Marks and Spencer, says, "Everybody wants to pick the low-hanging fruit." Get good at something that lets you pick the higher-hanging fruit—fruit that it is difficult for your competitors to reach.

Build a long-term advantage that:

Capitalizes on an aspect of your company that is unique. By doing this, you make it difficult for your competitor to copy you. If you are a small business, tying to your local geography can make you different from national competitors who can't compete as nimbly locally. Garland's supermarkets in Los Angeles does this with a uniquely Californian décor scheme—reinforcing its local roots and ownership.

Builds something that takes time to get good at. Anyone who has implemented a high-tech customer management system will report that the first step is just the first step. There are many steps to follow. Learning takes time. First, you learn your leverage points—what can you tell or communicate to your customers that they will react to. The process of "learning" takes years. When it is done, companies from Nestle to Tesco report, what they *know* about their customers, and how they can take *action* on that knowledge, is a unique strength.

Leverages a strength from another part of your business. Acquisitions are one way to do this. When Yahoo bought online photo-storing site Flickr, it was for the knowledge about "social media," practiced by Flickr, that Yahoo could transfer to all of its organization. With $30 billion in sales, Albertsons bought Shaw's markets, which had $3 billion in sales. Albertsons took Shaw's loyalty-card marketing practices and spread those back through the entire Albertsons organization. Those marketing practices were far more advanced and effective compared to what Albertsons was practicing at the time.

Cost can be a unique capability. But if it is easy for competitors to copy, it won't survive. Frequently, companies with a strong cost advantage develop it across a couple of dimensions. That adds to the competitive insulation. Even so, cost-based capabilities are among the most transparent and generally require scale to deter copycats.

Southwest famously started the low-cost airline industry. They offered a significantly simplified operation—a standardized fleet of planes, no first class, and no reserved seats. And they added nonunion, lower-wage people (who seemed to actually enjoy their jobs). But all of that could be equally said now about JetBlue as well, and a variety of smaller low-cost airlines like Frontier. Others followed the same formula.

Similarly, dollar stores (Dollar General, Dollar Tree, 99 Cent Stores, etc.) all take advantage of

1. Cheap production in China (a highly disproportionate share of sales comes from Chinese manufacturers),
2. Lower-rent strip mall or rural locations, and
3. Minimal in-store labor.

They are a strong competitor to many other retail formats, but they also tend to be highly interchangeable and cannibalistic with each other.

Take Advantage of Changing Markets

For many, success has come from taking advantage of a strength in a way they had not originally planned. Cisco grew to be the world's largest maker of Internet networking equipment as the Internet itself grew. This strength was built on the business-to-business market. But as the Internet grew, the consumer market for Internet networking also grew. First, in wired houses for people who had the means to afford that luxury. But like many stories in electronics and technology, the technology for Internet networking a house came down in price. And as that became wireless as well, the home market grew significantly.

Cisco, the business-to-business provider of this service, decided the home market was its next opportunity. Said Cisco, "Consumer electronics companies have been able to compete on a stand-alone device but the dynamics of the market are changing. The Internet and new networking requirements are enough of a disruptor for us to enter a new market." Said one analyst, "The home network is the last piece of territory up for grabs in the networking space and it makes sense for Cisco to try to dominate that." Cisco's success in the business-to-business space has prepared it for possible success in the home market as well.

PetSmart is the country's largest pet-food supply store. It has been through several twists and turns in its history. In the 1990s, it was a fast-growing company with good margins. It had a popular line of products. In particular, the Hills Science Diet and Iams pet food brands were strong draws. These brands were only available through the "specialty pet-food channels." That meant veterinarians, mall-based pet stores, smaller pet-food stores, and the chains of pet-food stores—of which PetSmart was the largest.

That changed. First, Hills Science Diet began to experiment with selling its product through supermarkets. Then Iams was bought by Procter & Gamble. Procter & Gamble wasn't aligned with the specialty pet-food channels and quickly expanded the brand to mass merchants and supermarkets. PetSmart's biggest advantage had vanished. The stock price fell significantly. Management changed.

Many people treat their pet like a member of the family. So PetSmart and the category continued on. After all, the specialty pet-food retailers let you bring your animal into the store with you to do your shopping. And the retailers in this channel eventually built private label and other offerings that let them rebuild some margin.

But the greatest innovation was in services around the core strength of caring for your pet. PetSmart started by building veterinarian centers in their stores. Similar to how LensCrafters and others, years ago, began to compete with the local ophthalmologist by putting eye doctors in their own stores. Vertical integration, some might say.

Now, PetSmart has over 400 veterinarian centers in their stores through their partnership with Banfield. Pet grooming is another area that PetSmart has grown into. Virtually every PetSmart has a pet grooming center. And most recently, PetSmart has gotten into animal boarding. These pet hotels are also located right in your local PetSmart, and are cleverly marketed to have "all of the comforts of home." And, of course, you can buy extra services for your pet while you are away. An extra walk. Maybe an extra treat. All to soothe your mind that your pet is happy while you are soaking up the sun. In just a few years, these PetsHotels have expanded to PetSmarts in fifteen states.

A classic "consolidation" strategy was used—taking industries (veterinarians, pet grooming, and pet boarding) where there was very low market consolidation and using a strong brand to establish leadership.

This worked because, as the pet-food market changed, PetSmart had a clear strength in a brand that was trusted by pet-food owners. And it leverages that strength as it continues to build its business from just selling products to selling services as well. These and other services have grown to just under 10 percent of PetSmart sales, from just 5 percent in 2001. And these services contribute to a margin growth of almost 1 point per year. Long-term advantage in money-making segments should be particularly valued. If you are a small or medium-sized company, identify emerging niches and gain an advantage in them early. Ride these niches as they grow. Long-term advantage is most efficiently built with time, and long-term trends, as your ally.

EXPERIENCE MATTERS

Execution Rules

- Stability of talented leaders is a huge advantage.
- Hire people who have "owned" something.
- Build experience in something you have a passion for.

> Those who do not know the conditions of mountains and forests, hazardous defiles, and marshes and swamps cannot conduct the march of an army. Those who do not use local guides are unable to obtain the advantages of the ground.
> —Sun Tzu

For many great leaders, their greatest victories came at the end of their career after they had gained a lot of experience. Trafalgar was Nelson's last battle and his greatest victory. Most World War II generals had military experience in World War I; many U.S. Civil War generals had experience in the Mexican-American War. Before getting to a big stage, most successful leaders have honed their skills on a smaller stage.

Experience matters. In the United Kingdom, Tesco has come to dominate mass merchant and food retailing. It is bigger than Wal-Mart's UK entry, Asda. And it maintains a strong leadership over the other leading food retailer, Sainsbury. And Tesco's historical rate of growth has been so strong, industry watchers wonder how much more business it can take from its competitors. The UK press occasionally wonders if Tesco is on the verge of becoming a monopoly in British retailing. Tesco has done this under one leader and with a stable management team. On the other hand, its competition has been through a parade of managers with a variety of backgrounds—four at Sainsbury from 1998 to 2005, and four at Asda from 1999 to 2005.

Look for the Right Kind of Experience

A former boss of mine used to ask the following question regarding experienced job candidates: "Does he have 20 years of the same experience, or 20 different years of experience?" Essentially, doing the same thing over and over, in the same way, doesn't teach you anything new.

Great experience for developing leaders is to be in charge of something or to own a process. Some jobs inherently have this:

- Store manager jobs inherently give a breadth of experience. At some big box chains, a store manager runs a $75 million-per-year business. And managers handle the same issues as any CEO—sales, costs, and HR. These jobs can give people good experience, sometimes early in their career.

- Chef jobs can give similar experiences as they are responsible for a staff of people, the quality of the product, and costs. Chefs must also have to have a bit of an accountant and market researcher in them as they develop future menus—menus they use to manage costs and deliver the right profits.
- At a higher level, division manager jobs give a broad and full perspective. These jobs are responsible for the short- and long-term success of the business.
- Owning and operating your own business, even at a small level, can build ownership. To pay his way through college, financial consultant Steve Doner operated a mobile DJ business. He bought equipment, did sales and marketing, and worked the weddings and parties that he booked. With each decision, he tried to figure out how to make a little more money at the business. It proved to be great experience for the decisions required in building his future financial consulting business.

These are all jobs in which daily execution is important, but in which short-term execution is also done in the context of longer-term responsibilities. Successful leaders know how to manage a variety of priorities—they know how to keep multiple balls in the air. They also know how to manage risk. Jobs that let people fail on their own in small ways are great for teaching people how to balance priorities and manage risk. People who have had jobs like these are good candidates to promote and to recruit. Their prior experiences give them a chance to be very good at execution.

Find Leaders with Passion—Let Them Build New Strengths

Lee Iacocca said simply, "I loved cars. I couldn't wait to go to work in the morning." Sometimes with hard work and experience, deep passions can develop. Many of the *Fortune* 100 Best Companies to Work

For in America are privately held companies. In many of them (Timberland, Wegmans, S.C. Johnson, to name a few), the first-generation family member isn't running the company anymore. The baton has passed to seasoned people who, literally, grew up in their business and developed a passion for keeping it successful and growing.

Says Oprah Winfrey, "What I know is, is that if you do work that you love, and the work fulfills you, the rest will come."

Frank Perdue worked hard to make a great chicken. He developed proprietary breeds. But more than anything, he seemed to truly believe he made a great chicken. Frank Perdue talking about his chicken on TV is a timeless piece of advertising. What made those ads work was Frank. Says Joe Nocera in the December 25, 2005, issue of *New York Times Magazine* on "What comes through most of all in those ads is that whether or not his chickens were better than his competitors, Frank Perdue believed they were."

When food merchant and former chef David McInerney is involved in product development, he has a lot of people taste the new food products he is working on. When someone likes the item, he frequently asks, "Did you like it or love it?" David is looking for the products you love. It is at this early point in execution—when the product is still in development—that a lot of work goes into making sure that the product being developed is one customers will love.

This makes a lot of sense. Customers will go out of their way to get a product they love. And if they buy that product from you, maybe they will buy something else at the same time. Think of your favorite restaurant. There is probably a particular dish there that you love. That's what brings you there. And you likely don't go there alone. Maybe you bring your spouse along. Perhaps you meet friends there. That one item you love brings the restaurant a lot of business.

Products you love also lead to strong word of mouth. Any advertising person will tell you word of mouth is the best advertising that there is. None of us tell our friends about products that are just okay. We tell people about items we have developed a passion about. When we feel that passion, we tell people.

This is the way great brands grow. You could almost call it "organic"—though frequently strong word-of-mouth brands have teams of people working to keep that word of mouth going.

Harley-Davidson is a great brand among its customers. Harley-Davidson customers talk about their motorcycles. Emeril Lagasse is a great brand—his fans talk about his show and visit his restaurants and buy Emeril-branded products at their local store. Starbucks isn't a big traditional advertiser. But Starbucks fans will seek out Starbucks coffee whenever they are traveling.

Remember: Passionate customers aren't shy—they will talk about your product and service. Why? Because advertising only goes so far—their experience with your product or service is what matters most.

MAKE YOUR WORK MATTER

Execution Rules

- Ask many questions on your journey.
- Commission many in your organization to help.
- Use intelligence to build constant feedback.

> What can subdue the hostile neighboring rulers
> is to hit what hurts them most.
> —Sun Tzu

A critical tool in making your work matter is defining what advantage you want to build versus that of your competitors. Market research is a key tool behind this—it doesn't necessarily have to be expensive. Market research can help you do this by identifying gaps where you can perform better than the competition.

Most market research looks at shortfalls and short-term changes. And businesspeople go to work fixing what isn't working well. Momentum starts moving in that direction with the thinking before the research. Retailers look at basic service scores. Consumer packaged-goods companies look at price image and product performance. And most of this stems from a traditional view of the business.

Building a towering strength starts with a view of what strengths could be built, what competitive advantages could be grown. That leads to market research questions that are different from the norm—and a willingness to ask some questions in advance of a company's emerging competence. Ultimately, this pays off in building strengths that are different from the competition's—strengths that are uniquely yours.

Good market research breaks down results into *actionable* segments. That means that the market research ties to the organization of the business. If your company is organized by sales territory, the market research should be organized by sales territory. This allows accountability for the results of the research, accountability that is easy to "enforce"—the results will speak for themselves. Businesspeople who want to be successful, and want their business to be successful, will take action to make their business better. The only way you make more money by spending money on marketing research is if the results are organized in an actionable way—and the more people who can take action based on those results, the greater and faster an organization will make the desired changes.

To use market research to build a towering strength:

Write down who your target customer is. Who does your company want to buy your products? The more clearly your target is defined, the more relevant will be the strengths you build. Clear definitions of target customers inherently exclude some people. If you are not excluding some current customers, rethink the level of targeting you are building.

Identify the gaps you might want to build. What can your company be better at than the competition? What could you own? Where do your strengths seem to match some products or services customers want? What are they already buying from you more then they do from some competition—how do you turn that into a unique strength?

Ask customers what they think. And use this process to narrow down the gaps you want to develop. Focus on two key issues: Are your potential gaps, potential future strengths, important to customers (would anyone care if you were the best in these areas?)? and Where do you stand versus your competitors? Ask enough questions, in enough different ways, that you can see the issue clearly. Bracket it with different questions to ensure you gain a clear understanding.

Track your performance against filling that gap, and communicate those results across the organization. Results will come slowly at first. But by tracking your results and improvements, an organization can see—and get excited about—the results.

Celebrate success. Focus, finish, and celebrate. Every team wants to win—and wants to beat the competition. Marketing research gives you a way to celebrate some wins. And to motivate a team to go out and win again.

This process works for executing change, and creating new strengths, for two reasons. First, it inherently breaks down work into actionable pieces. As you go through this, you will assign responsibility for building new strengths—ownership. People will take pride in this work—it will feel important to them.

The second reason this process works is because it lets you see the progress against building strengths. Progress will be uneven. If you work to create multiple strengths, you will be able to see the first successes. Use these successes to make people feel good about their work and even more committed to building new strengths.

No industry is easy. So as you work to build strengths, look at future trends you can own. Look at the margins of the industry. And look at industries near yours. Generally, you will not find any *one* strength that you can build that will trump the competition's. Frequently, you will find a series of small strengths that *deeply* matter to a few people. Building several of these strengths ends up mattering to many people—and a strong business is built.

Don't Hit Your Competitors Head-On

Hitting competitors where it will hurt the most is not hitting them head-on at their strengths. That won't hurt them.

- You don't hurt American Express by attacking it on service—it owns that ("membership has its privileges"). But you might hurt it by attacking it on breadth of acceptance, annual cost, or with a different rewards program.
- You don't hurt Domino's pizza in the pizza-delivery business by telling people you arrive on time. People know and trust Domino's delivery service. But you might hurt them by coming up with a better pizza and telling people about that product. That is the attack Papa John's has tried in this business.
- You don't hurt Maytag by telling people your appliances work well— they built reliability. But you might be able to undercut them on price and value.

Sun Tzu sums it up, "Now, the art of employing troops is that when the enemy occupies high ground, do not confront him uphill, and when his back is resting on hills, do not make a frontal attack."

REDOUBLE YOUR EFFORTS

Execution Rules

- Figure out what you are willing to give up to be successful.
- Practice and prepare.
- Persevere through the uneven advancement of building better execution.

> In difficult ground, press on.
> —Sun Tzu

Little that is worth winning comes easy. Steve Ballmer of Microsoft says, in the February 2001 issue of *Fast Company* magazine, "I like to tell people that all of our products and business will go through three phases. There's vision, patience, and execution." Patience is the time when persevering is most critical.

Don't Expect Wins to Be Easy

Mike Eruzione, the captain of the "Miracle on Ice" hockey team of the Winter Olympics, is now a motivational speaker. He's got a great story to motivate with. That team's victory in the Olympics has been called the greatest sports upset of the century. But it didn't get off to a good start. The opening game for the U.S. team of that Olympics was against Norway—a team the United States was supposed to beat. That game ended in a disheartening tie. Coach Brooks made the team do an hour and a half of intense skating. From the backboard to center ice and back again for an hour and a half. At the end, Coach told them if they didn't win the next day, they would have to do that again. The team won that game 8 to nothing.

Mike sums up his Olympic experiences with, "People who are successful make sacrifices." That 1980 "Miracle on Ice" team trained like no other U.S. Olympic Hockey team before them. That team practiced together for six months before the Olympic games.

Figure out what you will give up to be successful, but don't lose balance with family. Less golf, giving up a couple of nights of TV, getting up earlier every morning are all appropriate sacrifices to make. These are the kinds of conscious trade-offs that, if you are willing to make them, can free up time to invest in future success.

Beware Lurching

Many publicly held companies dash into a new strategy with great enthusiasm. Generally, it is this year's management trying to make their mark. It is almost predictable:

Auto companies will swear off their dependence on rebates every few years. And after a short time, they will return to rebates (they trained their customers to shop that way, after all).

Competitors of Wal-Mart will say, "There is more to shopping than price," and then fail to offer a shopping experience or product selection that offers a better–than–Wal-Mart alternative (after all, developing a point of difference to Wal-Mart requires vision, then patience—and many publicly held companies have a difficult time sustaining either).

Manufacturing companies will declare they are "customer driven," and then will introduce "me too" products that don't stand the test of time (15,000 new food products are introduced each year, as just one benchmark).

These are generally not strategies that shift execution. So they don't stand the test of time. Generally, the next management team signals some different, equally obvious, shift. And these kinds of shifts can happen at all levels of an organization—at a division, at an individual store, or in a particular geography.

A company needs a consistent vision that all team members execute against. And corporate visions can change.

But be careful about lurching—be careful about making sweeping changes to execute a new strategy (in times of severe economic challenge, of course expect some lurching, some fast change. And respond to, and lead, that change. But think of that as more of an exception in your career, rather than something you should execute frequently). Find where a new corporate vision and consistent execution find common ground. Where does the new corporate vision naturally create change in an area of the company? That's probably a good place to start. Where does the new strategy build on areas of current executional or market success? That's another good place to start. Don't just change areas of weakness—build your areas of strength.

The Advancement of Change Will Be Uneven

Most of us are trained to think linearly about change and progress. As you improve execution, change will be uneven. It will be uneven in three ways:

1. The level of execution. Since major changes are executed through people, the advancement of execution will be uneven. Initial training programs, new benchmarking, or a new technology may take time for people to gain a level of comfort with. Those investments (of time or money) may take time to sink into the organization. Some people will adopt the new ways before others will. People who are early adopters will likely buy into the change, and will have a tendency to execute well.

2. Lagging perception. A lot of change we will create will be so some-one notices a difference—maybe customers, maybe our own people, maybe distributors. None of these groups will wake up each morning to see if you have changed something. It will take time, it will take some

experience, before they notice a change. In my experience, in consumer goods, customer perceptions can frequently lag months behind a change in reality. Unfortunately, customers will notice changes for the worse much quicker than they notice changes for the better.

3. Initial failures. Frequently, when trying to build significant new executional strength, the first challenge is figuring out what to change. Where is the failure point that is causing the execution to lag expectation. And what will be effective at improving the situation? Since money is always limited, finding a cost-effective way to improve execution is always part of the equation. That means that frequently (1) the first thing you fix might not "move the needle," and (2) you may fix a couple of things, and benchmark each one of them, to figure out which fix moves the needle.

As we build execution, we will benchmark our success. Generally, people will use some sort of a "run" chart—the basic chart that has one series of numbers up the side and another series of numbers (or time) along the bottom. A very solid, linear chart.

Expect, as you benchmark against new execution, to see some limited successes before that level of execution settles in as the new standard. Essentially, that is what you are working to accomplish—a new executional standard. Celebrate early wins, but don't become unsettled if you occasionally give back some of those early successes.

PART THREE

SunTzu

FOR SUCCESS

Chapter 9

Personal Characteristics for Success

The question "Who are you?" is the foundation for a never-ending journey to success. One can look to Sun Tzu's *The Art of War* for short- and long-term guideposts on this quest. Sun Tzu emphasized knowledge as the pillar of our life plans. In applying his concepts and principles for success, Sun Tzu prescribed specific behaviors that could be learned, practiced, and integrated into daily life.

Sun Tzu's philosophy rests on deep foundations that cannot be fabricated or changed easily. His prescriptions start from questioning and discovering who you are. To achieve the full value from Sun Tzu and his thoughts, you need a solid foundation. This first section is therefore about the personal characteristics that are the foundation for success.

As a moral teacher, Sun Tzu expected the same moral values in his students. Our challenge in today's world is to program consistency into "who we are." From deep within us, we need to avoid "just fake it" and turn on the internal automatic pilot of "just do it" the right way for the right reasons.

KNOW YOURSELF

Success Rules

- Be who you are.
- Be enlightened—know who you are.
- Self-knowledge is the foundation of success.

> Know the enemy and know yourself, and you can fight
> a hundred battles with no danger of defeat.
> If ignorant both of your enemy and yourself, you
> are sure to be defeated in every battle.
> —Sun Tzu

A famous cartoon possum named Pogo said to his friend Albert the alligator: "We have met the enemy and he is us."

Perhaps he read Sun Tzu.

How many times have you made the observation, "They are their own worst enemy?" It is difficult to perceive ourselves as "the enemy" in any situation. Yet accurate self-perception is the golden key to success.

No one can tell you who you really are; everyone can help in the search. The problem lies not only in your perception, but also in your confidence in your perception. The more accurately you understand your real strengths and weaknesses, the more effective you can be in every endeavor.

Each of us is perceived as three different people:

1. Who we think we are
2. Who others think we are
3. Who we really are

The most important of these is "who we really are." This search for identity can be the quest of a lifetime.

Identify Your Personality

Our ability to identify ourselves is apparent in the administration of the widely used personality test, the Myers-Briggs Type Indicator. During this process, participants are asked to self-select individual preferences in four categories prior to completing a questionnaire that automatically measures their preferences and personality type. The match is often close between self-selected preferences and preferences measured by the instrument. When the two differ, people are advised that only *they* can know their real preferences.

Among the personality differences identified by Myers-Briggs are thinkers and feelers:

- Thinkers tend to base their decisions on logic. They are interested in analyzing factual data concerning the situation.
- Feelers make their decisions based on personal values and emotions. Feelers are less concerned with objective data and more concerned with how the decision affects people.

Although each of us makes some decisions based on emotion and some decisions based on logic, we do have a tendency to frequently act one way or the other. In general, whatever way we tend to favor in making decisions is the same method we favor in convincing others.

Base your arguments on the decision preference of the person you are trying to convince, not your own. To know their preferences, you must first know your own.

Knowledge of your preferences can be obtained by thinking about the people with whom you associate most comfortably. Often they have the same personality preferences and arrive at decisions in the same manner as you do. Looking at your closest friends can provide a mirror image of yourself.

The more you know about yourself and the reasons for your own preferences and actions, the more you know about others. Self-knowledge breeds a universe of knowledge about human dynamics.

As a young manager, I visited an organization that administered tests, interviewed me, and gave an oral review and written report of my qualifications. At the time I did not believe or understand all of their observations. Over a period of years, I saw my actions mirrored in the written report and developed a greater confidence in my strengths.

A review of this kind has three benefits:

1. You learn about yourself more quickly—eventually, time will reveal your true identity.
2. You achieve a deeper understanding of where your compass should point.

3. You can share the experience with employment interviewers who will be impressed by your efforts to learn more about yourself.

In contemporary management circles this idea of self-analysis is given life in how employers develop their people. Yesterday, the annual performance review was the vehicle for providing self-knowledge in the business world. During the review, your supervisor advised on where you needed to improve and grow. Today, performance is evaluated with 360-degree feedback from peers, subordinates, and bosses who provide information on how you are perceived and what you need to fine-tune in order to achieve objectives.

Head for the Next Level

Here is an overview of ingredients that can start you on the path to applying self-knowledge in your journey to the next level.

- *Determine your values.* At the core of your beliefs, what are the values that drive you? What has driven you to achieve success and what has influenced your failures? What are your priorities? Every decision you make reveals something about yourself. Finding common links is a powerful way to uncover "who you are." Write down your observations.

  At age twenty-six, Ben Franklin outlined his own list of personal values.

- *Show commitment.* The core values that make you who you are seldom change. This commitment establishes your identity and determines your future.
- *Accept the help of others.* It is the assistance of others that helps you determine your true identity. Finding out "who you are" is best achieved with the help of someone who can be a sounding board.

- *Think positive.* You have faults that need to be recognized and minimized. Be humble, but not to the extent that humility makes you set your goals too low. Success is achieved by focusing on, and taking advantage of, your inherent strengths. One wins by leading with strength.

An experiment conducted years ago at Hawthorne laboratories is recognized as revealing the beneficial effects of positive psychology. In short, "The Hawthorne Effect" says people who believe good things are happening are motivated to do better. That is, the more strongly you believe things are going well, the more likely you are to be motivated to excel. Conversely, the more you believe things are getting worse, the lower your motivation will be to improve.

Plan Self-Improvement

Everything on earth is either green and growing—or ripe and rotting. As long as you are green and willing to learn new things you are growing. You either get better or you get worse. You grow or decay. It's when you think you have all the answers that you are ripe and rotting.

In his classic book, *How to Win Friends and Influence People,* Dale Carnegie wrote: "[Improving yourself] is a lot more profitable than trying to improve others."

Ancient Chinese philosopher Lao Tzu reveals an important truth when he states:

One who knows others is wise.
One who knows one's self is enlightened.

At every Winter Olympics we see athletes standing at the top of the hill mentally rehearsing their route to victory—with no spills or misses.

These champions are not deluding themselves; they simply believe in what they have practiced and have confidence in their abilities.

Grow Through Relationships

Relationships are one of the most important vehicles for self-growth. Relationships—be they with your boss, your colleagues, your spouse, or your family—are a mirror of your strengths and weaknesses, as well as your values and desires. We all want to be involved with people with similar interests and values. We all want to create relationships that reflect our best qualities back to us.

Honest sharing builds "closeness." When you sincerely express emotion you build intimacy and camaraderie. More importantly, you engage others in your personal development. "Opening up" and sharing personal experiences builds feelings of closeness with others and, in the long run, fosters intimacy with yourself.

Take a sincere interest in others. If you can't be sincere, don't bother. But don't miss the opportunity to "follow your gut" when an opportunity arises and take the time to help. Although you may know many people, you can't know each of their concerns. But when someone needs your help (whether they ask for it or you just "pick up on it"), that is an opportunity.

What makes it challenging is that people generally don't need help at a time of your choosing. Offering help is often inconvenient and gets in the way of other plans. Think about assistance as "caring about one individual at a time." You can't continually care about every person you know. But when the need arises, one person at a time, you can care about that person at that time.

Share values. Some of us easily and comfortably share our values in conversations, interviews, and how we ask questions. Keeping alert can help you identify people with whom you can share a common purpose. These like-minded people will be "attracted" to you and you to them.

When you want help reaching a goal, start with a group of people who share your common values and who can become a committed team.

In your quest for personal success you have to make decisions. You won't always make the right ones along the way but strong relationships can help you overcome setbacks en route to your goals.

HAVE MORAL INTEGRITY

Success Rules

- Integrity is a powerful force.
- Moral integrity is the bedrock of your reputation.
- Either you have integrity, or you do not have integrity.

> The commander adept in war enhances the moral
> influence and adheres to the laws and regulations.
> Thus, it is in his power to control success.
> —Sun Tzu

The strength of moral influence is at the heart of Sun Tzu's ability to lead an army. Moral integrity is a characteristic of successful leaders.

Develop a Sense of Moral Integrity

Former Prime Minister of Israel Benjamin Netanyahu states the fundamental importance of "moral clarity" in describing key components necessary to winning the war against terrorism: Moral clarity is simply being clear about what is right and what is wrong.

We saw this when American national leaders made America's moral stand clear by declaring there is no excuse for terrorism. It is a "given" in conflict that both sides think "right" is on their side. By being "right," leaders are simply following Sun Tzu's advice on the role of moral influence in getting people in harmony with their objectives.

Netanyahu states the following moral imperatives for victory:

- A military victory cannot be secured until it has been secured as a political victory.
- A political victory cannot be secured until it has been secured with public relations.
- A public relations victory cannot be secured until it has been secured in a sense of justice.

Netanyahu built his argument for Israel's position by starting with a sense of justice. He tells of having dinner one night with the prime minister of Spain, who questioned him about Israel being on land that at one time belonged to others. The prime minister asked Netanyahu, in this historical context, how could Israel have a right to exist?

Netanyahu responded, "Why does Spain have a right to exist?" Startled, the prime minister of Spain asked him to explain this question. So Netanyahu pointed out that for centuries, all of Spain was controlled by the Moors, except for one little piece of land in the north. From that base in the Northern Iberian Peninsula, over a span of decades, Spain succeeded in retaking its country and expelling the Moors.

No one has ever questioned the Spaniards' right to their land, because the Spaniards never gave up that right. Netanyahu asked why would it be any different for Israel, which has a clear claim to the land going back to the Old Testament, and is a claim no Jew or Israeli has ever given up.

You may, or may not, agree with Netanyahu's line of reasoning. But, one can only imagine the power that argument had with the prime minister of Spain! Obviously, this logic has great moral influence in motivating the people of Israel and those who support the Israeli position in the

Holy Land. Note that this argument for the State of Israel is not rooted in power, guns, or pity, but rather in logic that has a moral base.

On the flip side, throughout history, some of the greatest evils have been perpetrated in conjunction with a sense of moral right. Leaders gained support for their actions by justifying a supposedly moral position to their people—often at the expense of integrity.

Harness the Power of Integrity

In our interactions, the word that most clearly sums up moral influence is integrity—defined as adherence to a code. We can have integrity in adherence to a variety of codes—artistic, legal, or moral. In our culture, people who "do not have integrity" generally are viewed as not having adhered to a moral code. Lack of integrity destroys "moral influence."

Integrity is the bedrock of personal reputation. Personal reputation is based on others' perceptions of our behavior. A strong base of integrity gives you the leverage to build your reputation and execute a plan for your personal success. To strengthen your position on an issue, look to the power of moral integrity.

The value of integrity shows up in many different thoughts:

> Integrity without knowledge is weak and useless. Knowledge without integrity is dangerous and dreadful.
> —Samuel Johnson

Morality and integrity influence us into "going the extra mile." These same virtues influence relationships in both overt and subtle ways. Often, it's the subtleties of morality and integrity about which we lack understanding. These same subtleties drive so much of our success and interactions in life. Depending on the moral influence present in a relationship, consequences can be either good or bad. When the bad catches up with you, a setback can occur. Here's an example:

Some time ago, Notre Dame lost a football coach who arguably "fudged" on his integrity. Officials at Notre Dame knew that hiring the head football coach from Georgia Tech was a somewhat controversial call. This head coach had been accused of abusing a football player only a year earlier. The story was that a player had been gang tackled by four other players for missing a blocking assignment. The Notre Dame officials supposedly pushed hard on this point during their interviews with the head coach from Georgia Tech. Eventually, they came away impressed and publicly praising him for his integrity offered him the position at Notre Dame.

Yet, just five days later the new coach was forced to resign over a series of old lies. Not really big lies—he's a football coach after all and his win-loss record is what counts. The new coach claimed to have a master's degree he clearly had never earned. This "degree" had apparently been on his resume for years. The Notre Dame athletic department responded with the following statement, "We understand these inaccuracies represent a very human failing; nonetheless, they constitute a breach of trust that makes it impossible for us to go forward with our relationship." In resigning, the new coach could only say, "The integrity and credibility of Notre Dame is impeccable, and with that in mind, I will resign my position as head football coach."

The story ended unhappily for everyone. The lie probably did not win the coach the new position but it did cost him the job.

Is this an extreme story? The consequences are extreme but the situation is all too common. When a professional executive-search consultant checked my background and college degrees on my resume, I casually inquired how often someone lies about college degrees on their resume. The consultant replied "In my experience, about 1 in 10!"

In building personal success, the foundation is your personal integrity. Although integrity does not guarantee success, lack of integrity is a prescription for failure. We all know successful people whose integrity is in doubt and will, like the Notre Dame football coach who had to resign, pay a huge price. Building your personal success on a base of integrity is a much stronger, firmer, and better place to start.

We all want to influence people. This influence should not be in a Machiavellian way, but rather with the idea of achieving a win-win. This mutual win is the bedrock of many relationships such as: Who should we date? Who might we select to be on our team? These types of decisions are built on trust. The most effective backbone of any communication is the answer to the question: "Does the communication come from a trusted source?" If not, the entire message is in doubt.

Harold Denton, who served as the president's representative to the nuclear incident at Three Mile Island, was in the difficult situation of determining risks and handling the press. He offers this set of rules for managing any crisis with moral integrity:

1. Tell it like it is.
2. Admit uncertainties exist.
3. Don't make statements you'll have to retract later.
4. Act on the best estimate of a situation.
5. Refrain from "value judgments."

Introducing former president Gerald Ford at Harvard, Senator Alan Simpson encapsulated the moral influence of integrity in President Ford's administration:

If you have integrity, nothing else matters.
If you do not have integrity, nothing else matters.

LISTEN WELL

Success Rules

- Listening is learning.
- Practice active listening.
- Questions provide the answer.

> It is the business of the general to be quiet and
> thus assure depth in deliberation.
> —Sun Tzu

One doesn't think of any general as being quiet to assure depth in deliberation—certainly not General Patton, whom we see portrayed delivering famous lines in movies and on television.

But actually, many generals well understand the importance of being quiet. When General Curtis LeMay was repeatedly interrupted by a young lieutenant, he gently admonished the officer. The lieutenant responded that listening quietly was not how LeMay got to be a general. LeMay is reported to have answered the lieutenant, "No. But it is how I got to be a captain."

Engage in Active Listening

Good listening is an active process. It is how you can achieve the level of listening that Sun Tzu promises will "assure depth in deliberation."

Here are a few rules for active listening:

- *Play back what you are hearing.* The fundamental component of active listening is clarifying and confirming the other person's dialog with paraphrasing comments such as, "What I heard you say was . . ." or by simply repeating the person's statement. This helps make sure you understood correctly and aids in getting additional information.

- *Ask questions.* Frequent questioning is another important component of active listening. Asking questions keeps you actively engaged, yields new information, and enables you to have a positive influence in the discussion. Be sincere with your questions and you will get more information flowing.

- *Acknowledge the other person's thoughts and feelings.* This engaging response can be with words or body language such as an occasional nod. Indications that you are receiving the commentary will help those talking to move past their own feelings and get to deeper issues. Conveying that you are indeed listening will help clear away the "baggage" others bring to the conversation. Acknowledging the "baggage" with a nod, or comment of understanding, can encourage him or her to move on in the conversation.

- *Focus on the other person's needs.* Listening provides information that enables you to build off the needs of others. If you can sincerely listen to and understand the needs of others, you are a powerful listener. The positive interactions of active listening give you a complete picture of the logic and emotion of the conversation. People will judge you to be empathetic.

- *Build the other person's self-esteem.* Smile, be helpful and positive. If you can be the kind of listener who builds the self-esteem of others, people will want to talk to you and feel comfortable confiding in you.

- *Be aware of your own listening "derailers."* Do you listen well to people whose values you do not share? Can you listen well to a variety of topics? Many things can affect our willingness to listen. If you know what derails you from listening well, you can achieve a more active listening stance.

- *Stay in the present.* A wandering mind is the opposite of good listening. Don't make assumptions or drift to future implications of what you are hearing. Keep your mind tuned to the present.

- *Take notes.* Whether or not you do anything with the notes, taking them helps keep you focused on the conversation.

The Role of Questions

Listening in the present can be a challenge. The best way to keep active in a conversation and influence the outcome is to ask questions.

Here are several benefits from properly worded questions:

- *Persuading.* Asking questions is a great way to help people convince themselves of the right or wrong status of a position. A question can make a point more clearly and influence the other person more deeply than any statement you make.
- *Staying engaged.* Asking questions helps both parties stay engaged. Two-way conversations are always better than a monologue. Asking questions keeps more of your brain invested in listening.
- *Maintaining control.* Questions guide the discussion and keep the conversation on track or lead in new directions. When asking questions, you are in control. The person who is in control wins.

People are more convinced by what they say than by what you say. Don't expect immediate acceptance of your ideas. People are often convinced more by time than by the truth.

Whenever executives ask my advice about how to prepare for an important visitor, my response is "prepare a list of questions." Why is it that we are always thinking of how we are going to respond and what we are going to tell rather than what we are going to ask? Don't play defense by responding to the other person's questions. A list of questions prepared in advance is your strongest weapon.

In any conversation, the more the other person can tell you about his or her situation, the smarter you are. He or she knows you are smart because they delivered information to you. The more questions you ask, the more you listen; the more information you gather, the more you know.

Use the Power of Silence

Although questioning is a great tool, silence can be a powerful way to get the other person talking. Because we are uncomfortable with silence, we have a tendency to move into a conversation vacuum. Good salespeople know that when they ask a question that should be answered by the customer, the salesperson should "shut up" and wait, and wait, and wait for an answer.

Wait for the other person to respond. If you step into the vacuum first, you will not get the information you want. For example, if you ask a person if they will do something, give the other person time to think—the silence will often help pressure a positive response. If you talk first, you often give them an excuse for not taking action. For example, if you step into the conversation vacuum and say, "Perhaps you are too busy," the other person will often latch on to the excuse you offered and say, "That's right, I am just too busy." If you talk, you lose.

Sun Tzu encouraged his generals to be quiet "to assure depth in deliberation." Listening is a great tool to assure this depth and achieve the next level of personal success. By listening you get more information from each conversation.

BE CONSIDERATE

Success Rules

- Don't abuse power.
- Don't burn your bridges.
- Do unto others as you would have them do unto you.

Pay attention to the soldiers' well-being and do not fatigue them.
Try to keep them in high sprits and conserve their energy.
—Sun Tzu

Another translator points out how Sun Tzu's consideration for humanity extends beyond his own troops:

Treat the captives well, and care for them. Thus, command them with civility and imbue them uniformly with martial ardor and it may be said that victory is certain.

Although we usually do not find ourselves in this position of power over captives, a power hierarchy exists in many of our relationships. Our positions of "superior" power can range from hiring and firing, to whether we return phone calls, to the amount of the tip in a restaurant.

In these daily power relationships we are sometimes tempted to abuse our power and take advantage of the inherent inequality in the power balance. Whether consciously or subconsciously, we often make a decision that works to our advantage—perhaps not returning a phone call when we have nothing to gain. In one such example, the president of a large financial group bawled out one of his senior executives for making a delivery person wait in the lobby for twenty-five minutes to deliver lunch. The president knew that the waiting time reduced the delivery person's income. This incident became a corporate legend.

Sun Tzu's words about being considerate are appropriate for the way relative power in relationships shifts from situation to situation. In the new "knowledge worker" information age, we sometimes find ourselves in control of information. At other times we are in need of information. Treating others with magnanimity when we are in control sets up the potential for a winning situation again when we are not in control.

Imagine the opposite scenario, where someone has alienated people across an industry. When that person goes to look for another job, is there a positive "buzz"? Also, as time goes on, alienated people rise to be peers or superiors. Often we run into these people in other parts of our life—at professional gatherings, a restaurant, or local school events. Don't burn bridges—ever.

Treating people well is a building block for the kind of success that sticks. The world is a series of complex relationships where we need to interact across industries and communities in a variety of roles. Being considerate of others, as Sun Tzu advises, will bring the most benefit.

BE COURAGEOUS

Success Rules

- Balance confidence with wisdom.
- Take action to do the right thing.
- This is courage.

> The principle of military administration is to
> achieve a uniform level of courage.
> —Sun Tzu

Sun Tzu's concern was getting his men to have the courage to engage in battle. We too have a need for courage in our everyday battles.

Everything we do involves risk. There is also risk in doing nothing. In fact, trying to maintain the status quo can be the greatest risk of all.

People who assume risk and take action seldom claim to be courageous. They talk about "just doing what anyone else would have done" in that situation. They do not profess any lifelong ambition to be courageous.

When impulse is required they may say something like "I didn't think" or "it was the only thing to do." They simply did what they felt had to be done.

Build Self-Confidence

Confidence is the father of courage—taking action to do the right thing. We take action not just because of the impulse based on values but also because our training gives us confidence that we can succeed—or be mentally satisfied that we "gave it our best shot."

Self-confidence is great as long as it has a sound foundation. While lack of confidence is at one extreme of the scale, overconfidence is at the deadly other extreme. Overconfidence creates situations where you will be defeated by the unexpected. It's when we are sure everything is going well that we are in the most danger of being surprised.

Stevie Wonder put it this way:

When you begin thinking you are really number one, that's when you begin to go nowhere.

Physical self-confidence involves the body. Mental self-confidence involves the mind. In many cases, the physical and mental self-confidence generates mutual reinforcement. A quarterback who has learned to pass accurately believes in his skill. The mental belief in his skill helps him keep a cool head and perform well on the field.

General Wavell said,

A bold general may be lucky, but no general can be lucky unless he is bold.

That is, we've got to have courage to take risks and if we do not take calculated risks we can't win. Concerning General McClellan at Antietam, biographer Stephen Sears writes of McClellan's cautious mindset stating that the general was ". . . so fearful of losing that he could not win."

Put Courage Into Action

Courage surfaces in many forms:

On September 11, 2001, in the sky over Pennsylvania, when Todd Beamer uttered the now famous "Let's roll," he and fellow passengers became heroes. They certainly did not board the plane planning to become heroes. Understanding the circumstances, they did what they needed to do. Trying to overtake the hijackers cost their lives, but it's very likely the crash in a Pennsylvania field saved lives at a target where the terrorists intended to crash the plane.

At the time Betty Ford was the First Lady of the United States, she was also secretly battling alcoholism. At first, she sought treatment con-fidentially. Eventually she demonstrated true courage by going "public" with her disease and founding the Betty Ford Center.

If courage is taking action, we all have the ability to be courageous. What we call courage is people taking action on something in which they believe.

Sun Tzu says,

He kicks away the ladder behind the soldiers when they have climbed up a height.

Climbing to success in life often requires having the courage to take a risk and kick away our own ladder.

However, courage must also be balanced with wisdom. Field Marshal Montgomery wrote:

Many qualities go to make a leader, but two are vital—the ability to make the right decisions and the courage to act on the decisions.

PRACTICE DISCIPLINE

Success Rules

- Discipline is a friend.
- Discipline makes good people great.
- It takes discipline to practice self-discipline.

> If discipline is not enforced, you cannot employ the troops.
> —Sun Tzu

Some of *The Art of War*'s most famous sections suggest strong discipline. The story of "the concubines" demonstrates how Sun Tzu uses discipline to achieve performance. This stress on discipline is consistent with winners everywhere.

Discipline Helps You Win

All great achievements are won through discipline. When home run king Henry Aaron was asked the difference between a good team and a great team his answer was one word, "discipline."

The Japanese have a word for the discipline of rebuilding a process—it's *kaizen*—meaning continuous improvement. *Kaizen*, as a discipline, also has its place in personal improvement.

After dominating the 1997 Masters, Tiger Woods studied videotapes of his performance, and went back to his coach to rebuild his swing so he could get even better! It's the discipline of continuous training and practice that makes Tiger Woods a champion among champions. He is known for being the last to leave the practice tee. Tiger excels—yet still improves—and so can we.

The day after being the youngest quarterback to win a Super Bowl and the second youngest to earn MVP honors, the New England Patriots' Tom Brady exclaimed, "There's so much room for improvement, I don't know where to start."

Discipline is getting up early every morning to study how we can improve our profession—or exercise to improve our physical health. Mornings are best for practicing good discipline because putting "it" off until later in the day means that "it" can be put off until the next day, and the next day. Without consistency there is no discipline.

Discipline is a friend—not an enemy. Excuses for not practicing good discipline are the real enemy. Discipline keeps us doing the right thing and puts us on the path to achieving our goals.

Discipline Generates Power

In an overview of Colin Powell's "Seven Laws of Power," author Oren Harari identifies several of the general's key disciplines—perhaps Powell is a latter-day Sun Tzu:

1. *Dare to Be the Skunk.* Says Powell, "Every organization should tolerate rebels who tell the emperor he has no clothes . . ."
2. *To Get the Real Dirt, Head for the Trenches.* "The people in the field are closest to the problem. Therefore, that is where the real wisdom is."
3. *Share the Power.* "Plans don't accomplish work. It is people who get things done."
4. *Know When to Ignore Your Advisors.* "Experts often possess more data than judgment."
5. *Develop Selective Amnesia.* "Never let ego get so close to your position that when your position goes, your ego goes with it."
6. *Come Up for Air.* "Anybody who is logging hours to impress me, you are wasting time."

7. *Declare Victory and Quit.* Powell advises about the importance of timing in withdrawing from a position.

Great rules! The problem is that following these rules, or any other set of rules, requires discipline. Self-discipline starts with doing small things that eventually become habits. Set a realistic number of goals. You can then move on to bigger challenges and more productive self-discipline that will generate increased success.

BE CREATIVE

Success Rules

- Brainstorm.
- Think outside of the box.
- Unleash your creative energy.

> In battle, there are two kinds of postures,
> extraordinary force and normal force.
> Their combinations give rise to an endless series of maneuvers.
> —Sun Tzu

Creativity is also important for managing our personal success. In the business world, new products have a "half life" of five years—that is, in five years, half of them will be obsolete. The success of most organizations results from a sustained succession of successful creativity—not a single product or lone creative effort. So, it is with the creativity of successful people.

Too often, we think of others, but not ourselves, as being creative.

Creativity is not a mystical thing; it is simply people searching for alternate solutions to problems. Creativity is a key component in our search for strategies for personal success.

Like so much of success in life, creativity appears to revolve around hard work, or "knowing our stuff." This is good news. Everyone has the opportunity to apply their own "creative genius" and tools in the search for success.

Unleash Creative Energy

Edward H. Land, the inventor of the Polaroid camera, explained the creative process this way:

True creativity is characterized by a succession of acts each dependent on the one before and suggesting the one after.

Obviously, a path we can understand and follow. Darwin tells us the route is not easy. He says:

At no time am I a quick thinker or writer; whatever I have done in science has solely been by long pondering, patience, and industry.

These descriptions of creativity do not suggest that great ideas come as "lightning bolts from the sky." Indeed, creativity involves rational advancements. Creativity arises out of what we know and the focus of our interests. Its fire is kindled by our passions.

A small Texas restaurant company constrained by its small lot size looked for ways to grow their sales during the 1950s. Located on a busy thoroughfare, it searched for a creative way to get more business from the cars driving by daily and hung out a simple sign saying, "Drive Thru," a novel approach at the time. Their business exploded and others copied the idea. This creative idea has become so common we would be surprised to find a fast food restaurant that does not offer "Drive Thru" service.

Sun Tzu's quote on endless combinations is from a chapter in *The Art of War* titled "Energy." This energy is the creativity of human beings trying to be successful in tackling problems by looking for the extraordinary.

Sun Tzu's 2,500-year-old advice involves using simple weapons and limited resources. The extraordinary does not necessarily mean the newest and latest or the most expensive. Often the extraordinary lies in the simple, the mundane, the everyday things we look at with a fresh perspective. Sun Tzu suggests we tap into a creative reservoir of options others may not have considered.

Think Outside of the Box

> We are all taught what is known, but we rarely learn about what
> is not known, and we almost never know about the knowable.
> —Ralph E. Gomory

When the leader of an organization wanted to impress upon his people the need to search for the "not known" and "knowable," he drew a series of boxes on a flip chart:

He labeled the first box "Our Professional Expertise" and acknowledged that all had a high degree of knowledge.

Around the outside of that box, he drew another box labeled "Our Suppliers and Customers." He recognized a relatively high level of knowledge about this group.

Around these boxes, he drew another box labeled "Organizations in our Industry." Here, he expressed a concern about a lower level of knowledge by his people.

The next box encompassing all others was labeled, "Organizations Outside of our Industry." He expressed real concern about the existing level of knowledge.

The final box outside was labeled "Any Organization in the World" and further concern was expressed about the lack of knowledge.

He said, "Our task is to 'think outside of the box' and into new areas that enhance our value and assure future income. This requires getting out of the box and finding new opportunities away from the box."

Discovering new strategies outside of the box is not a case of "I'll know it when I see it," but rather: "I'll see it when I know it." That is, only when we know about it do we see it as a new opportunity.

Use the Tools of Creativity

If we understand that creativity is a thought process, enhanced by tools and aided by interaction, we can then understand how to use creativity to build our own personal success. Here are a few basic tools for creative thinking:

- On a "blank piece of paper" develop a list of options.
- Construct a "Ben Franklin Balance Sheet" by making two columns on a sheet of paper, heading one column "yes" and the other "no." Write down the "yes" and "no" reasons, compare them, and make your decision.
- Set up a structured brainstorming session where a small group gathers around a flip chart observing simple rules as they generate input. In one recorded instance of brainstorming, the group developed over 2,000 uses for parts of a chicken.

Most experts in creativity maintain that all of us are creative in our own way. In Sun Tzu's description it's the attainable creativity we all can achieve. It's not "inventing" new "musical notes," "colors," or "flavors." Creativity is simply combining the known in useful variations.

AIM FOR HIGH STANDARDS

Success Rules

- Aim high.
- Work upstream.
- Set new standards.

> The commander must create a helpful situa-
> tion over and beyond the ordinary rules.
> —Sun Tzu

Success is not doing what needs to be done. Success is going "above and beyond" what needs to be done. To succeed you must break "the ordinary rules" and set new standards of performance. Then you must break your own records.

What has been successful in the past, may continue to work in the future. But somewhere, sometime, someone will set a new standard of performance.

New standards result from changes in process. Examination of a century of records in the simple sport of the high jump reveals changes from the Scissors to the Western Roll to the Straddle to the Fosbury Flop. After the new and better methodology was introduced, no one could compete effectively with the old methodology. Today, every high jump champion uses the Fosbury flop. Tomorrow, who knows what the methodology will be. No one even knows whether that tomorrow is today or another day.

Look at the Process

When we think about excelling, we look at the results because that's where the measurement is made. However, it is the improvement in the process that creates the results.

Everything we do involves a process—a series of steps, a chain of activities. Building a fire is a process, preparing a meal is a process, and our work activities involve dozens of processes. In the performance of every process, we can identify three different types of standards:

- Input standards: Ingredients that go into a process.
- Operating standards: Process activities.
- Output standards: The results of the process.

For example, in preparing a meal:

- Input standards determine the quantity and quality of the ingredients—to end up with a tender steak, you must have a good cut of meat; to make a good salad, you must have fresh ingredients.
- Operating standards determine the method of preparation—this is how long you cook the food and at what temperature.
- Output standards are concerned with the serving temperature, taste, and appearance of the meal.

WORK UPSTREAM

When thinking about preparing a meal, it's easy to see that input standards (ingredients) and operating standards (preparation) have a significant effect on the output standards (results). To achieve better results in any process, work upstream on input and operating standards.

To excel in any event requires a process of preparation and practice. A last-minute scramble to improve on the day of the event is too late. Only by improving the preparation and practice standards can we improve the results.

The higher the aim, the greater the stretch required to meet the standards, the more likely we are to achieve improvement.

Whatever you do, strive for the big changes in process that improve performance. These changes require more effort but they produce bigger rewards.

SEEK SOUND COUNSEL

Success Rules

- Quality beats quantity.
- Eloquent ignorance is deadly.
- Get a guru, a coach, and a sponsor.

> Enlightened rulers must deliberate on the plans to go to battle.
> —Sun Tzu

As you develop plans and strategies for success, you can expect plenty of advice—often more than you want or need. Nevertheless, feedback from mentors and advisors who can give you ideas, support, and "course corrections" on your path to success is critical. Achievement is rarely accomplished in solitary practice without the aid of coaching.

Create a Counseling Staff

What you want from your staff of counselors is guidance that helps orient your internal compass to success. You will learn the most from people of good will who will be honest with you.

Listen carefully to your advisors and keep score of the usefulness of their advice. A few advisors of high reliability are more important than a large quantity of advisors.

Here are key counseling positions to fill:

- *A guru.* This is a wise person not directly involved in your activities who will listen and give good positive input. Gurus are traditionally sought out for their wisdom and can be great for exploring new ideas. With a good guru, one never feels threatened and is often inspired.
- *A coach.* While gurus are selected for overall wisdom, coaches know your profession or business. He or she can go beyond your own defenses and ego so you can truly "know yourself."

    What top professional athlete doesn't use a coach? Whether you are at the top of your profession, or on the way up, the tweaking and ideas from an outside coach can help raise the level of your success.

    Although you may not have access to a professional coach, the underlying idea of feedback from others can be applied—someone who can highlight the "blind spots" in your understanding or approach. A coach can be a friend who can help analyze what's happening and why. Mutual candor is the most valuable component of this relationship.
- *A sponsor.* This is someone at a high level in the organization who will act as your mentor. If that person moves on, cultivate another. One young man told me that about a year after he was hired, the three next senior people up the chain of command left. Since the young man had lost all of his original sponsors, he soon left the organization.

Sponsors can also be valuable in outside activities. If asked to sit on a local board of a civic organization, ask the person inviting you to be your mentor in the workings of the team. This assistance can help you get up to speed faster, make you more effective, and deepen your relationship.

Beware of Eloquent Ignorance

I can recall a meeting at a consulting organization where several people were reviewing the content of a seminar. An individual who was visiting for the week was invited to the meeting. Wanting to exhibit his knowledge, he participated actively. His input, though well-intentioned, had little validity.

A room full of well-meaning people who have no knowledge of the situation will often come to the wrong conclusion. Eloquent ignorance yields deadly contributions.

I have found the easiest thing to do in any consulting situation is to give advice. Beware: good answers come only from a blend of prior experience and local knowledge.

Among people who know how to evaluate information flow, a common statement regarding an opinion is simply "that is one data point." This is a polite way of noting that "more than one data point" is needed to make an informed decision.

Follow these admonitions at your meeting tables:

1. The ability to carry on a meaningful and intelligent discussion decreases with an increase in the number of people attending.
2. All advice is not sound advice. All voices should not be considered equal. Keep counsel with advisors who know the situation.

The most frustrating meetings I attended were the twenty-two-person board of directors sessions of a national trade association. The group was too large for interchange and much advice was given by people impressed only with the sound of their own voices.

Avoid using meetings as a decision-making forum. Use meetings for input and then make your decision. Although it's good form to poll everyone in a small group to get their opinion, avoid voting. It polarizes people.

Small support groups of like-minded individuals, who may or may not be in your field, provide a good opportunity for exchanging information and networking. Noncompetitive relationships provide an ideal sounding board for testing ideas and solving problems.

Chapter 10

Strategies
for Success

Strategy and tactics perform different roles in our quest for success.

- Strategy is thought seeking its means of execution.
- Tactics is the means to carry out the thought.
- Strategy determines the allocation of resources. It is the plan.
- Tactics deals with the use of resources. It is the implementation of the plan.
- Strategy is doing the right thing.
- Tactics is doing things right.

Compare the roles of strategy and tactics to a boat race. Strategy is the rudder—it determines direction. Tactics is the power that propels you to your goal.

All planning activities are strategic; all implementation activities require contact and are tactical. For example, if your strategy is to find new employment by personally contacting people, your tactic is the process of making the actual contacts.

When the president of a company is determining the course of action, that activity is strategic. When the president of a company is talking to a customer, that action is tactical.

Action, any action no matter how seemingly small or insignificant, follows a plan or intention. Strategy is the creation of "right action." Strategy comes before tactics—always.

KNOW YOUR BATTLEGROUND

Success Rules

- Know your stuff.
- Expand your learning horizons.
- Time invested in learning brings big rewards.

One must compare the various conditions of the antagonistic sides in terms of the five constant factors:

- Moral influence
- Weather
- Terrain
- Commander
- Doctrine

These five constant factors should be familiar to every general.
He who masters them wins; he who does not is defeated.
—Sun Tzu

The first step of great strategy is research—the gathering of information. The first section of this book is devoted to the most important area of information collection—knowing yourself.

Accurate information allows for better use of your resources. The information derived reduces risks because you have data that gives you better odds. Only a gambler with inside information can rationally bet his entire stake on a single race. What warnings we are going to get, we probably already have. Analysis of information available prior to the World Trade Center disaster proved that point once again.

Knowledge of a situation helps separate the useful from the useless. Your own interactive experience will help you evaluate the information.

The Boy Scouts say it most succinctly, simply "Be Prepared."

Seek Knowledge

In the first sentences of *The Art of War*, Sun Tzu says,

War is a matter of vital importance to the state; a matter of life and death, the road either to survival or to ruin.

Hence, it is imperative that it be thoroughly studied.

He further advises:

Analyze the enemy's battle plan so as to have a clear understanding of its strong and weak points. Agitate the enemy so as to ascertain his pattern of movement.

Here are active ingredients that will help you build a strong knowledge base:

- *Learn your subject well enough to teach it.* The subject content is mastered if you feel able to teach it—a simple standard to establish. This search for expertise will make you ask deeper questions and anticipate questions that might be asked. Continuous searching for knowledge reveals new questions and information you did not know existed.
- *Ask the "five why's" to get to the root cause of a problem.* In the quality management arena where the "five why's" are considered an important tool, the questioning series might go like this:

Q1. Why was the delivery late?
A1. The delivery was late because the truck broke down.
Q2. Why did the truck break down?
A2. The truck broke down because it had not been lubricated.
Q3. Why wasn't the truck lubricated?
Q3. The driver had not been trained.
Q4. Why hadn't the driver been trained?"
A4. The training was canceled.
Q5. Why was the training canceled?
A5. The budget had been cut.

Now you are at the root cause of the problem. The late delivery was not caused by the driver, it was a result of a failure of funds to provide training on how and when to lubricate the truck.

If you can't ask and answer "why" five times, you probably haven't gotten to the heart of an issue.

- *Break your subject into pieces.* Sun Tzu often advises segmentation as means of study. Segmentation puts order in analysis. This is known as "eating the elephant" one bite at a time. Dissecting a subject into smaller units helps us understand each component and see how they meld into "the whole."
- *Study information close to time of use.* Because immediate application increases retention, training should take place close to time of use.

Expand Your Knowledge Horizons

Humorist-philosopher Mark Twain said,

I have never let my schooling interfere with my education.

This wise observation points us to widening our knowledge horizons. Limiting your knowledge to a narrow focus keeps you from seeing new and creative solutions. Leave yourself open to unexpected and perhaps unwelcome discoveries.

Here are a few ways to gain input beyond your area of operations.

- *Have a networking mindset.* Develop a network of bright people who can give you information that is important to your success. Know the thought leaders in your profession and in other areas of interest. Create situations where these people can be comfortable with you. Strive to be a contributor as well as a recipient of important information and your relationship will be secure.

- *Take advantage of learning opportunities.* Too many people claim they do not have time to attend trade shows or industry meetings (and not because they don't think they are important). This failure extends to volunteer organizations—such as, not attending the church council annual retreat. These people are saying they are "too busy chopping wood to stop and sharpen their ax." There never is enough time for all of the things we want to do. So concentrate your efforts. Take the time to learn something new. Do it now.

- *Spend time with people with different interests.* If you only spend time with people who know the same things you do, you won't learn new things. Even worse, you may become more certain that your information, ideas, and point of view are the most important or correct. Take courses in other fields; join organizations with other interests; go to a trade show in a different industry. You will gain new insights and find lots of new ideas to "steal" and apply.

- *Seek new experiences.* Don't let yourself get stuck in a rut! Explore the world; take a ride in a balloon; sign up for a raft trip; have new people over for dinner or attend a new civic activity.

- *Learn new questions.* Observing by wandering around is a good way to discover questions that need answers.

A recent consulting assignment in the grocery industry did not require me to visit any retailers, but I decided that on-site knowledge would be helpful. My travel schedule made it convenient to visit four of the five largest retailers—two of which are the most respected industry leaders. This hands-on experience enabled me to know the retail store component of the assignment better than anyone else. I arranged the information into a presentation for my client. He reported outstanding success—"kicked butt" was his exact phrase.

You are not in control of what challenges you will confront—you are in control of your response to those challenges. The broader your knowledge, the better your ability to react in a winning way to new challenges.

Sun Tzu writes:

The general who understands war is the controller of his people's fate and the guarantor of the security of the nation.

To achieve his personal success, Sun Tzu studied war. The subject of your focus may be different. Your ability to affect your own personal success will be enhanced if you have access to many universes of knowledge.

BUILD A PERSONAL NETWORK

Success Rules

- Set stretch goals.
- Solidify every contact.
- Actively work your network.

Foreknowledge must be obtained from men who know the enemy situation.
—Sun Tzu

Our existing network of friends and business associates is an outstanding source of "foreknowledge."

Sun Tzu says,

Those who do not use local guides are unable to obtain the advantages of ground.

When we meet new people, we instinctively look for some common ground in order to establish a closer relationship; for example:

- At a conference in Helsinki, a Finnish manager told me how he searched America for a town to build his factory. Since the town he selected is my hometown, we developed a common bond.
- The stranger next to me at a luncheon turned into a friend when we discovered that we had been at the same New Year's Eve party.
- The passenger in the seat next to me on an airplane became an important contact when we discovered that both of us had lived in the same neighborhood in a distant city.

The foundation of your personal growth is the size and strength of your network. Chances are you probably do not have a very big or strong network unless you actively manage it. If you are too frugal about whom you call or the time you spend developing relationships, your network will be limited.

Tom Gunnels, author of *Keep Your Lights On*, gives good advice on the three types of knowledge critical to your success:

What you know!

Whom you know!

Who knows you!

Grow Your Network

A solid network grows from continuous investment of time and resources. It is a combination of new acquaintances and deep friendships. Good networking involves both meeting new acquaintances and actively moving these relationships to a closer friendship.

- *Set Contact Goals*: It's one thing to go to a meeting or conference and try to meet people; it's quite another to have a more specific goal in mind.

    The contact goal need not be large. Any reasonable goal serves as a gentle reminder to keep you moving from a comfortable circle of friends to seeking new relationships. If you do not feel a little uncomfortable when meeting new people and extending your network, you probably are not reaching enough people.

Yes, the quality of contacts is important. However, I know of no one who has a high-quality network who also does not have a high-quantity network. As your contacts advance in their careers, they become high-quality resources—provided you keep in touch with them. That's the second part of networking—working the network.

The Transition Team, an outplacement organization, offers the following goal-oriented advice for getting started on networking for a new job: "Make a list of the first twenty people you can think of who might be able to help you with your search. Don't be concerned with how comfortable you are calling upon them, or how long it has been since you have talked. List both the name and the person's relationship or role. For example: Mrs. Lawson—retired librarian (friend). Push yourself to reach the goal of twenty names! The next step is to inform your contacts of your situation in a positive way."

- *Solidify the Contact*: When you meet someone new, find out his or her interests and promise to send something he or she might like to have. For example, you might keep a file of interesting articles for this purpose. Get their business card, write down the promised action along with date and place you met. Then keep your promise to send something and be sure to include a handwritten note. Reason? A handwritten note is a personal touch and you want a personal relationship.

- *Use the Phone*: The telephone is an obvious networking tool. My traveling companions say that I've never been able to walk past a phone in an airport without using it. Their statement is quite accurate.

    Whenever you place a call, it's in good taste to ask if he or she has a moment. Otherwise, you will be embarrassed by being cut short if the person is in the middle of a conference.

When I am contacting someone I do not know well (or at all), I never leave a message. This approach keeps me in control of my networking and solves several problems:

1. When I leave a message, I abrogate my right to call back because if the call isn't returned, then when is it appropriate to call again? If I do not leave a message, I can call anytime—even a few minutes later if I am told that my contact is on the phone.
2. Because I keep control of the time when the call is initiated, I can call when I am mentally prepared.
3. I avoid the embarrassment of receiving a return call and not remembering why I called.

- *Use the Internet*: A great networking tool if you use it wisely. Keep messages brief and informative.

Keep Your Network Active

Be active. The more people you know and the more friendships you cultivate, the more people you will know well. Some of your contacts—hopefully, many—will breed other contacts.

When you plan to visit a city, call people in your network and ask to meet them. Your contacts will be flattered by your interest. Whether or not you do meet, the offer breeds a stronger relationship.

In some cities, I've had three breakfasts with three different groups of people—although you need to watch your diet, there is no rule against this. A friend facetiously commented that the way to "do New York" is to plan three lunches on the same day. Because many New Yorkers commute, breakfast or dinner meetings are inconvenient.

The bad news about networking is the continuous investment of time and energy. The good news is that it is fun and generates results.

Statisticians say only four contact links separate you from anyone in the world. That is, if you know the name of the person you want to reach. And, if you don't? What if you are looking for someone who can help you solve a problem and you do not know precisely who that person is? Then you really need a network—and the broadest base yields the best responses.

DEVELOP GREAT STRATEGIES

Success Rules

- Develop a vision.
- Express as a vivid image.
- Drive success with strategic initiatives.

> Their aim must be to take all under heaven
> intact through strategic superiority.
> —Sun Tzu

Another translator of *The Art of War* describes in very simple terms that winning strategy achieves victory before the battle:

A victorious army seeks its victories before seeking battle.
An army destined to defeat fights in the hope of winning.

Without strategy, success is left to chance. With strategy, we have direction and goals.

Tactical considerations can influence your strategic plan. You may need to direct your efforts in an area that is tactically possible, instead of one that is strategically preferable. Financial or family considerations will influence your selection of strategic goals. You may want to be president of the United States; however, a high political office may be a more practical goal.

It is a fundamental truth that the strategy must be correct to succeed in any endeavor. There's no chicken and egg problem here. The strategy must be right first; then the tactics can support the strategy. Excellent strategy can sustain many tactical failures.

A bad strategy supported by good tactics can be a fast route to failure. Sustained tactical success—even continuous brilliant execution of tactics—seldom overcomes an inadequate strategic posture.

The best personal strategies cascade from a vision of the future. The vision is not a flash of insight. It requires the sweat equity of careful consideration.

Have a Vision

A "vision" is not just a vision statement. Visions are not words, they are discoveries of "what we will be." Without a vision, we perish mentally.

A friend who headed a consulting organization stated clearly that:

Visions are the vehicles that transport us across the boundaries of current reality to the boundless hopes of a future seemingly beyond our grasp. What once we deemed impossible becomes not only possible but probable when we live out our vision through actions.

Here are guidelines for establishing a vision of your success.

1. *Identify your core competencies.* What is it that others say you do best? What do you like to do? Ask trusted advisors to comment on your identification of core competencies.

2. *Determine applications.* Think about how you can be most productive using these core competencies. Where can you best apply your talents and skills?

3. *Establish a direction.* Develop a clear mind-picture of where you want to go and what you want to be. Explore factors critical to achieving your vision.

Express the Vision as a Vivid Image

A vivid image is an energetic and vibrant description of what your world would look like if your vision was achieved or manifested.

Transform your mission into word pictures:

Write a vivid image of your vision in a single session. Start with a sentence like "Five years from now I will . . . " and let thoughts flow out of your head and onto a sheet of paper. Continue without stopping until you have covered several sheets of paper. Set your comments aside for a day or two and then simplify this vivid image into a short paragraph or two. The mental exercise is more important than the words on paper. Now you are ready to transform the vision into action.

The value of exploring the vision is in the mental exercise. The process of exploring crystallizes your thoughts and takes you one step closer to realizing your mission.

Develop Personal Strategic Initiatives

A strategic initiative is strategy on paper. In a few words, the strategic initiative provides your compass and states your goals.

Think about existing opportunities. Review threats and blockers to your vision. Consider optional courses of action. Then write out your strategic initiatives using statements like the following:

Career: I will get a degree at night school that makes me eligible for promotion.

Family: I will send our children to college.

Renewal: I will go on an educational trip overseas for a week.

Health: I will train and attempt to run a marathon.

Now, move on to implementation. Prioritize the most important three to five initiatives. Do not select more than this number or you will be attempting too much. Develop a plan of action for each initiative. Be diligent in your follow-though. These steps will ultimately create your individualized pathway to personal success.

WIN WITHOUT FIGHTING

Success Rules

- Great strategy is better than great combat.
- Innovations yield great strategies.
- Great strategy wins.

To win 100 victories in 100 battles is not the acme of skill.
To subdue the enemy without fighting is the supreme excellence.
—Sun Tzu

That offensive strategy should be aimed at winning without major conflict is a principle often repeated throughout *The Art of War*.

Find Victory in Your Strategy

Your strategy should be so good that you will not have any competition; if you do encounter able opponents, your tactics should be so good you will win anyway.

It is in the formulation of strategy that victory is determined. The person who wins will probably be the person who has already won. That is, the winner will have developed a great strategy prior to engaging the opponent.

Those who win without fighting are often so well prepared to fight and win that they avoid battle by intimidating their opponents. The potential opponent decides to expend his or her energy elsewhere because they are afraid of losing or do not like the cost of winning.

Phillip Fulmer, national-championship-winning football coach at the University of Tennessee says,

I constantly coach our players about having the intensity to be able to intimidate our opponents. This doesn't mean to play outside the rules. It means that our players should be fundamentally sound and in such good physical condition that they can outlast and outwork their opponents.

In this sense, Coach Fulmer is talking about being so good that our performance is, in itself, intimidating.

In every part of Switzerland are streets, plazas, and statues honoring generals of an army that did not fight. Switzerland wins a lot of wars (that it never fought) using the Porcupine Strategy:

**You
roll up into
a ball in place and
brandish your
quills.**

The Swiss army is composed of many hundreds of thousands of civilians who train regularly and keep weapons in their home. Switzerland does not have an army; Switzerland is an army.

Sun Tzu reinforces his belief in the strength of strategy by saying:

Those skilled in war subdue the enemy's army without fighting. They capture the enemy's cities without assaulting them and overthrow his state without protracted operations.

Capture the Strength of Innovation

Sun Tzu says that if you are not doing something unique, you have not really attained a victory:

To foresee a victory no better than ordinary people's foresight is not the acme of excellence.

Neither is it the acme of excellence if you win a victory through fierce fighting and the whole empire says, 'Well done!'

Sun Tzu goes on to confirm that easy wins are not victories. The real victories are where you "conquer an enemy already defeated" (by strategy).

Innovation often gives you the kind of strength that, in itself, declares victory. Winners innovate to find new ways to victory without encountering competition; for example, the youngster entering a science fair with an exhibit that is clearly at a higher level than other students. Think of Dick Fosbury innovating the Fosbury Flop in the high jump, or Dell selling computers direct to customers and ignoring traditional distribution channels.

Thinking up new ideas is easy; the test for success lies in the ability to implement the ideas. Here are steps that will help energize your mind to see a different reality and find new possibilities.

1. *Define the challenge.* Use words or draw pictures to state essential elements of the challenge. For example, Fosbury wanted to jump higher so that he could win competitively.
2. *Develop "How about ..." statements.* These statements should lead you to the radical and unusual. Go beyond the boundaries of the normal. Fosbury's statements might have been:

   - How about using a different type of pole?
   - How about using a pogo stick?
   - How about a different take-off style?
   - How about radically changing the way I go over the bar?
   - How about talking to other coaches?
   - How about looking at the techniques of divers?
   - How about being shot out of a cannon?

3. *Visualize action.* Select several ideas that are intriguing and visualize putting them into action. Imagine what happens, moment by moment. Focus your interests on the action, not the results. Observe what is interesting as the scene takes place.
4. *Innovate.* Diagram input from these ideas and look for a new way to fulfill the challenge.

A successful biologist said,

Discovery consists of seeing what everybody has seen—and thinking what nobody has thought.

Among the orchards of Northern Michigan, Bob Sutherland saw what everybody has seen—cherries—and thought what nobody has thought. The result: his unique store is themed around a fictitious nation—the Cherry Republic. Today, in the tiny town of Leelanau, shopping is fun among the décor spoofing the fictitious Cherry Republic. Here throngs of tourists choose from hundreds of cherry-related products.

APPLY STRENGTH AGAINST WEAKNESS

Success Rules

- Know your strengths.
- Concentrate strengths against weaknesses.
- The concentration is always at a decisive point.

> The law of successful operations is to avoid the enemy's strength and strike his weakness.
> —Sun Tzu

Concentration of strength is one of the major principles of military success—and of success in any endeavor. Every successful attack has succeeded because somebody concentrated.

Concentration is not a mere mass of numbers, but rather the focusing of strategy and tactics where you want to win. The key to success is not how much strength you have, but how and where you concentrate your power.

Use Many to Strike the Few

Although more than two millennia of time and thousands of miles separate Sun Tzu from the European general Carl von Clausewitz, look at the following similarity of advice.

If we are able to use many to strike few at the selected place, those we deal with will be in dire straits.
—*Sun Tzu, fifth century* B.C.

Where absolute superiority is not obtainable, you must produce a relative one at the decisive point by making skillful use of what you have.
—*Carl von Clausewitz, nineteenth century* A.D.

Although some suspect that Clausewitz could have read *The Art of War*, there is no proof that this happened. It is clear that Sun Tzu's Eastern strategy and Clausewitz's Western strategy agree on concentrating strength against weakness. Sun Tzu says to concentrate "at the selected place." Clausewitz says concentrate "at the decisive point." Clausewitz further admonishes that this tactical concentration must be achieved by "making skillful use of what you have"—definitely the situation facing most of us.

Find a Weakness

Again, Sun Tzu says,

His offensive will be irresistible if he plunges into the enemy's weak points.

People recognized for expertise have concentrated their quest in a narrow area where the weakness is lack of competition.

Jim King parlayed his corporate specialty in analyzing environmental risk into a position of expertise by writing the 1,290-page *Environmental Dictionary*. From this base he launched a new consulting career.

King's fame is confined to the world of environmental management. On any street in every town are niche entrepreneurs who are "experts" in narrowly defined areas where there is limited competition—or none at all.

The essence of the daily task of winning is to operate from a base of relative superiority in a specific field. That is, you must select a niche where you can apply your strengths against weaknesses.

When you think about where you are going to concentrate, look for the weakness of your opponent's strength. For example, in 1704, Peter the Great arrived at the Russian town of Dorpat to assist 20,000 Russians who had forty-six cannons firing at the besieged garrison. He found his commander's concentration faulty. They were firing at the town's strongest bastions. Peter switched the artillery to the most vulnerable walls and a breach was made for Russian troops to enter. Victory came five weeks after the siege began but only ten days after Peter arrived to focus the strength of his cannons against the weakest walls.

Obtain Relative Superiority

Organizational Superiority: Often we can obtain a relative superiority with an organizational strength. That is how the Greeks fighting in a phalanx won the Battle of Marathon against the Persians who were fighting one to one.

Organizational superiority is what helps sports teams win, and makes business franchises successful. Organizational superiority is achieved by any individual who marshals his or her personal resources—often known as "getting your ducks in a row."

Technological Superiority: Another avenue to relative superiority is through technology. Today, this winning strength is most often found in hi-tech organizations. Each of us can derive the advantages of applying the latest technological knowledge in our chosen areas of endeavor.

It's critical to keep up with the rapid pace of change in technology. Distinct advantages accrue to those who keep on the leading edge. Not only can technology help you look like a leader, it can help you be a leader. People want to associate with knowledgeable leaders.

Reinforce Strength—Not Weakness

The best odds for success are achieved by spending time, money, and energy reinforcing what is working. Then you are leveraging off what you do well.

When you spend time and resources shoring up what's not working, you are reinforcing weakness—this is diametrically opposed to the concept of reinforcing strength.

It's not that you shouldn't pay attention to weak areas, the problem is that reinforcing weakness denies time and resources to areas of strength. The best results are obtained when strengths are reinforced.

A regular system of deliberately and continuously reinforcing strength is alien to many organization cultures. Too often, managers think they must be involved in day-to-day operations. Because they get so involved in giving support to the weak, they end up defending instead of attacking.

In the world of success, coaches coach and players play. When coaches try to play and players try to coach, the results can be disastrous.

The key to success is making sure that all resources are focused on predetermined strategic initiatives. A military adage warns:

Guns that have not fired, have not attacked, no matter how long they have been in position.

AVOID THE AVOIDABLE

Success Rules

- Correct predictable components first.
- Then devote resources to the unpredictable.
- Sloppy form destroys the content of substance.

> By taking into account the unfavorable factors, he may avoid possible disasters.
> —Sun Tzu

Victory and success go not always to the most brilliant, but to those who make the fewest mistakes. This task is not easy; mistakes are often visible only in hindsight.

The process of avoiding the avoidable is one of understanding that physical hazards are identifiable obstacles concerning which specific measures can be taken. In contrast, the human element is completely unpredictable. Consequently, you must take specific action to reduce the possibility of defeat by physical conditions in order to devote your full resources to dealing with the unpredictable human elements.

Here are examples of how to avoid the avoidable and increase the odds of attaining success:

1. Schedule regular training that increases your professional skills or prepares you for an alternate career.
2. Always arrive early for appointments so that you do not have to begin with the negative of an excuse for being late.
3. Understand that every document presented to another has both form and substance. Go for the ultimate quality in the physical element of form so that it does not distract from the more psychological and

important elements of substance. For example, errors in spelling and language usage can detract from the content of any presentation.

In your work life, avoid the avoidable by never allowing your plan to fail because of quality of the product or service, or delivery time, or any physical element.

There are many other simple rules to follow in everyday life that can keep us from disasters—large and small. Here are a few:

1. Take an aspirin prior to a long plane flight and walk around during the flight to reduce the risk of blood clots—known as economy class syndrome.
2. Never send a letter on the day you write it. An amazing amount of wisdom results from the passage of time and a second look.
3. Carry two credit cards in different places. If you lose one, you have another.
4. Don't drink and drive.

BUILD A STRONG POSITION

Success Rules

- Be who you really are.
- Build sound relationship positions.
- Strengthen expertise to strengthen your position.

It is a doctrine in war that we must rely on the fact
that we have made our position invincible.
—Sun Tzu

Our personal strength is the foundation of our position. It encompasses the way we act and what we do best.

We perceive our position by the way we see ourselves. Others perceive our position by the way they see us.

The perception is indeed the reality.

We can change ourselves and we can cause a change in the way others perceive us. Although our actions can change our position, the change is permanent only if our actions are "for real." Attempts at false positioning are destructive.

We are all actors on the stage of life. Our best role is to act out our part based on who we really are. One of the greatest compliments I've heard about another person is, "He is who he says he is!"

Today, our position is determined by what we do with the strengths we have. Tomorrow, our position is determined by how well we have applied our strengths today. Strong positions provide stability and direction to life. Weak positions are destructive.

Find Strength in Relationship Positions

Margaret J. Wheatley and Myron Kellner-Rogers in their book, *A Simpler Way*, make a strong true statement:

Relationships are all there is.

A position with strong relationships is an invincible position.

Here are the major positions one can occupy in life's families:

Home family position: For married persons, the nuclear family is well defined by marriage or birth. For singles, the surrogate family often is a circle of friends. For all, our family includes some circle of close relatives who give support. How we fulfill our roles determines our ability to contribute to the strength of the family and receive strength from it.

I recall a young lady telling me that she worked every day on being happily married. Like our job at work, our home life requires that we practice the give-and-take of making our relationships successful.

Here are the major positions one can occupy in life's families:

Religious family position: To many, this position is much more than a Sunday thing. Religion can be a great source of position strength. It is the only strength that stretches into infinity. Of all strengths, it is the most deeply personal.

Career family position: The educational process points us to a career position. In careers, there is a ladder that can be climbed and climbing the ladder determines the goals for new positions—or we may choose to move to a different career ladder.

"Other interests" family position: This is what we do in our spare time beyond family, religion, and work. This position may be intertwined with, and supportive of, other positions. For example, a parent (nuclear family) may coach a child's sport (other interest's family).

In each family, you need to devote time and energy to your role; when you excel in the role, your position becomes invincible.

Clearly Define Your Position

To be perceived as more than just another person, develop a personal brand. Define that brand identity narrowly so you can own it. For example, "The author who writes mystery stories involving black Persian cats."

A key to discovering your personal "brand identity" is to imagine a good friend, with a sense of humor, introducing you to an audience using a descriptive middle name. What is the middle name that describes your major interest or area of expertise? That is your personal brand identity.

Reinforcement of a position is possible only after you clearly determine what that position is. This reinforcement is an evolving process.

For example, when I decided to become an expert on the application of military strategy to business, I spent time between appointments and in the evenings visiting bookstores and libraries to find books on the subject.

I climbed over students reading in the aisles of bookstores in Cambridge, Massachusetts. I visited the Library of Congress as well as stores specializing in military books. I gained access to military libraries at West Point and the Infantry school at Fort Benning. Every city I visited offered new opportunities for expanded knowledge in my chosen field of concentration. I applied the knowledge of military strategy to my first book: *Winning the Marketing War*.

I developed a platform presentation on the application of military strategy to business. Eventually, I addressed audiences on five continents on the application of both Eastern and Western military strategies. When I spoke at seminars, I met other prestigious speakers and broadened my world of contacts. The national network became an international network. My credentials provided access to business and military leaders who provided an information flow in my chosen field of expertise.

During my search for information on military strategy, I redefined my focus to accumulating expertise about one specific Chinese strategist—Sun Tzu. The only place in the world where you can find every English translation of *The Art of War* is in my personal library.

Almost every success I experience today can be traced to contacts from my quest to becoming an expert in the application of military strategy to business. When asked if I achieved that goal, my answer is, "Probably not, but I am still learning and improving from life's new experiences."

In the course of this journey to expertise, I twice visited China to understand the Chinese view of Sun Tzu's lessons and lecture on my views of applying Sun Tzu's philosophy.

When the opportunity arose for me to consult internationally, I set another goal of developing expertise on the differences in service quality around the world. Since I would be staying at some of the finest hotels in the world, I decided to interview the general managers of these hotels. These professionals are a knowledgeable source of information because hotels are the world's stage for service quality. The interviews yielded valuable insights on service quality and served as a basis for my book, *Building Bridges to Customers*.

Here are a few rules for building expertise:

1. *Select a particular niche.* The narrower the field, the more limited the competition.
2. *Support your native expertise.* Develop expertise in an area that reinforces your current strengths. Anything else is a hobby.
3. *Be an explorer.* Get out of town and meet new people. Network. Go to the source.
4. *Build a reputation.* Experts aren't chosen, they are announced. Be your own announcer.
5. *Get more expertise.* The quest never ends.
6. *Answer the phone.* You know you are arriving when people start calling you.

Form Alliances

Get allies to help secure your position. This is where networking and teamwork unite to generate personal power. Spending time with others who have similar interests opens the opportunity for new knowledge.

You can't do it all. Every golf professional has a coach, an agent, and a caddy—who does much more than carry his clubs. Get a coach, empower agents, and find other advisors who can discuss the approach for each shot at a better life.

Don't be a bore, but do use every opportunity to communicate about your chosen position. The Internet puts you in touch with the world.

Warning! It's an axiom that the more secure you feel about your position, the greater the danger. It is when you feel most secure that you become most vulnerable to surprise.

ORGANIZE A TEAM

Success Rules

- Form teams.
- Share a common purpose.
- Working together gets better answers.

> When the troops are united, the brave cannot advance
> alone, nor can the cowardly retreat.
> —Sun Tzu

Determined to succeed, we are too often focused on applying our own skills to solving a problem. We jump from "our idea" to implementing "our solution" without soliciting assistance. We have been conditioned to work as individuals, not as team members.

Form Teams to Win

To make the point about how teams succeed, I often use the following exercise in workshops:

I ask people to count the number of times the letter f appears in the box labeled "f" Exercise.

Try it for yourself now. Count the number of times you see the letter f. Do this before you read the answer in one of the following paragraphs.

"F" EXERCISE

The necessity of training farm hands for first-class farms in the fatherly handling of farm livestock is foremost in the minds of farm owners. Since the forefathers of the farm owners trained the farm hands for first-class farms in the fatherly handling of farm livestock, the farm owners feel they should carry on with the family tradition of training farm hands of first-class farms in the fatherly handling of livestock because it is the basis of good fundamental farm management.

Count the number of "f"s in this exercise.

Often, participants will offer a wide range of answers ranging from the low twenties to the mid thirties. As responses are solicited, the audience chuckles because it seems ridiculous that such a simple question could have so many different answers. Yet, when participants completed the exercise, they were certain they had the correct answer.

Participants are then asked to work in small teams of three or four individuals to determine the correct answer. Usually, someone on each team suggests that one person count the number of fs on a specific line. Often, every team now gets the right answer—proving that better results are arrived at by working together as a team than trying to solve problems as individuals. Because these individuals have determined a team process for getting the correct answer, they now have the tools to get a correct answer on a similar exercise. (The correct answer is 39.)

We cannot achieve the level of success as individuals that we can as members of a team. We cannot compete as individuals against others who are functioning as a team.

Some may think that time consumed in teamwork is inefficient. So is defeat.

About 100 years ago, a French strategist stated the value of teams:

Four brave men who do not know each other will not dare attack
a lion. Four less brave, knowing each other well, sure of their reliability and consequently of mutual aid, will attack resolutely.
This is the science of organization of armies in a nutshell.
—Ardant du Picq

Knowing others well and being sure of reliability and mutual aid is the essence of teamwork in a nutshell. Successful teams are made up of people who know and trust each other. To operate effectively as a team, members must spend time learning team skills and working together as a team. It takes time to build the productive interaction and mutual trust of a team. Successful teams are not made up of people who have been lectured to about teamwork; successful teams are made up of people who have shared experiences working towards a common goal.

Bo Schembechler, as football coach at the University of Michigan, said,

You will never get the same effort from one man seeking glory as from a group of men pulling for a shared goal.

Share a Common Purpose

Being involved in a common, unifying purpose energizes and excites us towards a goal. A purpose helps us commit with our hearts and not just our heads. Sun Tzu advises he whose ranks are united in purpose will be victorious. Building towards a common purpose has a lot to do with how "who we are" is integrated into our personal style. This spirit of common purpose builds team consistency. Teams of motivated, mature people will accomplish amazing things.

GO FOR A BREAKTHROUGH

Success Rules

- Be pleasantly disruptive to capture attention.
- Be intrusive with real benefits.
- Go for it big-time.

> Use the normal force to engage; use the extraordinary to win.
> —Sun Tzu

Nowhere does the simplicity of Sun Tzu's ancient wisdom ring more clearly than in the advice of employing the extraordinary to win.

Strive for a Big Win

Thinking big helps focus your strategy on meaningful gains. It's not that small goals are not important; it's that the best small goals are steps to a larger goal. In life, we tend to lose interest in small goals that do not lead to major results.

Little victories can be just as time consuming as the big victories. Wherever you are going, plan a strategy that achieves a big goal.

It is easy to do a lot of nice things. The real issue is to focus your energy where you can make a difference.

Years ago, when General MacArthur headed the American Olympic Committee, he advised the athletes, "We are here to represent the greatest country on earth. We did not come here to lose and lose gracefully, we came to win and win decisively."

With these few words, MacArthur took advantage of the opportunity to merge a big responsibility, representing America, with a big goal, winning decisively. Inherent in supporting most big goals is the opportunity to declare an energizing reason for justifying the effort.

Eighteenth-century strategist Carl von Clausewitz stated simply:

Only great battles produce great results.

A supporting corollary would be:

Only the prospect of great results can produce the means to fight great battles.

It's the prospect of great results that generates great enthusiasm.

Plan Breakthroughs

Often, we attempt to achieve breakthroughs by searching for more resources—if only we had more time, more funds, or more support in our projects. We fail to recognize that "just a little more" is not enough. As we achieve incremental increases, so do our opponents. The result of two opposing forces inputting the same amount of energy is another stalemate with no clear winner. The cycle repeats with each exerting "a little more effort" thus creating another standoff. The problem is "just a little more" doesn't work.

Too often we ignore the strategist who advised:

Do not renew an attack along the same line (or in the same form) after it has once failed.

The message is: Trying harder is not the solution, trying smarter is. Breakthroughs don't simply happen, they are planned.

Generals say that in order to win in war, you must:

Dislocate the enemy and exploit that dislocation.

Think of battles as mental ones where you must capture mindshare for your idea, service, or product. Disrupting the mind gets the other person's attention. To gain mindshare, think of how you can disrupt the mind and then intrude into that disruption.

The disruption cannot be crass or obnoxious. It must be in good taste. However, to break through the clutter, our message must disrupt the mind—that is, we must gain attention.

When I wanted to sell a product licensed with the Pink Panther brand name, I gave away six-foot-high stuffed Pink Panthers as premiums with the purchase of a quantity of the product. The sheer size of the Panther was disruptive. The intrusion was achieved by appealing to the desire to own this unique item. Everyone wanted a six-foot Pink Panther as a gift for a child and the more children you had, the more Panthers you needed, and the more products you needed to purchase to get the Pink Panther. Wow! A breakthrough.

I've used a messenger to deliver six-foot Pink Panthers with a pink tag reading, "You'll be tickled pink with the opportunity I have for you." (signed) Gerald Michaelson. The recipient may never have heard my name, but that's okay because I'm not asking him to call. I initiate a phone call a few days later and identify myself. Responses from the receptionist have been comments like, "He wants to talk to you." That is the introductory atmosphere I wanted to create. The next step is to intrude into that disruption with a personal visit and a benefit-laden message. Wow! A breakthrough.

When a person who received informational material from me could not recall receiving the material, I sent the brochures again in a box with a chocolate chip cookie the size of a pizza. The message written in frosting on the cookie said, "Here's the cookie with the message." When I called again, the lady said, "You made my day. When are you coming to see me?" Wow! Another breakthrough.

When I wanted to promote a book dealing with the problems of business overcapacity, I sent twenty-five different boxes of chocolate-chip cookies to business writers—along with a copy of the book. When my newest product was featured in a contest on the back of a Kellogg's cereal package, I sent every salesperson a case of the cereal to pass out to retailers selling the product. Wow! More breakthroughs.

When a young man in Australia wanted to apply for a job with an advertising agency whose principal client sold athletic clothing, he didn't just send his resume. He got a "foot in the door" by arranging with the building custodian to wedge a running shoe in the owner's office door one morning with his resume and an appropriate message. He got the interview and the job. Wow! Another breakthrough.

At a national trade show, I arranged to stack a display of $1 million in one-dollar bills to illustrate a profit opportunity. Objections from a few naysayers disappeared when the company president declared in favor of the promotion. The money was banded together in packages of 1,000 dollar bills, stacked seventy-two bills high, and fourteen bills wide in a glass case that towered high in the air. The effort was costly, but the resulting increase in sales was overwhelming—we tripled the sale volume. Wow! A breakthrough.

As orders poured in and results became evident, no one inquired about the cost. Proof that great efforts produce big wins and the strength of big wins overpowers criticism. Incremental improvements are important; the big win comes when you plan for a breakthrough.

Use Extraordinary Effort

Extraordinary effort generates extraordinary results. Sun Tzu says,

> *To a commander adept at the use of extraordinary forces, his resources are as infinite as the heaven and earth, as inexhaustible as the flow of the running rivers.*

The reference to infinite resources simply means the creative mind can find an inexhaustible variety of ways to do the extraordinary.

HAVE A PLAN

Success Rules

- Think of every plan as a plan of action.
- Planning without acting is a waste of time.
- Acting without planning is a recipe for defeat.

> The commander who gets many scores during the calculations in
> the temple before the war will have more likelihood of winning.
> —Sun Tzu

Too often, planning is simply a mental process. An idea that is only in our head as we simply look at the past and adjust for the future. Sailors call this "steering by the wake."

In war, generals say that no plan survives the first battle. The same is often true in life—outside events influence the success of our plan. Do not let this possibility of disruption defer you from planning. Without a plan of action, you may never get started. Simply consider plans as a basis for change. President Harry Truman said,

> *When I make a dumb decision, I go on and make another dumb decision.*

Put Your Plan in Writing

The plan exists only when it is a written document. If you do not have a plan in writing you may have a dream, a vision—or perhaps a nightmare. You do not have a plan unless it is a written document.

Kipling wrote:

I have six honest serving men.
They taught me all I knew.
Their names were what and where and when,
And why, and how, and who.

Answer the questions posed by the six honest serving men and you have a simple format for putting your plan into writing.

Why am I taking this course of action?
What am I going to achieve?
How am I going to proceed?
When am I going to do it?
Where will it happen?
Who is going to be involved?

It's so easy to answer these questions in our head and so much better to put the answers in writing. Tom Monaghan, founder of Domino's Pizza, says,

Writing is the key to my system. I carry a legal pad with me every-where I go. All my thoughts, my plans, my dreams, and my analyses of problems are written down in my pad. I sometimes have several pads going at once for different kinds of thoughts. I have accumulated dozens of these pads—although I never look at them again. What's important is the thinking that goes into the writing, not the words that wind up on paper. I set long-range goals, annual goals, monthly, weekly, and daily goals. The daily goals take the form of to-do lists. The long-range goals are dream sheets.

Instead of Monaghan's yellow pad, I prefer an attractive bound journal that can be purchased for $10 at a bookstore. Others prefer notebook planners with calendar pages. Whatever you use, a single place to record everything is the kind of organization that will make you more productive.

Adapt to Circumstances

Your plan must be flexible and adaptable to circumstances. A plan like a tree must have branches if it is to bear fruit. A plan without options is like a barren pole.

Sun Tzu says:

Tactics change in an infinite variety of ways to suit changes in the circumstances.

No single plan works well for everyone and everywhere. If your plans are too rigid, you will not be able to adjust to circumstances. Planning is a process of understanding what is happening in constantly changing situations and adapting with energy and determination.

The intuition that breeds great strategies and great plans can only come from being in touch with the situation. Your planning cannot be done in a vacuum. The winning plan incubates in the warmth of knowledge of where you want to go and how you are going to get there.

Moses brought down from the mountain just ten commandments to live by. The U.S. Army sets forth only nine principles of war. At Gettysburg, Abraham Lincoln's speech lasted less than ten minutes. Often, very often, less is more. Your plan for success does not need to be complicated. A simple plan is easier to translate into action.

Here are three simple, basic rules for implementing your plan.

1. Set a goal and timetable. Although you cannot be number one in everything, you can be number one in something.
2. Get started. The greater your initiative, the greater your momentum, and the faster your journey to success.
3. Leverage every gain. Use each success to attain the next level.

Develop a contingency plan to provide for the next step following a success or failure. Good planning considers the alternatives available. Don't rely on crystal-ball assumptions. Examine the worst that can happen and provide for such a contingency. Frederick the Great said, "There is no dishonor in a hard fought defeat and no excuse in being surprised."

Chapter 11

Tactics for Success

In any hierarchy, strategy at one level will often be tactics at the next level. That is how the master plan becomes increasingly more focused as action cascades through an organization.

Strategy and tactics must be woven together. When we separate planning from implementation we are separating thinking from doing, and responsibility is diffused.

Francisco Pizarro coordinated strategy with tactics when he conquered the empire of the Incas with four dozen horses and a few hundred men.

- **Strategy**: Establish a method of communication.
- **Tactics**: Francisco got hold of an interpreter—Felipillo.
- **Strategy**: Communicate effectively.
- **Tactics**: Through Felipillo, the Spaniards cooed winning speeches to the Indians.
- **Strategy**: Implement activities to support your communication.
- **Tactics**: Trinkets were exchanged for gold and food. Smiles were the order of the day. To his men, Pizarro ordered, "Touch nothing, respect the inhabitants."
- **Strategy**: Play off one tribe against the other and fuel a civil war between the chiefs.
- **Tactics**: Attack the Incas' enemies (so they won't think you are the enemy).
- **Strategy**: Select the place and time for the decisive battle.
- **Tactics**: The Incas' "Waterloo" was the battle of Cajamarca.

Some claim it was the horse that conquered Peru. The Indians were confronted by well-armed men on horses—animals they had never seen before. How interesting it is that good fortune always seems to come to those who coordinate their strategic planning with tactical implementation.

TAKE THE OFFENSIVE

Success Rules

- Take the initiative of action.
- Develop an offensive spirit.
- Keep on the move.

> The possibility of victory lies in the attack.
> Generally, he who occupies the field of battle first
> and awaits his enemy is at ease.
> —Sun Tzu

Keys to a successful offensive are information, preparation, and skill. Often, the norm is the confusion of not enough information, not enough time to prepare, and not enough skills training.

Initiate Action

The most effective and decisive way to reach the objective is to seize, retain, and exploit the initiative. Being on the offensive puts you in control, and forces the foe to react rather than to act. An ancient proverb proclaims that "the first blow is as much as two."

Only by acting on the offensive in achieving your goal can you preserve freedom of action. Get too far behind and many of your actions must be a reaction to the leader. Get out in front and you are the leader.

In any offensive, mental action precedes physical action. Consequently, the offensive is often a great mental leap in the dark made at gut level. There are two mental approaches to launching an offensive:

1. Plan everything in detail and then get going. Too often, preparation is an excuse for procrastination. Although preparation should not be neglected, decisive action should not be delayed.
2. Determine general objectives and then get going. Details can be filled in as your offensive gains momentum.

It would seem that the choice is either to get ready or get going. Your greatest odds for success lie on the side of action.

I recall the dean of a prestigious law school telling me that in law school, you are trained to look at both sides of the situation and that is not good training for business. His observation is that people are better off deciding to do something rather than spending a lot of time analyzing the situation.

Keep on the Move

Inactivity causes more loss of opportunity than mistakes in the choice of methodology. Generals say:

If you want to determine the shape of the situation, fight and find out.

The offensive originates in our mind and then moves on to become a physical act. When I've been in the office for a week, I've generated enough activity to keep me in the office for another week. Similarly, when I've been in the field for a week, I've generated enough activity to keep me in the field for another week.

However, there is a dramatic difference between the useful productivity of results from office-generated initiatives and field-generated initiatives.

I saw this problem when working at the corporate headquarters of a Fortune 500 company. The president, who spent weeks in the office managing from his desk, made decisions based on his historical experience.

On the few occasions when the president did physically visit our customers, he would return to the office with new ideas. Unfortunately, the new actions were often misguided because they were based on conversations with a few customers in the same market.

Develop Spirit of the Offensive

An offensive spirit must permeate everything you do.

I've seldom found opportunity calling on me; instead, I've found opportunity outside the office. Even more important is the fact that being on the offensive visiting my market provides me with the timely information that keeps me on the cutting edge. When I've waited for information to be filtered through the bureaucracy, the offensive has been launched too late.

Schedule face time with people who are on the route you must travel to reach your goals. That helps put you in position to be master of the situation. Decisions about what to do become a matter of course when you spend time "where the action is."

Consider Alternative Routes

Sun Tzu says,

The army must know the five different attack situations and wait for appropriate times.

Here are a few different ways to take the initiative:

- *Launch a head-on attack.* This is often not the best route to your goal. It works only if you have overwhelming strength.

- *Use an indirect approach*. Instead of telling someone what to do, present facts, ask questions, and let the other person suggest a solution. That is, you help him or her think the solution is their idea.

  Taking a different type of indirect approach, fund-raising organizations will schedule events to raise money instead of asking for donations.
- *Be a guerrilla*. The guerrilla warrior carefully selects a point of attack where he can have an advantage. Guerrillas win with a series of minor coups that tip the scales.

Heed Rules for a Successful Offensive

Here are a few basic rules that will help you keep on the offensive:

1. *Be Professional*: In his book, *The Exceptional Executive*, Harry Levinson identified the importance of knowledge to a professional:

   A professional is a person who can understand and apply scientific knowledge. Given knowledge, the professional can choose a course of action; he remains in charge of himself and his work.

   Knowledge is critical. The heartbeat of success is your knowledge in your area of expertise.
2. *Circulate to Percolate*: Network often and with people with different interests.
3. *Be Disciplined*: Plan your work and work your plan.
4. *Be a Difference Maker*: In sports, difference makers are players who cause good things to happen. Focus on making a positive difference.
5. *Keep on the Leading Edge*: Use the newest technology. For example, a digital video camera is a neat tool for showing visual images that excite people.

6. *Extend Every Contact*: A handwritten thank-you note is the extra step that shows appreciation and gets attention. Follow up with copies of articles that will interest the other person.

7. *Be Action-Oriented*: Keep things going by developing ongoing action plans. Involve others in your planning process.

MOVE RAPIDLY

Success Rules

- Set timetables for action.
- Develop a sense of urgency.
- Get going and get done with it.

> Speed is of the essence in war. What is valued in war
> is a quick victory, not prolonged operations.
> —Sun Tzu

Speed is of the essence in war and winning.

Get Started

All of the positive consequences of speed accrue to the early offensive. The less you delay:

- The less apt you are to be surprised.
- The less ready will be your opponent.
- The greater the opportunity for surprise.

General Patton declared that a partially developed plan violently executed is superior to being late with a perfect plan. Too often, what impedes our progress is a lack of urgency. The problem is not just doing "it" rapidly, but rather deciding to do "it" at all.

While we are procrastinating with our decisions, someone else is getting going. Although it is important to examine the problem and potential solutions before proceeding, beware of paralysis by analysis. Napoleon said that two-thirds of the decision-making process is based on analysis of information and one-third is a leap in the dark.

Although more data may be desirable—we never have enough data and neither does our opponent. Winners get going and fight their way through to the finish. Losers continue their search for the always elusive "more." Time is the enemy. That is why many decisions must be made at gut level. Not making a decision is a decision. Not charting a course is a decision. In our lives, opportunities appear and disappear—in careers, in relationships, and in every thing we do.

When you know that Napoleon's troops marched at a rate of 120 paces per minute while his opponents marched at the more orthodox 70 paces, you know a fundamental advantage that contributed to his success. Think of the advantages that accrue if you are able to reduce by 50 percent the time required in initiating action.

Achieving the initiative by moving rapidly has a positive effect on morale. An ancient writer explains the morale factor this way:

> *Attack inspires the soldier . . . and confuses the enemy. The side under attack always overestimates the strength of the attacker.*

The speed of the Mongol hordes invariably gave them a superiority of force at the decisive point, the ultimate aim of all tactics. By seizing the initiative and exploiting their mobility to the utmost, Mongol commanders were almost always able to select the point of decision.

Solve Differences Rapidly

The concept of rapid movement also applies to personal disagreements. It's important to get started solving the problem. The odds for mental well-being in any altercation lie on the side of getting through the difference. Sun Tzu advises,

While we have heard of stupid haste in war, we have not yet seen a clever operation that was prolonged. There has never been a case in which a prolonged war has benefited a country.

The historic feud between the Hatfields and the McCoys is a classic example of carrying an altercation to the extreme. Every disagreement has two dimensions: time and depth. The longer the disagreement, the deeper the resulting emotional depth. Hatred grows over time. A common statement in arguments is "the more I thought about it, the madder I got." The advice is always, "get over it and go on with your life."

GAIN MOMENTUM

Success Rules

- Decision time is the enemy.
- Momentum preserves freedom of action.
- Keeping on going is easier when on the move.

When torrential water tosses boulders, it is because of momentum. The energy is similar to a fully drawn crossbow. The momentum of one skilled in war is overwhelming.
—Sun Tzu

Success requires not only the initial speed of the attack, but also a continuation of the initiative—it's called momentum.

Offensive action must be a continuing process. When you have momentum, you also have freedom of action—the opportunity to make the right decisions for the long term.

Here are key components of momentum:

- One may feel protected from falling only when one is rising. It's not difficult to understand that any positive action or degree of success generates positive emotions. Clausewitz says the pursuit is as important as the attack. Keep on the move.
- Rapid decision-making produces rapid execution. The shorter the decision time, the sooner a decision can be communicated. This allows everything to proceed more rapidly and leads to a greater probability of success. In contrast, delayed decisions inevitably lose their positive quality. When you wait too long, your opponents have had time to prepare and your friends have lost patience.
- Rapid action is simultaneous action. When swiftness is at a maximum, it is easier to coordinate all actions into a simultaneous thrust.

TAKE ADVANTAGE OF OPPORTUNITIES

Success Rules

- Achieve the first success.
- Then leverage to the next level.
- Use leverage at every opportunity.

A skilled commander sets great store by using
the situation to the best advantage.
—Sun Tzu

Success breeds success. Key to any successful equation is getting the first successful step and then leveraging additional success from each new victory.

Get Leverage

The first rule of good leveraging is that you must give leverage in order to get leverage. One-sided leverage produces the kind of pressure that destroys relationships. The person who gives no leverage gets none in return.

Airline frequent-flyer programs are examples of productive leverage. They succeed because they give the customer an opportunity to leverage his relationship. The more the airline gets what they want (the flier on their routes), the more benefits the flier accrues.

You can take advantage of leveraging opportunities in many of life's activities—for example, volunteer work in charitable organizations. The opportunities are endless, but your time resources are limited, so make choices that support personal objectives. David Thiel, founder of Auragen Communications, participates in charitable organizations to aid in pursuing political interests. Active membership in organizations like the United Way helps Thiel understand how the community works. By helping his community, he is leveraging his time to gain knowledge and contacts that can advance business and personal goals.

All you need to do to be a leader in these organizations is raise your hand and volunteer. Leaders give more to volunteer organizations and leaders get more from volunteer organizations in personal satisfaction and contacts that can be leveraged into other opportunities.

Wherever you have a relationship, your success can be leveraged. In sports, the team athlete knows that his success will be recognized by the coach and the greater the athlete's success, the greater his playing time in the game.

Advancement in your career is all about leverage. Going to the right school gives you leverage for getting your first job. Getting hired by the right company, gives you leverage for applying for a position with another company. Getting promoted gives you leverage within the company and in the job market.

One component of every decision concerning your career should be "does this move give me leverage?" Staying with a company and getting promoted can be great. However, at some point you may want to look for a new position.

A respected college professor advised that we should have five different jobs in the first five years—and be fired from one of them. Good advice? Perhaps. Let's dissect his overstatement:

1. Five different jobs in the first five years: The advice is to get different experiences with different companies. Moving around that much may not be a good idea, but looking is a good idea. A few years out of college, I found myself in a position where the seniority of peers hampered opportunities for advancement. The professor's advice encouraged me to look for another job. I found a better one very soon.

2. Be fired from one: Horrors! Why would anyone want to be fired? The point here is that you should be willing to be aggressive enough to put your job at risk. On select occasions, we need to make a decision that can result in a big win. Success requires calculated risks.

Being successful without building a broad base can make you vulnerable in your career. The answer is to get the right kind of leverage.

When you get the new position, think carefully about what you are going to do the first day and the first week. The impression you make establishes your base for leverage. The most important activity may not be taking action, it may be attentive listening as you meet your new coworkers.

When the new director of a hospital stood at the employee entrance on the first day of his employment to meet everyone and shake their hand, he established the first link in communications. Having a video camera running during this welcoming event provided a method for learning names and faces. This simple action signaled the beginning of building the new relationships he needed to leverage his leadership position.

Leverage is a device for successful communications. It's getting the person you are trying to convince to agree on minor issues and pyramiding that agreement into acceptance of a major issue.

Develop an Opportunity List

A friend who went into business with a partner said that after losing a sale, his partner commented on the action necessary to succeed:

> *The opportunities we lose are often due to circumstances beyond our control like loss of funding or the buyer changing jobs. It seems that we need ten sure things for one to work.*

Ever since then, I've developed a list of "ten sure things." Sometimes, I do not have ten prospective opportunities on my list. However, the search for additional opportunities to add to my list keeps me on the offensive. This keeps me from being discouraged when something doesn't work out. I know that I have other alternatives and simply go on to the next opportunity on my list. At the same time, I search for a new one to replace the one I lost.

Do It Now

Timing is of great importance in taking advantage of opportunities. The problem often is not that the time span is of a really short duration such as days or hours. It's things that can be done either this year or next that never get done.

Once again, the solution is a lifelong goal and timetable for accomplishment.

BE PERSISTENT

Success Rules

- Sequential implementation requires step-by-step persistence.
- Cumulative implementation requires random persistence.
- Simultaneous implementation requires short-term persistence over a wide front.

> Pursue one's own strategic designs to overawe the enemy.
> Then one can take the enemy's cities and overthrow the state.
> —Sun Tzu

After deciding on a course of action, stick to it. This gives your plan the strength of consistency of action.

Determine an Implementation Methodology

You can roll out your plan sequentially, cumulatively, or simultaneously.

Sequential Implementation: A sequential approach to any project is a series of reinforcing steps. Success at each level sets the stage for moving to the next level.

General MacArthur's island-hopping drive up the Pacific is an example of the execution of a sequential operation.

A sequential job hunt would be to send out a resume and wait for a response before sending out the next one, obviously not a good idea in most instances. In contrast, your career path is a series of sequential steps, each making the next one possible.

Cumulative Implementation: A cumulative approach to any project is a multipronged approach with unconnected or dissimilar activities that eventually reach a critical mass.

The American submarine force attack in the Pacific is an example of a series of unrelated events accumulating the planned effect.

An exercise program involving diet and several exercise regimes is a cumulative approach to better physical well-being.

A cumulative job search would be characterized by taking a series of actions over a period of time such as, inquiries at a trade show, sending out resumes, checking with friends and calling headhunters. This is the type of activity where you "test the waters" to see what's available.

Simultaneous Implementation: This is a mass attack where a concentrated effort is launched across a wide front in a limited time span.

The German blitzkrieg across the Low Countries during World War II is an example of a simultaneous effort.

Any project where you concentrate multiple contacts in a short time is a blitz. For example, you could launch a phone blitz to get job interviews. Direct mail and phone blitzes are common actions by politicians just prior to election day.

What Counts Is Persistence

Admiral Rickover found that getting the backing for a nuclear submarine was almost as difficult as designing and building it. Rickover reminds us that:

Good ideas are not adopted automatically. They must be driven into practice with courageous patience.

Sports coaches state simply, "When you are knocked down, get up!" Moreover, if your ideas fall flat, get up! If you are dead wrong, get up! Your personal mission is to storm the next barricade.

All implementation is goal-oriented. It's important to select the implementation process that works. For example, an athlete training for an event would probably succeed best with sequential implementation—that is step-by-step improvement. A manager trying to build a stronger organization might find that a cumulative approach works best—that is, continually looking for good people. However, if he or she needed to move rapidly to fill positions, a blitz might be the right ticket to success.

OCCUPY THE HIGH GROUND

Success Rules

- Head for the mental and physical high ground.
- It takes a plan and discipline.
- Start your engines.

In battle and maneuvering, all armies prefer high ground to low ground.
—Sun Tzu

Some 2,000 years later than Sun Tzu, Frederick the Great said:

The first rule that I give is always to occupy the heights.

The real question is not whether occupying the high ground is a good idea, but rather: "What is the high ground?"

In any endeavor, the high ground is both mental and physical. Improvements in either the mental or physical position are mutually supportive. For example, more security in the physical high ground makes for a healthier mental high ground. In turn, sound mental health leads to activities that build physical health.

Establish a Mental High Ground

The foundation of your mental high ground is in areas such as moral beliefs, personal integrity, and motivation towards success.

Moral beliefs: Most of all, the mental high ground is a moral position. It is where we have a belief "in the right" of our position. We have discussed moral strength earlier and recognized how emotional inputs can strengthen or destroy moral outputs. The battle for the moral high ground is waged in our minds and the minds of our opponents. Much of life is a battle of the mind because the best entries to the mind are often through emotions. Logic can sound great to the persuader, but emotions play a powerful role in determining courses of action.

Personal integrity: Here is another view of this personal quality we discussed earlier. I recall a young man telling me how easy it was to develop successful business relationships with customers. He said, "All you need to do is to tell them the truth." Good idea! The problem is that truths are elusive. What might be recognized as a truth on one day can be dispelled as a myth on another. Look at the constantly evolving world of medical advice as proof. Regarding certain treatments, medical doctors are often heard to say, "We don't do that any more." Truths change. Facts can be quicksand.

The wise man said long ago that "all generalizations are false, including this one." Certainly, one way to avoid making a statement that could later be proven inaccurate is not to make any statements. Obviously, this approach is a nonsolution.

It's okay to take a position, but be open-minded. Finding "the best" is a continuous search.

Motivation: How many times have we heard "if you do not know where you are going, any road will take you there." Often, the problem with lack of direction is lack of motivation. When we are going nowhere, we are obviously in no hurry to get there.

Maxwell Maltz examined motivation and goal-orientation in his classic book, *Psychocybernetics*. The word "cyber" is derived from the Greek word for "steersman." Since "psycho" deals with the mind, psychocybernetics considers "steering the mind" or mental directions.

In his work in plastic surgery, Maltz discovered that some people who had reconstructive surgery were changed and others were not. For example, some who had a facial scar removed had a new self-image; others did not.

Maltz determined that the way we perceive our present and future has a great effect on how we act. People who are goal-oriented and moving towards that goal have more stability just as the person who is on a bicycle achieves stability by pedaling—and has none while standing still.

To state it simply: to keep going towards a goal is more important than reaching the goal. That is, being motivated towards success is what keeps us successful. Goal-directed actions produce dramatic results.

There are mountains of materials available to help us get better. A fast reader, who could read a book a day on self-improvement, could not read them all in a lifetime.

When interviewing people for new positions, I often ask the question, "What are the last five books you have read?" This unusual question often produces a chuckle and a variety of responses ranging from a comprehensive list of books to "I only read magazines." The answer gives me a snapshot of the interests of that person. What I'm looking for is that one of the books is on some topic that indicates a thirst for self-improvement. The books can be focused on improvement of any aspect of the personal or professional life. I want to employ someone focused on getting better and one way that can be measured is by knowing the candidate's reading preferences.

When interviewing salespeople, I always ask the question, "How did you learn how to sell?" One candidate replied, "Mr. Michaelson, I'm a natural-born salesman." Baloney! I believe that we are all "natural-born" and everything else is learned. I want to work with people who are willing to learn how to get better.

Secure Physical High Ground

The battle for the high ground in life is more mental than physical. However, without being able to actually see ourselves progressing toward, or reaching, the high ground, we lose confidence in our compass.

Position strength: In all of our families (nuclear, religious, career, and other interests), the position we hold identifies where we are on our climb to the high ground. Position is a source of identity and reward. The process of continually improving our position gives us stability in the uneven terrain of life.

Career security: Career paths can be crowded and disrupted by outside events over which we have no control.

A friend who had his company acquired by a new conglomerate sought a new position and received an excellent job offer which he accepted.

In counseling him on the move, I suggested that he not burn any bridges and that corporate exit interviewers should be considered a potential future employer. He later reported that the day after his exit interview with a senior manager, he received a phone call from another division asking him to come for an interview. Following advice, he politely declined stating that he had already accepted an offer. (To do otherwise would undermine his integrity.) He further indicated that he could consider offers only after spending time in his new position—a way of stating his loyalty and leaving an opening for opportunity.

By carefully orchestrating his exit, he strengthened his career security. The new job will give him new experience that will make him more valuable to any employer, including his old company. He is in the proverbial catbird seat for a while—he has a great new job and potential future opportunities with his previous employer. The path to the high ground is paved with stepping stones that we carefully place in position.

Physical health and fitness: Good mental health is a byproduct of being on the mental and physical high ground. Following advice on achieving the mental high ground does not assure physical health and fitness. A sound body is a product of physical conditioning.

Nothing epitomizes physical fitness more than a gold-medal winner in the Olympics. The names and feats are legendary. The focus of training for sports victories has moved from training harder to training smarter.

Sport-specific training doesn't mean performing the exact event. It does involve working the right muscles and training in the right pattern of movement to stimulate the neuromuscular systems needed to excel.

Bobsled racers practice sprinting in a shuffling style to learn how to impart take-off speed by keeping their feet on the ice. In contrast, a track sprinter's ideal practice attempts to keep feet in the air much of the time. Cross-country skiers work on upper body strength because scientists have found that upper body muscles are important in propelling racers forward rapidly. Luge racers work on torso strength and control as well as balance.

Winners in the high ground of life are in good mental and physical condition. The primary ingredient of a good exercise program is discipline. Get a schedule and then find the right types of exercise that work for you and your body.

BUILD ON YOUR SUCCESS

Success Rules

- You are a valuable resource.
- Consolidate your achievements.
- Success is a springboard to the next level.

> To win battles and capture lands and cities, but to fail
> to consolidate these achievements is ominous and may
> be described as a waste of time and resources.
> — Sun Tzu

The master is talking about a win that breeds the conditions that cause a loss. This is another case of "we have met the enemy and they are us."

Why is it that 95 percent of the people who lose weight gain it all back—and often more? Is it because they accepted the challenge and won—and then in winning they became complacent and lost?

In every task, we must project our vision tape to the end. That is, what do we want to accomplish long term? How do we transition from success in the short term to success in the long term?

We see the failure to pyramid success in sports teams who vanquish a very tough opponent. The exhilaration and sense of relief at winning the tough victory seems to temporarily dull the fighting edge. The loss of the strong drive to win often means the next game involves defeat by a less able opponent.

It is a military maxim that:

The greatest cause of defeat is victory.

The more successful we get, the more we tend to stop doing the things that made us successful. The deterioration of our own efforts opens the door to motivated opponents.

Business acquisitions can be a victory that leads to defeat because the different cultures fail to mesh. If you have ever been in a company that is being acquired, you have seen and felt the effects of internal clashes.

International economists talk about "the curse of resources." For examples, they point to countries such as:

- Argentina, which was a rich nation a century ago, thanks to its abundance of cattle and beef production. That prosperity bred a social-welfare system that eventually brought it to financial ruin.
- The oil-rich states of the Middle East have never weaned themselves from the dependence on oil income.

We see a similar decline caused by "the curse of resources" in the later generations of wealthy families.

A sad example of not taking advantage of victory is the person who gets a great education and then fails to use that knowledge base to leverage success.

Using Sun Tzu's words, our "consolidating of achievements" is taking inventory of our personal strengths and resources and determining how we can use these "weapons" to achieve the next level.

If this "consolidation of achievements" is only a mental exercise, chances are we will not move on. By putting a plan of action in writing, we take the first step on the road to success.

Chapter 12

Competitive Success

Setting priorities is an essential element of every competitive engagement. Sun Tzu gives great advice:

1. *The best policy in war is to attack the enemy's strategy.*
   Attacking strategy means to "win without fighting." This is a mental battle that seeks to win through psychology. For example, "kill 'em with kindness" or achieve a level of excellence that discourages opposition.
2. *The second best way is to disrupt his alliances through diplomatic means.*
   "Diplomatic means" is, of course, negotiations. For example, "let's sit down and talk."
3. *The next best method is to attack his army in the field.*
   Attacking the army in the field would involve battle strategies like an indirect approach or blitz. This could be finding leverage or action that forces the issue in your favor.
4. *The worst policy is to attack walled cities. Attacking cities is the last resort when there is no alternative.*
   This is definitely a head-on attack. In life, it could be "taking the case to court," or expending a lot of resources to try to win.

It's clear that winning with strategy is better than winning by fighting—attaining competitive success does not always require conflict.

PICK YOUR BATTLES CAREFULLY

Success Rules

- Don't fight battles you cannot win.
- Get the overwhelming odds on your side.
- Winning too often in office politics can invite calamity.

> If you are not sure of success, do not use troops.
> If you are not in danger, do not fight.
> —Sun Tzu

Sun Tzu's math lesson for determining odds of success is quite simple:

> *When ten to the enemy's one, surround him.*
> *When five times his strength, attack him.*
> *If double his strength, engage him.*
> *If equally matched, be capable of dividing him.*
> *If less in number, be capable of defending yourself.*
> *And, if in all respects unequal, be capable of eluding him.*
> *A weak force will eventually fall captive to a strong one if it simply*
>   *holds ground and conducts a desperate defense.*

When Allied forces staged an invasion in America's island-hopping campaign in the Pacific, they tried to achieve a minimum of three-to-one superiority when their forces staged an invasion. If the Allied forces had invaded Japan, the planned strength was one-to-one. The atom bomb made the invasion unnecessary.

In today's world, technological strength can be more important than numerical strength. The important issue is that overwhelming strength succeeds. If not, you may be better served to look elsewhere for better odds for victory.

Avoid Political Battles

In Sun Tzu's ancient time, another Chinese warlord wrote:

> *To win victory is easy, to preserve its fruits, difficult. And therefore it*
>   *is said that when all under heaven is at war:*
> *One who gains one victory becomes the Emperor;*

One who gains two, a King;
One who gains three, Lord Protector;
One who gains four is exhausted;
One who gains five victories suffers calamity.
Thus, he who by countless victories has gained empire is unique,
while those who have perished thereby are many.

This quotation offers a special warning for political battles in the office or other activities. Don't fight if you do not have to fight. The danger is winning too many battles and making too many jealous enemies.

Know How to Win

Sun Tzu states a list of simple points that assure victory. Analysis after any battle reveals a few simple basic reasons why losers lost. The problem is not knowing why battles are lost; the problem is being smart enough to do the correct analysis prior to the event. Sun Tzu offers a simple plan for analysis that applies today.

There are five points in which victory may be predicted:

1. *He who knows when to fight and when not to fight.*
   Control your temper. Approach problems clinically.
2. *He who understands how to handle both superior and inferior forces.*
   Superior forces win; inferior forces lose unless they can achieve a relative superiority.
3. *He whose ranks are united in purpose.*
   Believe in what you are doing.
4. *He who is well prepared and lies in wait for an enemy who is not well prepared.*
   Do your homework.
5. *He whose generals are able and not interfered with by the sovereign.*

Think Vietnam, where President Johnson picked bombing targets.

Following these simple rules for winning will keep you on the road to success.

KNOW YOUR OPPONENT

Success Rules

- Identify the opposition.
- Understand his or her style.
- Make sure you are not the enemy.

> He who is not sage cannot use spies.
> —Sun Tzu

Again, Sun Tzu says,

> *When you know yourself but not the enemy, your chances of winning and losing are equal.*

Do the math. According to Sun Tzu's statement, equal chances of winning and losing means your chances of winning are reduced by half if you do not know your enemy.

Sun Tzu devotes his entire Chapter Thirteen to the employment of secret agents. The type of "spying" most of us might do today is quite different from that envisioned by Sun Tzu.

Sports coaches do not spy by sneaking in to watch a competitive team practice, rather they spy by purchasing film of the competitor playing a public game and seriously study play action. Using this information, the coach develops offensive and defensive plans and sets up a practice session against a team modeled after the opponents system. Is this an effective way of spying and using the information secured? Just ask any winning coach with an extensive library of films of opposing teams.

Build a Creative Information System

Every successful competitive endeavor, whether in business, sports, or politics, requires a flow of incoming information. Here are key steps in building that system.

Cultivate your contacts: With your own informal, organized information flow, you gain advantages in both time and accuracy. Close personal contact guards against filtered reports.

Responses to your inquiries must be nurtured with a message of appreciation to keep the information flowing. Contact information systems work only when the outgoing flow matches the incoming flow.

Snapshots build pictures: Our world of available information is vastly expanded by contacts on the Internet. For example, when I wanted to find out business conditions in another industry, I e-mailed a contact made playing golf in Hawaii. His reply gave me a snapshot of the current situation in another city. Other contacts gave me a series of snapshots to get the big picture.

When a retailer told me his business was unusually slow, I sought other snapshots in order to build my own financial picture of an impending downturn. This encouraged me to adjust my stock portfolio. When the adjustment turned out to be the right decision, I kept in touch with my sources because their information would be valuable for future decisions.

Validate your sources: Although number of contacts is important, seek to validate who is the best of your information cadre. Some will simply provide data while others will provide analysis and insights that are of great value. As you work the system, you will determine which sources are the most reliable and provide the best insights. Cultivate and nurture these relationships. This is where the gold is buried.

Put it all together: First, you must develop a network. Then you must evaluate the usefulness of information from your sources. Finally, you must cultivate the best of your network. Only then, will you have an information system that aids in your solutions.

Identify the Enemy

The enemy is anyone with the power to keep you from winning. Be sure to clearly define who is and who is not "the enemy." To the business person, the enemy is the competitor. In sports, it is the opponent. To the teacher, it may be some blocker in the educational process. In many situations, the enemy will be the system and not the people who must work within the system.

The enemy is never a close friend or marriage partner. The mental set of viewing someone who can be an ally as an enemy leads to actions that destroy the relationship.

The struggle with ourselves as the enemy often requires overcoming some personal weakness or lack of confidence. We need a close relationship with personal gurus and coaches to overcome these weaknesses. How often have we seen people held back, not by lack of ability, but rather by a lack of confidence in their ability to grow.

Understand Style

Frederick the Great said:

A great advantage is drawn from the knowledge of your adversary, and when you know his intelligence and character you can use it to play to his weakness.

Learning about your opponent involves both knowing what he or she is doing now and what he or she has done in the past. Go beyond the issues to look at personalities. Analyze the situation in terms of its history—who did something like this before and what happened. Look at the personalities in terms of their background of experience—where did they acquire their expertise and what have they done in similar situations.

For example, if you want to know the style of a new employee, supervisor, preacher, or club officer, look at the style where they were previously. All new arrivals bring their personal strengths and weaknesses with them. Each will tend to clone the style of his or her previous organization. When a new leader introduces change, that person is merely introducing the system with which he or she is comfortable. Accept the change and rally around the new leader.

SKILLFUL ATTACKS WIN

Success Rules

- Focus.
- Plan a surprise attack.
- Keep on doing what works until innovation works better.

> Take advantage of the enemy's unpreparedness, make your way by unexpected routes, attack where he has taken no precautions.

> Against those skillful in attack, the enemy does not know where to defend.
> —Sun Tzu

Several issues are common to any skillful attack:

1. A focal point: Concentrate a critical mass.
2. Surprise: Be unpredictable.
3. Follow through: When it works, keep on using it.

Concentrate on a Focal Point

The first action decision is what are you going to do—that is, what is your plan and where should you focus the critical mass of resources?

- *A plan*: Put yourself in your opponent's shoes. How would he organize an attack? Use this analysis to organize your own attack.

  One of the most productive exercises in seminars I conduct is to ask participants to imagine they are now employed by their strongest competitor. Teams are asked to identify the strategies and tactics required for this competitor to win. Learning what their competitor would do yields valuable insight into their own plan of attack. The exercise also reveals where they are most vulnerable.

- *A critical mass*: When you have decided that the objective is worth winning, then you must allocate resources. It takes keen insight to determine the critical mass. A fog often masks what is really happening. Of all the things that need to be done to achieve success, many are good ideas, some are important, but only a few are critical.

A U.S. Army Chief of Staff for Plans and Preparations described the allocation of resources this way:

The efficient commander does not seek to use just enough means, but an excess of means. A military force that is just strong enough to take an objective will suffer heavy casualties; a force vastly superior to the enemy's will do the job without serious loss of men. —General Mark S. Watson, 1950

In other words: to be sure of winning you must apply more than enough resources. Attacks with overwhelming superiority suffer relatively few casualties. The greater the strength of your attack, the less likely you are to be beat up in the process. Of course, the reference to "strength of your attack" applies to all facets of strength: moral, mental, and physical. The concept of applying overwhelming strength applies to any attack whether it is against an opponent or for a personal objective—such as a career position.

Sun Tzu states the power this way:

An army superior in strength takes action like the bursting of pent-up waters into a chasm of a thousand fathoms deep. This is what the disposition of military strength means in the actions of war.

Plan Surprise

You are most vulnerable to attack when standing still. Keep moving towards your objective.

In 1747, Frederick the Great advised his generals:

Everything which the enemy least expects will succeed the best.

A sound principle of management is that the manager should be predictable so that his or her people can take action without asking for authority.

In contrast, in competitive situations the attack that is least predictable is the one most likely to succeed. You see this often in sports. It's the quarterback sneak or the fake pass in football. Instead of kicking a field goal, it's running or passing the ball for two points.

To achieve surprise it is not necessary that your opponent be taken completely unaware; it is only important that he becomes aware too late to react effectively.

Carl von Clausewitz writes,

Surprise achieves superiority almost as strongly as direct concentration of forces.

A report in *Newsweek* about the war in Afghanistan stated, "... as the Americans withdrew. A Taliban commander ordered his tanks to open fire but U.S. bombs destroyed them first. An observer commented, "What kind of an army are these Americans? It was amazing to see how they destroyed our tanks." The best kind of surprise is when the opponent doesn't know that he or she has been surprised. The deed is done without the opponent aware of how it happened. You see this scenario most often in office politics.

Follow Through

Anyone who has ever learned how to throw a ball knows the importance of follow through. The continued forward motion of the arm after the ball leaves your hand is not a separate step, it's a component of the entire process.

Understand that your opponent has weaknesses and be prepared to exploit them. Keep on doing whatever works. However, doing the same thing that worked before will not work forever. Eventually, your opponent will figure out how to counter your action. Long before that happens is when you need to think about innovation.

TIMING IS EVERYTHING

Success Rules

- Don't delay.
- Generate the mismatch.
- Use speed and maneuver to win.

> When the strike of the hawk breaks the body
> of its prey, it is because of timing.
> The timing is similar to the release of the trigger.
> —Sun Tzu

In achieving success, the role of timing has many components. Fast movement precedes "the strike of the hawk," great power is generated at the point of attack and, of course, all of this works best at the right moment.

Get Started

As a rule, earliest is best. Make a decision and get going.

The later you start, the more you require. The longer it takes to begin the action, the more speed will be required later.

If you wait for approval, you will be late. It is often better to seek forgiveness, than to ask permission.

Keep Ahead of Your Opponent

Among fighter pilots, "getting inside" an opponent requires maneuvering faster than your opponent. This increased agility allows you to get a good fix on your opponent.

"This mobility is key," says John Boyd, a retired fighter pilot and recognized expert on maneuvering. Boyd's key to success is generating a mismatch by getting inside your opponent's "observation-orientation-decision-action" time cycle. By the time your opponent "observes" what you are doing, "orients" his thinking to it, "decides" what to do and "acts," his response will be too late.

This competitive tactic, like many, is both physical and mental. Your mind is conditioned to generate the speed of physical actions that surprise and confuse your opponent. This places your adversary in the position of focusing his mind on what you are doing and reacting. In real life, the process of keeping ahead of your opponent can be a single action, but is most often a series of actions.

You see it in sports when teams are continually changing plays and presenting "different looks" to their opponents as they race to victory. You see it in competitive actions where innovation defeats an opponent mentally and physically.

Anytime you can preempt an opponent's action, you have a real possibility of generating a mismatch that works in your favor. A superior fighter doesn't just parry his adversary's thrust, he gets off one of his own as he operates within his opponent's ability to respond. Even if the opponent seems to have every advantage, a well-timed attack can uncover weakness.

Speed and movement are the first two essentials to this successful attack. They are key to generating the initial mismatch and beginning the cascading circumstances that keep you ahead of your opponent.

Chapter 13

Practical Applications

Way back at the beginning of time, two men wanted to test the wisdom of a country's oracle. They decided upon a plan. They would appear before the oracle with a bird in their hand with some of the feathers showing and would ask, "What is it I hold in my hand?'

Seeing the feathers, the oracle would respond, "It is a bird."

Then the men would ask, "Is the bird dead or alive?"

If the oracle said the bird was alive, they would crush their hand and let it fall to the floor dead. If he said it was dead, they would open their hand and let it fly away.

At the appointed time, they appeared before the oracle.

To the question, "What is it I hold in my hand?" the oracle responded, "It is a bird."

Then they asked, "Is it dead or alive?"

The oracle responded, "I do not know, you hold its future in your hand!"

Your future is your decision. The following examples illustrate how leading-edge thinkers and doers apply Sun Tzu's wisdom to enhance their future.

INVEST IN INTELLIGENCE

David Rich
President and CEO, ICC/Decision Services

ICC/Decision Services works with the largest retailers on the globe to measure, manage, and improve the customer experience. ICC strongly believes that ultimately the experience is the brand. And like any great brand, it needs to be repeatable and consistent.

We are in the information services business, so when Sun Tzu speaks of employing "secret agents" to collect good intelligence, it resonates with me. Good information is critical to success, but too often we work with organizations that either don't want to acquire good information or don't know how to utilize it once they acquire it. Some common mistakes include only using one source for gathering information: a customer satisfaction survey or a focus group. These are all very good tools to have in your arsenal, but when used individually or in isolation they do not lead to success on the brand battlefield.

Another common mistake is creating silos within a company, and not sharing valuable information across divisions. When management makes intelligence a commodity, it can lead to ineffective and poor results. A fragmented approach to intelligence gathering or using intelligence punitively rather than to provide incentive to management and sales associates can adversely affect your customer experience. Ultimately, the cost of doing it wrong will be much greater than the cost of getting it right.

ICC has developed our own six-step process for intelligence gathering comprised of:

1. Discovery: Initiate a process for improvement in an organization and identify customers' needs (key value and service attributes).
2. Design: Design a survey instrument and the survey methodology.
3. Delivery: Conduct measurement programs and analyze the satisfaction information collected.
4. Discourse: All insights and findings need to be internally evaluated to determine their true impact and meaning.
5. Direction: Communicate the insights discovered to management and employees. Acknowledge customers' participation.
6. Decisions: Develop improvement plans and monitor improvement progress.

A 400-store retailer employed a full-service intelligence system that employs weekly mystery shopping at its locations, daily customer satisfaction surveys, and a rolling employee-engagement survey program to measure success. Before rolling out the program, we did employee huddles and customer exit interviews to gauge where to begin. This data was then funneled throughout the organization, and all departments worked together to develop the mystery shopping (objective measurement), customer satisfaction surveys (subjective measurement), alongside an employee engagement program. The employee engagement program is critical because if employees are not engaged it will ultimately damage the customer experience, which will be reflected in the mystery shops and/or customer satisfaction surveys. We use the process above to work the program through the organization from bottom to top and back down again, while doing cross analysis of all metrics to make sure they correlate with sales and profits. It's an active intelligence system—and one of our best weapons for producing ROI for our clients.

SKIP THE FRONTAL ASSAULT

Angelo Vassallo
Senior Vice President, Pernod-Ricard Beverages
After World War II, veterans returning to the United States returned with a taste for a popular European spirit: rum. When combined with a native American beverage, Coke, rum and Coke became a popular beverage of the postwar boom. And the dominant brand was Bacardi.

Seagrams first tried to attack Bacardi's hold on that market with a classic frontal attack. Seagrams's first effort was a Bacardi-like rum, Ronrico. Ronrico was introduced in the seventies, and Seagrams invested heavily in its introduction, giving it a Bacardi-like flavor profile and "from the islands" imagery. It never became a strong seller, and Bacardi continued to dominate.

Seagrams tried a different tact a few years later. This time, we followed Sun Tzu's stratagem to "attack by an unexpected route."

First, the group decided to offer a different flavor of rum. We experimented with different rum-flavor profiles and created one that had a slight vanilla flavor that mixed well with other beverages—particularly orange juice. Second, a brand was developed that appealed to a younger drinker. Captain Morgan—the brand name picked—was actually a small brand the company owned in Europe. That brand name was Americanized and the Captain Morgan character was made a younger and more pronounced character.

And finally, a group hungry to introduce the brand was identified,—the Calvert's organization, traditionally only given niche or tired brands to sell, brands that were too small for the other divisions to handle. The group was given the product and challenged to show what they could do with it. Captain Morgan became a success.

After performing a variety of roles in different countries, years later I came back to a job that had this U.S. brand as part of my group. It had grown for a few years, and the owner of Seagrams challenged me to grow it even further, giving me two weeks to come back to him with a plan.

That plan took Captain Morgan to its next level of success. In a move few brands had made, we lowered the proof of the product ten points. Spirits are taxed based on proof content, so that move lowered the tax per bottle by $4. We also raised the price $5. We proposed significantly increasing the value of the product to our company—increasing the per-case profits by over 50 percent through those two actions. The result? The younger drinking consumer did not miss the alcohol and did not think the price increase was excessive. The first year we sold the same number of units as the prior year and profits went through the roof, giving us the margins to invest more in that brand. Captain Morgan has been a continual success ever since and today is the preferred rum amongst the over-twenty-one consumer.

BUILD ON STRENGTHS, ATTACK WEAKNESSES

Jeff Tripician
CMO/EVP Niman Ranch

As one of the premier niche Gourmet brands in the country in 2006, Niman Ranch had developed a truly unique live-side supply network consisting of over 400 U.S. family hog, cattle, and lamb farmers. This network of farmers produced a superior-tasting product, but suffered from inconsistency in quality from farm to farm due to the number of independent farms involved.

The company operated out of Oakland, California and from there ran a meat distribution facility that cut meat and managed delivery routes, food service sales, retail sales, Internet sales, feedlot operations, and farmer auditing. As a result, the company was overextended and geographically constricted.

After our acquisition of Niman in August of 2006, the company developed a more strategically focused business model built around its two core competencies: live-side procurement and branded sales and marketing. This leveraged the quality and the mystique of the brand name—two advantages larger national competitors could not easily emulate. As Sun Tzu advises, "That you are certain to take what you attack is because you attack a place the enemy does not or cannot protect."

The company closed the Oakland plant (stopped cutting and distributing meat) and switched to a distributor system. Niman established a centralized distribution hub in Iowa for all customer orders in order to efficiently supply all distributors nationally via one consolidated order for all Niman Ranch products (beef, pork, lamb, poultry, processed products).

The company developed a national retail and food service distribution network of over forty companies that would distribute Niman Ranch meats within their market area, using their trucks and their sales force. The change in Niman's business model allowed the company to focus on growing its live-side farmer network from 400 farmers to over 650—dramatically increasing supply and supporting the growth. It allowed the company to hone the live-side protocols for raising livestock, increasing the consistency and quality of the product. On the sales and marketing side, the new business model allowed the company to double in size over the same time period and increase gross margin by targeting the top customers in each market.

The brand is now on over 5,000 menus nationally and placed in niche/specialty grocery stores from Maine to Miami and Seattle to San Diego.

A MARINE OFFICER'S VIEWPOINT

Bruce M. MacLaren
Colonel, U.S. Marine Corps (Ret.)

I have always had Sun Tzu's *The Art of War* close at hand, especially during my thirty years as an officer of Marines. In 1953 when I was a cadet at Norwich University, Major General Harmon (Ret.) suggested that all cadets should start reading the Master's treatise as well as Clausewitz. His reasoning was that our nation was becoming more involved in unconventional conflicts. The Korean War focused my attention on General Harmon's suggestion. In 1954, as a new officer in the Marine Corps, my basic training company commander reiterated that all hands should make *The Art of War* required professional reading. In 1963, Brigadier General Samuel B. Griffith U.S.M.C. (Ret.) translated his version of *The Art of War*. He also translated Mao's *Chinese Guerrilla Warfare*.

Both of these treatises became pocket manuals in the field as well as in training during peacetime as far as I was concerned—especially during my many years of service in the Far East. Knowledge of *The Art of War* became a professional link between myself and other foreign officers, especially the Chinese, Korean, Thai, and Vietnamese. I recall many times in Vietnam where our major units would overreact to enemy efforts in the East, only to be struck unaware in the West. Reading Sun Tzu conditioned me to put myself into my enemy's thought process and to better anticipate events. It slowed me down and stimulated my own thought process—probably saving my life.

Even after retirement, I was able to apply the lessons of Sun Tzu in local civic endeavors to keep our town great. Also, as a middle school teacher in social studies, I imparted some of *The Art of War* theories to the best of the brightest who were headed to high school and on to college and corporate endeavors. Michaelson's great book, *Winning the Marketing War,* is still used. The local high school now has its own copy.

I must add that Confucius's analysis was better received by some of my less-than-dynamic middle-school students.

Militarily, I favor *The Art of War* translations of General Samuel Griffith, Thomas Cleary, and my old Chinese friend and mentor, Major General Tao Hanzhang P.L.A. (Ret.), whose input helped me earn a degree at the University of Maine. As far as applying *The Art of War* to the business world, Michaelson's work is that of a master! Those who read his advice as they enter the world of competitive business will win their corporate battles; those who don't will fall by the wayside.

SEIZE A MEANINGFUL ADVANTAGE

Peter Brennan
Retired President, Daymon Associates

Daymon Worldwide has a reputation as private-label experts throughout the world. Currently, the company represents over 5,000 suppliers in twenty-four countries and has over 5,000 employees. This private-label expertise developed over a forty-year history, through the development of insightful relationships with retail customers in hundreds of locations.

One of the early strategies of the organization was to dedicate teams of people to operate at each retail customer location and help develop a unique relationship with the end consumer. In part because of their location, these dedicated teams of associates working with individual customers evolved to become experts in the individual objectives and goals of those customers. Sun Tzu says, "Nothing is more difficult than the art of maneuvering for seizing favorable positions beforehand," and our strategy accomplished that. Our company headquarters became an intelligence center where more knowledge developed with universal applications to most areas of the business.

Our growth was affected by increasingly competent managers at the local level who were empowered to give headquarters input regarding support they needed. In turn, we could quickly develop systems and solutions needed immediately in the marketplace. These strong and savvy local entrepreneurs became a communication system to bring what was needed in the local markets to the headquarters and for us to be able to see emerging trends long before they became broadly accepted.

Throughout the history of our company, we have been faced with consolidation in the retail industry. This consolidation of retailers has necessitated appealing to a new corporate entity who acquired a successful customer with whom we had a relationship. In doing so, we have frequently faced competitors who had a pre-existing relationship with the consolidator. Our future became dependent upon demonstrating we had more to offer than the competitor with whom the surviving client had a long-term relationship. Thus, every consolidation scenario commenced with a complete diagnostic of what we needed to accomplish offensively at the larger customer. Or, as Sun Tzu would advise, that "the enlightened sovereign and the wise general conquer the enemy whenever they move and their achievements surpass that of ordinary men in that they have foreknowledge." Recognizing our former customer no longer existed and was now part of a larger entity was critical in this thought process. Consolidation in and of itself creates new complications for customer and supplier alike, and we were able to change our strategy from what it had been to servicing a far more complex, diverse organization. This normally made us the preferred choice when our customer was part of a consolidation.

REORGANIZING THE BATTLEFIELD

Jay Kurtz
President, KappaWest, Laguna Hills, California
As a student at Canada's Royal Military College, I became familiar with Sun Tzu. As a business consultant, I used the principles of Sun Tzu and other great captains to aid our clients. Here is an example.

State Bell (not its real name) is a regional telephone company operating in a remote area. The state public utility commission wanted to increase competition and advised State Bell that it expected the company to give up significant market share. New generations of technology were emerging and competition was invading. To satisfy the regulators and incur minimum impact to State Bell, we heeded Sun Tzu's advice: "Enlightened rulers must deliberate upon the plans to go to battle, and good generals carefully execute them."

Sun Tzu says, "Wise generals win because they have foreknowledge." State Bell undertook a market study and classified customers as:

- Green—would very likely stay with State Bell
- Amber—would not actively seek a competitive system, but would seriously consider another company's proposal
- Red—would aggressively look for a competitor to replace State Bell

State Bell persuaded the utility commission to define the reduction in terms of number of customers instead of number of lines. It then redefined the market using Sun Tzu's advice to "make use of both the high and low-lying grounds." "High ground" was customers with the greater number of lines. The "swamps" were smaller red and amber customers with fewer lines and lower revenue.

We organized around Sun Tzu's wisdom: "By taking into account the favorable factors, he makes his plan feasible." State Bell trained a team of sales personnel to convert the larger amber customers with more lines to the newest generation of technology. They also sought longer leases with large customers. In its strategic withdrawal, State Bell allowed competitors to "capture" smaller customers with fewer lines. Consequently, it did not allow any competitor to achieve the critical mass that would justify a full-time service center in any area. This gave State Bell an important service quality superiority.

State Bell lost enough customers—30 percent—to satisfy the utility commission's measure of customers. State Bell won this battle by keeping the bigger customers so that it lost only 15 percent of its lines and revenue.

WIN WITHOUT FIGHTING

Gregg A. Nathanson
Manager, Real Estate Practice Group, Couzens, Lansky, Fealk, Ellis, Roeder & Lazar
The Art of War speaks to sophisticated, twenty-first-century transactional real estate law practice. Consider Sun Tzu's central thesis that you can avoid fighting when you plan the right strategy before the battle. Strategy, Sun Tzu teaches, is the planning process, the war on paper. Tactics, in contrast, implement the plan. Tactics are the contract process, the battle.

Every smooth, successful real estate transaction is won or lost in the planning process. An artful purchase agreement bridges strategy and tactics. The buyer wants the seller's property; the seller wants the buyer's money. That is the essence of the relationship. With a well-crafted purchase agreement, each side's rights and duties are clearly defined. The essential elements of closing the transaction have been predetermined. So, the ultimate tactical point of contact, the closing, goes smoothly. Conflict and fighting are avoided.

Sometimes, a transaction does not pursue the smooth course anticipated by the purchase agreement. With today's depressed real estate economy, many property owners are "underwater," and have negative equity. Many property owners with negative equity engage in a "short sale." The mortgage lender agrees to release their lien on the property and come up "short" by accepting less than the full amount due.

In one recent transaction, we represented a homeowner with two lenders. We fought to convince each of them to accept a short sale. This was not your ordinary residential transaction; the amount of debt exceeded $1 million. We employed varied tactics with each point of contact—the individuals representing the lenders. Ultimately, we were successful in helping our client achieve victory by liquidating their underwater asset and walking away from two sizeable potential deficiency judgments. To a lesser extent, each of the secured lenders achieved a victory as well, since they received more money by compromising and permitting the transaction to close than they would have received otherwise.

In this scenario, the value of the property was already a loss to each side's original expectations. Sun Tzu advises, "If equally matched, be capable of dividing him, if less in number, be capable of defending yourself." Since there was more the lenders could have lost, the seller, with our help, was able to defend himself.

SUN TZU IN THE BOARDROOM

Domminick Attanosio
Senior Adviser, Young and Partners LLC, New York, New York
Some years ago, I served on the board of a public pharmaceutical company that was developing a new delivery system to provide adjustable dosing of oral medications. I suggested the board consider the following precepts of Master Sun Tzu in their deliberations.

Know the enemy and know yourself, and you can fight 100 battles with no danger of defeat. To better know our competitors, we developed a system that monitored the drug industry to track emerging technologies that could impact our dosing system. To ensure our own strength, we engaged the services of the best marketing research and development engineering people we could find.

Travel where there is no enemy. Since the smaller segments of the pediatric and geriatric markets were given limited attention by potential competitors, we guided development efforts into these smaller segments.

Pursue one's strategic designs to overawe the enemy. There were many financial temptations to deviate from our decided mission. We passed by potential investor windfalls in favor of maintaining our long-term objectives.

An army can be raised only when the money is in hand. Authorizing the balance of finances in product development with investor relations, we fulfilled the board's fiduciary responsibility for this emerging public company to assure the timely development of technology with adequate funding for the venture.

The general whose only interest is to protect his people and promote the best interests of his sovereign is the precious jewel of the state. We ensured that our senior managers had proven track records in their respective jobs and adjusted organizational responsibilities accordingly.

The enlightened rulers must deliberate upon the plans to go to battle, and good generals carefully execute them. The statutory responsibility of the board was to keep the company on the offensive with the appropriate management team.

We believed in the philosophy that makes Sun Tzu unique: "To subdue the enemy without fighting is the supreme excellence." Providing the public with needed technology enabled the board to guide the company to its ultimate victory.

The final chapter in the company's successful history was written when the organization was purchased and stockholders earned an equitable return on their investment.

TAKE THE INITIATIVE

Stan Johnson
President, Johnson & Company

Johnson & Company is a boutique human resources firm located in Connecticut. We offer executive search services as well as a range of organizational consulting. From the start, I positioned this business not just as an executive search, but as a full human resources partner for clients looking to build or optimize leadership teams. This differentiated view of partnering with our clients and immersing ourselves in their organization to provide executive search and related services has worked well.

I started Johnson & Company in the recession of the early nineties. I reasoned there was a very large demand for executive search that included looking at how a client's organization would have to be configured when the economy turned and an equal demand to fill holes in top management's skill set. Even in a recession, the demand for executive search would still be very large. I just needed to get my piece of it. And since my intent was to be a boutique firm, I only needed to get a modest-sized piece.

As Sun Tzu advises, "Know the enemy and know yourself and your victory will never be endangered." I knew the competitive landscape from my time as the senior partner of one of the largest executive search firms, so I also knew where a smaller company could find success, since we would have very few client or candidate conflicts and I would be involved in every engagement.

Since then I have built a steady business. Even in the most recent, and deeper recession, my business has been very strong. There are a couple of ways I have been able to do this:

1. I am fortunate to have come out of one of the great executive training schools—Procter & Gamble. During my time there and in the executive search firm, I had a chance to build relationships with successful business leaders at many of our largest corporations—decision makers for the kinds of services Johnson & Company offers.
2. I have built the business on strong service and long-term successes— word of mouth has been my best advertising and my clients are the people, not the corporations. When they moved, I went with them.
3. While I continue to successfully complete searches for *Fortune* 500 companies, I have particular success with privately held companies— companies where a smaller firm can serve a broad range of needs.

These are generally also companies where the smaller amount of total business available doesn't attract larger competitors.

Knowing the business and the potential clients and their businesses gave me the pieces I needed to achieve initial success and to continue to build a successful business.

COACHING CHALLENGES

Lou Sartori

History Teacher and Girls' Varsity Basketball Coach, Seneca High School, Louisville, KY

My first contact with *The Art of War* and Sun Tzu fell upon deaf ears. It was in the early 1980s when attending a basketball coaching clinic. I wanted to learn the X's and O's and become a successful teacher/coach. The speaker was Bobby Knight. He mentioned how Sun Tzu's book was full of philosophy and practical applications. Needless to say, I ignored the book upon this first encounter.

Several years later, after attending numerous other clinics and hearing the same description from time to time, I finally decided to purchase *The Art of War* and read it. My eyes were finally opened and I have tried to follow certain guidelines and principles ever since.

Sun Tzu undoubtedly was a master teacher and would have had many undefeated "teams." The themes that keep pounding at me from the book are many. They have helped me to mature and grow as a teacher/coach. Although I could go on, the themes of preparation, discipline, and communication are the major ones I have applied.

Preparation. As a teacher/coach today, I have many different roles that I must play. Sun Tzu's early warning "know your enemy and know yourself" (Chapter 3) teaches us that preparation and planning is vital. This precept encourages me to make plans—lesson plans for the classroom, and practice plans for the court. Many people, including colleagues, have been complimentary of my organizational skills. I owe it all to Sun Tzu, who points out the calamities of not planning or being prepared. I believe that "failing to plan is planning to fail." Too many teachers today consider lesson plans a necessary evil, if they do them at all. Some schools require that lesson plans be turned in every week. Although our school has no such requirement, I draft a set every week. It keeps me on track.

Discipline. A proverbial problem for most teachers is classroom discipline. I recommend that teachers, coaches, and managers apply Sun Tzu's idea that soldiers must be treated with humanity but kept under control by iron discipline. In twenty-nine years of teaching and coaching I have had my share of problems, but they have been kept to a minimum. My teaching evaluations have stressed that a learning atmosphere exists in my classroom based upon firm, fair discipline.

Another principle from Sun Tzu affects how I discipline. He constantly stresses that orders (directions) must be clear and distinct. I've tried to use this technique throughout my career. Communication is very important in any endeavor and I have used the K-I-S-S (Keep It Simple Stupid) approach effectively in my role as a coach.

Communication. When I arrived at my present school, female students had very limited experience trying out for basketball. Effective, distinct communication was the biggest adjustment I had to make. It is critical to speak in a manner that your students comprehend. There is no need to show off your education and intelligence by using words that are not understood. You will immediately know if they "get it;" or, "don't get it." The blank, dazed looks speak volumes. My directions may seem very elementary; however, they have been followed completely for all assignments.

I owe a debt of gratitude to Sun Tzu. My career has been very rewarding. Teaching today's youth is very challenging; yet the task has been pleasant and the journey is one that I would not trade.

WINNING BATTLES

Terri D. Nance

Vice President—Business Intelligence, Ingram Book Company

Sun Tzu advises to fight only battles you can win. This advice is very useful in making effective choices when dealing with conflicting initiatives.

As a young woman I was faced with a difficult choice: borrow extensively to attend college or work to support myself and go to school part-time at night. Following Sun Tzu's advice to make an assessment, I determined that my best strategy would be to work during the day and go to school at night. I was now focused on the goal and my ability to commit my resources. As Sun Tzu says, I had kicked the ladder away.

By following Sun Tzu's advice to "fight only the battles I could win," I was able to accomplish much more than originally planned. I've gone on to complete a master's degree. As I entered a career with a large corporation I found new applications for Sun Tzu. My intuition told me that the wisdom behind Sun Tzu's words would ultimately prove applicable in dealing with internal corporate politics and constraints. However, one cannot really afford to apply Sun Tzu's advice too literally when dealing with internal business associates. Using deception and employing spies would be suicidal to one's career, at least in most companies.

Two previous attempts to implement enterprise-wide project management ended in failure. My breakthrough in analyzing Sun Tzu's application to business came as an epiphany. Imagining the enemy as organizational obstacles helped me in my daunting task of building a project management system for a large information technology division.

The following key concepts were applied to remove organizational barriers.

Apply extraordinary force. Despite the general resistance to another try at project management, I knew from my reconnaissance at the coffee machine that several managers were frustrated at the inability of the department to get projects completed on time and within budget.

I recruited an "extraordinary force" to help slay the enemy of organizational malaise. These managers proved invaluable in overcoming the most fortified pockets of resistance.

Plan Surprise. The little pilot project we started had no resistance in the hinterlands of the division we chose for this first small step. However, once the methodology proved both simple and robust, we asked the head of the division to present it as a mandated initiative at the next general staff meeting. We moved from a pilot to a full divisional mandate before naysayers could organize resistance.

Reinforce strength not weakness. Once the surprise worked, we pursued a rollout. My initial inclination was to attack the most resistant departments first, but Sun Tzu's advice to reinforce strength not weakness turned my mind. Instead of attacking the bastions of negative thought, we identified the allies and the uncommitted. We kept a careful accounting as department after department adopted the new methodology.

Be flexible. Sun Tzu consistently emphasizes the need for flexibility in the face of changing circumstances. Allowing flexibility in the method but enforcing great discipline in the output gave us a winning system. This approach proved informative to the executive leadership, improved our relationships with internal customers, and avoided saddling managers with unnecessary bureaucracy.

Consider tactical options. Sun Tzu advises there are some roads which must not be taken . . . some cities which must not be assaulted. We had one such citadel in our division where we decided to forego full-blown project management implementation. We simply asked this group to provide estimates of the project hours on each of their major projects. This accomplished about 80 percent of the goal without having to lay siege to the manager.

Consolidate your gains. As we made progress with our project management methodology, we began to see real gains in our performance and our relationships with the business units we supported. Regular updates made it easy for the leadership to see where their projects stood in the overall scheme. As satisfaction grew, we were able to trumpet our successes and build better relationships. Some of the naysayers became strong allies and acknowledged that the methodolgy was "working better than I thought it would."

Whether the enemy is a virus or failing public schools or tobacco use among teenagers, it is not necessary to attack the people—one can attack the problem quite successfully with a 2,000-year-old military strategy.

LEADERSHIP LESSONS

Mark Davidoff
Executive Director and COO, Jewish Federation of Metropolitan Detroit

What is leadership? Leadership is the art of communicating vision. It is about the design of strategy. It is the establishment of objectives and marshaling of resources to realize these objectives. Leadership is about making difficult decisions that impact the lives of those you serve and those with whom you serve.

In Sun Tzu's writings, he delineates the common flaws of leadership as recklessness, cowardice, hasty temper, delicate honor, and over-solicitude. It is in the last of that he warns those who love people can be troubled. I have transformed this teaching into a basic rule of leadership that I am reminded of on a daily basis. Get your love at home.

Business leaders must make difficult decisions on a constant basis. In making decisions, leaders must always determine what is in the best interest of the "sovereign," as Sun Tzu would call today's stakeholders. Discipline "in the best interests of stakeholders" applies to all businesses, nonprofit service providers, and government agencies. Having held various leadership positions in nonprofit social welfare and health service organizations over the past fifteen years, I have often been faced with deciding which service to fund, program to cut, segment of the populations is in greatest need, and employees no longer add value. Absent a clear mind, no such decisions could be made correctly.

Leaders who look to the work environment for their deepest friend-ships, glory, ego boosts, and love will not deliver. The leader who can control his or her "over-solicitude" and get his or her love at home will function with a clear mind and a solid heart.

Institutions are permanent fixtures on the landscape of our communi-ties. The individuals who fill the offices of these institutions over time are no more than stewards for the next generation. As a community leader with this heavy responsibility, I approach each day with a deep breath and a steady pace, being mindful of the fatal flaws of leadership described by Sun Tzu.

RELEVANT PRINCIPLES

Les Lunceford, (retired U.S. Marine Corps officer)
President, The Transition Team, Inc., Knoxville Operations

I read *The Art of War* in college and several times as a Marine officer; its applicability to private enterprise came later in my life. Sun Tzu's treasure chest of knowledge made a significant difference in my military career and that of fellow officers. *The Art of War* makes a difference for anyone who takes the time to read, understand, and actively apply the strategies.

It is a major mistake to read Sun Tzu and walk away feeling merely enlightened. Enlightenment is of little value without wind in the sails provided by ACTION.

Victory on the battlefield or in business is seldom achieved with the application of a single principle. When it came time for me to transition into business, more than one of Sun Tzu's principles unlocked winning concepts and pushed me to exceed my greatest expectations. Sun Tzu's principles served as a force multiplier—a concept drilled into me and all other military officers. Force multipliers (using multiple principles) apply additional pressure on the competition and reinforce momentum. In particular, four principles have had an impact on our business's success:

Thoroughly assess conditions. Good assessment is the foundation of a successful operation. Before we developed a marketing plan, we had to thoroughly assess our competitors, the market area, our weaknesses, our strengths, and feedback from existing clients. We found 23 percent of our customers were providing 80 percent of our revenues. Had we not accomplished a thorough assessment, we were about to lean our ladder to success against the wrong wall.

We focused on better serving existing clients because the high cost of acquiring new customers depletes resources faster than the cost of satisfying existing ones. This produced record results. Preparing any plan without a thorough assessment is like building a house on shifting sands; the house won't survive.

People are a valuable asset. Sun Tzu says, "He treats them as his own beloved sons and they will stand by him until death." When we treat others with respect, dignity, and as we'd like to be treated, we're displaying a sincere regard for those we're entrusted to lead. Genuine regard for other people helps us produce desired results.

Do not read Sun Tzu thinking its primary purpose is to get more work out of people so you can have more success for yourself. The principles in *The Art of War* are about the power to support others and make differences in their lives. I am talking about the power that comes from personal conviction; the power to lead and the power to visualize the future. When you make positive differences in other people's lives, you will notice that the world relates differently to you.

Be Flexible. While strategies remain constant, tactics must be adapted to each new situation. Being successful in business or war requires simultaneous planning and action. While initial planning is important, too much planning can be disastrous. Any plan must be the basis for change. Plans must not be so rigid that adjustments can't be made as the situation changes.

Know Your Terrain. Know the needs of the customer, the strengths and weaknesses of your team and opponents. After the September 11 terrorist attacks, our clients' needs dramatically increased.

Following those tragic events, we further developed our executive coaching capabilities; established an executive search arm of our business; invested considerable capital and structure. We demonstrated to our customers that we understood their needs and stood ready to assist them.

"THE ART OF WAR" IS THE ART OF PEACE

Colin Benjamin
Managing Director, Intellectual Property Holdings, South Melbourne, Australia
The writings of Sun Tzu have consistently delivered practical wisdom in my personal search for a creative approach to personal conflicts and challenging opportunities. Sun Tzu continues to offer practical advice in my daily battles to balance business survival with the desire to undertake struggles for social justice around the world.

For more than forty years I have studied *The Art of War* as a source of strategic guidance. This study included the works of Niccolo Machiavelli, De Jomini, and Mao Ze Dung as I attempted to identify the differences between the mind of the military and civilian strategists.

In this extensive study, the practical wisdom of Sun Tzu shines like a beacon—the battle is not the war. The war is won in the mind of the opposing forces, not on the battleground. Peace, not war, is the key to best practices in strategy.

The works of Rudyard Kipling, Ian Fleming, John Le Carré, Arthur Conan Doyle, and J.R.R. Tolkien proved literary ammunition for an appreciation of the genius of Chapter Thirteen on "The Employment of Secret Agents." Here, in one short chapter, is a profound insight into the Art of Peace—the means of avoiding unnecessary loss of life with practical, down-to-earth instruction on the management of people in the world of spies and secrets.

As a student participant in organizing anti-conscription for Vietnam campaigns, while also serving as a member of the volunteer Citizens Military Forces, I was in a strategic double bind.

My service was as a member of a psychology corps responsible for officer selection. As a result, I was placed in charge of a psychological warfare resource designed to understand the mind of the enemy. This led me for the first time to Sun Tzu' s *The Art of War* and a lifetime interest in the mind of my opponent.

Australia entered the Vietnam War late in the campaign, much like it entered the war in Afghanistan. We adopted this position in support of the ANZUS alliance and in recognition of America's decisive role in defense against external aggression. My unit was in a psychology corps responsible for officer selection. As a clinician working in the field of mental health and clinical psychology, I was naturally interested in this field of study. I soon found the hidden genius in Sun Tzu. Here was a mother lode of wisdom, with passages such as "Therefore, the skillful leader subdues the enemy's troops without fighting," and "The supreme excellence is breaking the enemy's resistance without fighting."

Regular visits to China over the past twenty years have given me the chance to work with Chinese professors, entrepreneurs, and military leaders seeking to apply the thinking of Sun Tzu to the development of national enterprises. All have shared their view of Sun Tzu's work as a reference to the realities of commercial conflict with community goals.

It has been humbling to learn how to apply this ancient strategist's thinking to the construction of new community initiatives and government programs—all more than two centuries after *The Art of War* was written. Working for government ministers, multinational corporations, and my own firms offers a constant reminder of one of Sun Tzu's key rejoinders: "In battle, there are not more than two methods of attack—the direct and the indirect; yet these two in combination give rise to an endless series of maneuvers."

In summary, the struggle to apply Sun Tzu's wisdom has provided a valuable insight into the military and political mind. I see that every day it is necessary to survey the competitive terrain, identify the paths to success, and build a platform for achievement. The lessons learned are that peace is not just the absence of war. Peace is a measure of goodwill, personal trust, and freedom.

RULES FOR DAILY LIFE

Benefsheh D. Shamley
Captain, U.S. Army, Commanding

As an Army officer and commander of troops, the concepts in Sun Tzu's *The Art of War* are very applicable to me.

"Know yourself; know your opponent" is my favorite rule. Knowing yourself can be tricky. I don't know how many times I've sat in front of superiors and they've told me to tell them my strengths and weaknesses. I usually just stare back for a while and sputter out something unintelligible. Why is this so hard? For me, I think it's because I really didn't want to know my weaknesses. We are always comparing ourselves to others and thinking "she's skinnier, prettier, smarter, and happier than I am." Yet, this serves no purpose and is self-defeating.

Instead of focusing on what others may think or how I measure up to someone else, I've learned to rely on my own assessment of myself. Today, I look at myself and address my weaknesses and concentrate on improving those that I can. It is important to be honest with yourself and to assess your strengths as well. This is half of the battle. With a little bit of research I can attack any situation (opponent) that may cross my path. This is a continuous process that I go through almost daily.

"Develop effective internal communications" is the next rule I use quite often. I have been lucky to have a very open and loving family. I talk to my parents frequently about various subjects and ask for advice.

This strong bond is important in other life relationships. It goes without saying that it is important to communicate effectively with your superiors and subordinates at work. Simple problems get blown out of proportion because of miscommunication. Effective communication is also very important in dealing with friends and love relationships.

Several years ago, I had a very good friend with whom I failed to communicate. We were roommates for a few months and subtle things she did annoyed me. I never told her. Our relationship took a turn for the worse and one day I "blew up" and told her to move out. Afterwards, I regretted my actions and felt a tremendous amount of guilt. If I had told her what was bothering me as it occurred, we might still be friends today.

"Thoroughly assess conditions" and "compare attributes" are two principles I use in just about everything I do. These rules are key to major decisions such as buying a house or car, career choices, or planning a wedding. I assess the conditions of my situation using the five constant factors:

- Moral influence: What impact will taking this assignment have on my family?
- Weather: Are there outside circumstances to take into consideration?
- Terrain: Where will this assignment take me?
- Commander: What will be my job and for whom will I work?
- Doctrine: Do I have the knowledge to qualify for the job, or do I need additional schooling?

Adjusting these five factors to my personal situation allows me to make a good assessment. I then compare the positive and negative attributes in order to make an informed decision. This simple process helps make sure I have looked at all options.

"Discipline can build allegiance" is another rule no one should live without. My inherent sense of self-discipline was enhanced by my time at West Point. Discipline allows a person to achieve his or her goals in academics, career, sports, or personal life. The hardest thing is telling myself what to do to succeed. Many times, especially now that I'm in command post, I tend to ignore my own disciplinary needs and focus on my soldiers. This is okay, as long as I don't neglect what I need to do to stay on track career-wise—physically and emotionally. It may take my fiancée, parents, or a friend to make me see where I need to be. It hurts to realize that you're not trying as hard as you can, or that you can be apathetic, but it happens to everyone. What you do to solve your problems depends on self-discipline.

IMPLEMENTING STRATEGY

Ivan Larsh
Former Captain, U.S.M.C., Corporate President (Retired)

One would think that my education at the U.S. Naval Academy would have included the teachings of Sun Tzu. Since Sun Tzu had no Navy, perhaps this omission is understandable although I could have learned much about strategy from him. Oddly enough, not even my infantry training as a junior officer in the Marine Corps or flight training as a young fighter pilot included the study of Sun Tzu.

I first learned of the master from his most ardent advocate and interpreter, Gerald Michaelson, as he facilitated a strategic planning session for my company in 1998. The financial performance of the company had been strong compared to industry standards, but top-line growth was anemic. All strategic paths that diverged from our historical norm seemed littered with major hazards.

"Stick to your knitting" is a recurring theme of Tom Peters in his book *In Search of Excellence*, and was also the sentiment frequently voiced by the more conservative members of our management team.

"Identifying strengths." Michaelson's advice: listen to Sun Tzu. "Now an army may be likened to water, for just as flowing water avoids the heights and hastens to the lowlands, so an army avoids strength and strikes weakness." Simply stated, battles are won by concentrating strengths against weakness—always.

With Michaelson's urging, the team embraced a process for identifying our strengths that could be amassed to assure victory against the corresponding weaknesses of our competitors. This part of the process was invigorating! Team members were encouraged by their ability to reach consensus on several competitive advantages that we viewed as dominant and sustainable.

"Identifying weakness." Then came the hard part—being honest about our weaknesses and vulnerabilities to attack by competitors. Again, we listened to Sun Tzu. "Invincibility lies in the defense, the possibility of victory in the attack. One defends when his strength is inadequate; he attacks when it is abundant."

It had been more fun to talk about our abundant strengths; but we clearly had inadequacies. In business, as in battle, if you are not on offense, you are on defense. It seemed to us that the best way to defend our areas of weakness was to convert them to offensive actions. We brainstormed the various ways that we could mount guerrilla-like attacks from our weaker positions, capturing small footholds inside our competitor's circle of strength while avoiding major battles against a superior enemy.

We envisioned small outposts in foreign countries, strategic alliances with noncompeting companies, ways to broaden our market position, lower cost positions and systems integration. Suddenly, playing defense seemed more fun!

From analysis to strategy. Finally, a strategy was emerging that assured steady generic growth from our strengths and also held the promise of additional growth from guerrilla-like offensive actions into new territories.

There are clearly two distinct activities in all strategic exercise: firstly, the planning and preparation; secondly, the conduct or execution. History (and personal experience) demonstrates that an average strategy, superbly executed, is more effective than a superb strategy with average execution. Sun Tzu has plenty to say about execution, but timing is one of the most important, "Speed is the essence of war [or business]. Take advantage of the enemy's unpreparedness; travel by unexpected routes and strike him where he has taken no precautions."

None of us will become great leaders simply by reading the words of great leaders. However, we can become substantially better managers, better planners, better at execution, by studying the expert teachings that have stood the test of time. Whether one is seeking victory on the battlefield, in the world of business, or in personal life, the teachings expressed by Sun Tzu in *The Art of War* more than twenty-five centuries ago are still remarkably current and beneficial.

EFFECTIVE DECISIONS

Robert Jerus
Professor, Southeastern College

Sun Tzu says, "The quality of decision is like the well-timed swoop of a falcon . . ."

The distinguishing characteristic of effective people is their ability to implement high-quality decisions. Sun Tzu's concepts provide the tools for honing decision-making skills. The master strategist repeatedly refers to expertise in long- and short-term planning; information gathering, analysis, and action.

Sun Tzu indirectly points out that failure teaches. We need to learn from past performances. Lost battles have their place in winning the war.

Decision-making skills distinguish between people who really have a grasp on achievement and those who live in quiet disappointment. The final, critical component lies in the boldness to act. Most people have visions, develop ambitions, and make tentative plans for attainment, but fail to transform dreams into reality.

Dreams have their place. Life is hollow without aspirations and hopes for the future. Championships lie in the implementation of plans. Strategies and tactics provide the operational framework for winning. Success is in living.

There are always reasons to postpone actions. If life is spent waiting for the perfect opportunity and most advantageous time to capitalize on that opportunity, life will pass by with quiet regret. Those who wonder "what if" are doomed.

Consider Sun Tzu's falcon. The powerful swoop to capture prey is essential to survival. As a hunter, the falcon's sight and flight abilities are designed for action. The keen sight, speed, and patience culminate in success.

Quality decision-making followed by action is the core of Sun Tzu's teaching. Success in life, as on the battlefield, is the product of information, analysis, and critically, the decision to act.

Perhaps the most striking example of effective decision-making I have ever seen was when I met a most unusual college freshman. The gentleman, I'll call him Jack, explained that he intended to be President of the United States. I held back my laughter when I realized he was quite serious. He had decided to major in accounting, noting that the President would have vast financial responsibility. In college, Jack was actively networking in the community because he deemed this activity critical to his mission.

After four years, he graduated very high in his program and continued on to law school. Within a few years, he earned his CPA and graduated near the top of his class. Jack continued community service and joined a prominent law firm.

For a few years, I lost track of him. When I met him again, he was in his early thirties. At this point he owned a successful law firm and was married with two children. I asked him about his dream to become President. He thought I had forgotten as he responded with a wide grin and carefully explained the decision was the root of his success. By following Sun Tzu's advice, his powerful decision had given direction to his life and training—it generated opportunities. Jack advised me of the power of decisions, something I should have been telling him.

Sun Tzu teaches the value of decisions followed by action. When implementing your dreams, good things happen.

Complete Translation of *The Art of War*

Chapter 1: Laying Plans

THOROUGHLY ASSESS CONDITIONS

War is a matter of vital importance to the state; a matter of life and death, the road either to survival or to ruin. Hence, it is imperative that it be thoroughly studied.

Therefore, to make assessment of the outcome of a war, one must compare the various conditions of the antagonistic sides in terms of the five constant factors:

1. Moral influence
2. Weather
3. Terrain
4. Commander
5. Doctrine

These five constant factors should be familiar to every general. He who masters them wins; he who does not is defeated.

COMPARE THE SEVEN ATTRIBUTES

Therefore, to forecast the outcome of a war, the attributes of the antagonistic sides should be analyzed by making the following seven comparisons:

1. Which sovereign possesses greater moral influence?
2. Which commander is more capable?
3. Which side holds more favorable conditions in weather and terrain?
4. On which side are decrees better implemented?
5. Which side is superior in arms?

6. On which side are officers and men better trained?

7. Which side is stricter and more impartial in meting out rewards and punishments?

By means of these seven elements, I can forecast victory or defeat.

If the sovereign heeds these stratagems of mine and acts upon them, he will surely win the war, and I shall, therefore, stay with him. If the sovereign neither heeds nor acts upon them, he will certainly suffer defeat, and I shall leave.

LOOK FOR STRATEGIC TURNS

Having paid attention to the advantages of my stratagems, the commander must create a helpful situation over and beyond the ordinary rules. By "situation," I mean he should act expediently in accordance with what is advantageous in the field and so meet any exigency.

All warfare is based on deception. Therefore, when able to attack, we must pretend to be unable; when employing our forces, we must seem inactive; when we are near, we must make the enemy believe we are far away; when far away, we must make him believe we are near.

Offer a bait to allure the enemy when he covets small advantages. Strike the enemy when he is in disorder. If he is well prepared with substantial strength, take double precautions against him. If he is powerful in action, evade him. If he is angry, seek to discourage him. If he appears humble, make him arrogant. If his forces have taken a good rest, wear them down. If his forces are united, divide them.

Launch the attack where he is unprepared; take action when it is unexpected.

These are the keys to victory for a strategist. However, it is impossible to formulate them in detail beforehand.

Now, the commander who gets many scores during the calculations in the temple before the war will have more likelihood of winning. The commander who gets few scores during the calculations in the temple before the war will have less chance of success. With many scores, one can win; with few scores, one cannot. How much less chance of victory has one who gets no scores at all! By examining the situation through these aspects, I can foresee who is likely to win or lose.

Chapter 2: Waging War

MARSHAL ADEQUATE RESOURCES

Generally, operations of war involve 1,000 swift chariots, 1,000 heavy chariots, and 100,000 mailed troops, with the transportation of provisions for them over a thousand li. Thus, the expenditure at home and in the field, the stipends for the entertainment of state guests and diplomatic envoys, the cost of materials such as glue and lacquer, and the expense for care and maintenance of chariots and armor will amount to 1,000 pieces of gold a day. An army of 100,000 men can be raised only when this money is in hand.

MAKE TIME YOUR ALLY

In directing such an enormous army, a speedy victory is the main object.

If the war is long delayed, the men's weapons will be blunted and their ardor will be dampened. If the army attacks cities, their strength will be exhausted. Again, if the army engages in protracted campaigns, the resources of the state will not suffice. Now, when your weapons are blunted, your ardor dampened, your strength exhausted, and your treasure spent, neighboring rulers will take advantage of your distress to act. In this case, no man, however wise, is able to avert the disastrous consequences that ensue.

Thus, while we have heard of stupid haste in war, we have not yet seen a clever operation that was prolonged. There has never been a case in which a prolonged war has benefited a country. Therefore, only those who understand the dangers inherent in employing troops know how to conduct war in the most profitable way.

EVERYONE MUST PROFIT FROM VICTORIES

Those adept in employing troops do not require a second levy of conscripts or more than two provisionings. They carry military supplies from the homeland and make up for their provisions, relying on the enemy. Thus, the army will be always plentifully provided.

When a country is impoverished by military operations, it is because an army far from its homeland needs a distant transportation. Being forced to carry supplies for great distances renders the people destitute. On the other hand, the local price of commodities normally rises high in the area near the military camps. The rising prices cause financial resources to be drained away. When the resources are exhausted, the peasantry will be afflicted with urgent exactions. With this depletion of strength and exhaustion of wealth, every household in the homeland is left empty Seven-tenths of the people's income is dissipated, and six-tenths of the government's revenue is paid for broken-down chariots, worn-out horses, armor and helmets, arrows and crossbows, halberds and bucklers, spears and body shields, draught oxen and heavy wagons.

Hence, a wise general is sure of getting provisions from the enemy countries. One *zhong* of grains obtained from the local area is equal to twenty *zhong* shipped from the home country; one *dan* of fodder in the conquered area is equal to twenty *dan* from the domestic store.

Now, in order to kill the enemy, our men must be roused to anger; to gain the enemy's property, our men must be rewarded with war trophies. Accordingly, in chariot battle, when more than ten chariots have been captured, those who took the enemy chariot first should be rewarded. Then, the enemy's flags and banners should be replaced with ours; the captured chariots mixed with ours and mounted by our men. The prisoners of war should be kindly treated and kept. This is called "becoming stronger in the course of defeating the enemy."

KNOW YOUR CRAFT

Hence, what is valued in war is a quick victory, not prolonged operations. And, therefore, the general who understands war is the controller of his people's fate and the guarantor of the security of the nation.

Chapter 3: Attack by Stratagem

WIN WITHOUT FIGHTING

Generally, in war the best thing of all is to take the enemy's state whole and intact; to ruin it is inferior to this. To capture the enemy's entire army is better than to destroy it; to take intact a battalion, a company, or a five-man squad is better than to destroy them. Hence, to win one hundred victories in one hundred battles is not the acme of skill. To subdue the enemy without fighting is the supreme excellence.

Thus, the best policy in war is to attack the enemy's strategy. The second best way is to disrupt his alliances through diplomatic means. The next best method is to attack his army in the field. The worst policy is to attack walled cities. Attacking cities is the last resort when there is no alternative.

It takes at least three months to make mantlets and shielded vehicles ready and prepare necessary arms and equipments. It takes at least another three months to pile up earthen mounds against the walls. The general unable to control his impatience will order his troops to swarm up the wall like ants, with the result that one-third of them are slain, while the city remains untaken. Such is the calamity of attacking walled cities.

Therefore, those skilled in war subdue the enemy's army without fighting. They capture the enemy's cities without assaulting them and overthrow his state without protracted operations.

Their aim must be to take all under heaven intact through strategic superiority. Thus, their troops are not worn out and their triumph will be complete. This is the art of attacking by stratagem.

ATTAIN STRATEGIC SUPERIORITY

Consequently, the art of using troops is this:

- When ten to the enemy's one, surround him.
- When five times his strength, attack him.
- If double his strength, engage him.
- If equally matched, be capable of dividing him.
- If less in number, be capable of defending yourself.
- And, if in all respects unfavorable, be capable of eluding him.

Hence, a weak force will eventually fall captive to a strong one if it simply holds ground and conducts a desperate defense.

BEWARE OF "HIGH-LEVEL DUMB"

Now, the general is the bulwark of the state:

- If the bulwark is complete at all points, the state will surely be strong.
- If the bulwark is defective, the state will certainly be weak.
  Now, there are three ways in which a sovereign can bring misfortune upon his army:

1. By ordering an advance while ignorant of the fact that the army cannot go forward, or by ordering a retreat while ignorant of the fact that the army cannot fall back. This is described as "hobbling the army."
2. By interfering with the army's administration without knowledge of the internal affairs of the army. This causes officers and soldiers to be perplexed.
3. By interfering with direction of fighting while ignorant of the military principle of adaptation to circumstances. This sows doubts and misgivings in the minds of his officers and soldiers.

If the army is confused and suspicious, neighboring rulers will take advantage of this and cause trouble. This is simply bringing anarchy into the army and flinging away victory.

SEEK CIRCUMSTANCES THAT ASSURE VICTORY

Thus, there are five points in which victory may be predicted:

1. He who knows when to fight and when not to fight will win.
2. He who understands how to handle both superior and inferior forces will win.
3. He whose ranks are united in purpose will win.

4. He who is well prepared and lies in wait for an enemy who is not well prepared will win.
5. He whose generals are able and not interfered with by the sovereign will win.

It is in these five points that the way to victory is known. Therefore, I say:

Know the enemy and know yourself, and you can fight a hundred battles with no danger of defeat.

When you are ignorant of the enemy but know yourself, your chances of winning and losing are equal.

If ignorant both of your enemy and of yourself, you are sure to be defeated in every battle.

Chapter 4: Disposition of Military Strength

BE INVINCIBLE

The skillful warriors in ancient times first made themselves invincible and then awaited the enemy's moment of vulnerability. Invincibility depends on oneself, but the enemy's vulnerability on himself. It follows that those skilled in war can make themselves invincible but cannot cause an enemy to be certainly vulnerable. Therefore, it can be said that one may know how to achieve victory but cannot necessarily do so.

Invincibility lies in the defense, the possibility of victory in the attack. Defend yourself when the enemy's strength is abundant, and attack the enemy when it is inadequate. Those who are skilled in defense hide themselves as under the most secret recesses of earth. Those skilled in attack flash forth as from above the topmost heights of heaven. Thus, they are capable both of protecting themselves and of gaining a complete victory.

WIN WITHOUT FIGHTING

To foresee a victory no better than ordinary people's foresight is not the acme of excellence. Neither is it the acme of excellence if you win a victory through fierce fighting and the whole empire says, "Well done!" Hence, by analogy, to lift an autumn hare does not signify great strength; to see the sun and moon does not signify good sight; to hear the thunderclap does not signify acute hearing.

In ancient times, those called skilled in war conquered an enemy easily conquered. Consequently, a master of war wins victories without showing his brilliant military success, and without gaining the reputation for wisdom or the merit for valor. He wins his victories without making mistakes. Making no mistakes is what establishes the certainty of victory, for it means that he conquers an enemy already defeated.

Accordingly, a wise commander always ensures that his forces are put in an invincible position, and at the same time will be sure to miss no opportunity to defeat the enemy. It follows that a triumphant army will not fight with the enemy until the victory is assured; while an army destined to defeat will always fight with the opponent first, in the hope that it may win by sheer good luck. The commander adept in war enhances the moral influence and adheres to the laws and regulations. Thus, it is in his power to control success.

USE INFORMATION TO FOCUS RESOURCES

Now, the elements of the art of war are first, the measurement of space; second, the estimation of quantities; third, the calculation of figures; fourth, comparisons of strength; and fifth, chances of victory.

Measurements of space are derived from the ground. Quantities derive from measurement, figures from quantities, comparisons from figures, and victory from comparisons.

Therefore, a victorious army is as one *yi* balanced against a grain, and a defeated army is as a grain balanced against one *yi*.

An army superior in strength takes action like the bursting of pent-up waters into a chasm of a thousand fathoms deep. This is what the disposition of military strength means in the actions of war.

Chapter 5: Use of Energy

BUILD A SOUND ORGANIZATION STRUCTURE

Generally, management of a large force is the same in principle as the management of a few men: it is a matter of organization. And to direct a large army to fight is the same as to direct a small one: it is a matter of command signs and signals.

EMPLOY EXTRAORDINARY FORCE

That the whole army can sustain the enemy's all-out attack without suffering defeat is due to operations of extraordinary and normal forces. Troops thrown against the enemy as a grindstone against eggs is an example of the strong beating the weak.

Generally, in battle, use the normal force to engage and use the extraordinary to win. Now, to a commander adept at the use of extraordinary forces, his resources are as infinite as the heaven and earth, as inexhaustible as the flow of the running rivers. They end and begin again like the motions of the sun and moon. They die away and then are reborn like the changing of the four seasons.

In battle, there are not more than two kinds of postures—operation of the extraordinary force and operation of the normal force, but their combinations give rise to an endless series of maneuvers. For these two forces are mutually reproductive. It is like moving in a circle, never coming to an end. Who can exhaust the possibilities of their combinations?

COORDINATE MOMENTUM AND TIMING

When torrential water tosses boulders, it is because of its momentum; when the strike of a hawk breaks the body of its prey, it is because of timing. Thus, in battle, a good commander creates a posture releasing an irresistible and overwhelming momentum, and his attack is precisely timed in a quick tempo. The energy is similar to a fully drawn crossbow; the timing, the release of the trigger.

Amid turmoil and tumult of battle, there may be seeming disorder and yet no real disorder in one's own troops. In the midst of confusion and chaos, your troops appear to be milling about in circles, yet it is proof against defeat.

Apparent disorder is born of order; apparent cowardice, of courage; apparent weakness, of strength. Order or disorder depends on organization and direction; courage or cowardice on postures; strength or weakness on dispositions.

Thus, one who is adept at keeping the enemy on the move maintains deceitful appearances, according to which the enemy will act. He lures with something that the enemy is certain to take. By so doing he keeps the enemy on the move and then waits for the right moment to make a sudden ambush with picked troops.

Therefore, a skilled commander sets great store by using the situation to the best advantage and does not make excessive demands on his subordinates. Hence, he is able to select the right men and exploits the situation. He who takes advantage of the situation uses his men in fighting as rolling logs or rocks. It is the nature of logs and rocks to stay stationary on the flat ground and to roll forward on a slope. If four-cornered, they stop; if round-shaped, they roll. Thus, the energy of troops skillfully commanded is just like the momentum of round rocks quickly tumbling down from a mountain thousands of feet in height. This is what "use of energy" means.

Chapter 6: Weakness and Strength

TAKE THE INITIATIVE

Generally, he who occupies the field of battle first and awaits his enemy is at ease; he who arrives later and joins the battle in haste is weary. And, therefore, one skilled in war brings the enemy to the field of battle and is not brought there by him.

One able to make the enemy come of his own accord does so by offering him some advantage. And one able to stop him from coming does so by inflicting damage on him.

PLAN SURPRISE

Thus, when the enemy is at ease, he is able to tire him; when well fed, to starve him; when at rest, to make him move. All these can be done because you appear at points that the enemy must hasten to defend.

That you may march a thousand li without tiring yourself is because you travel where there is no enemy.

That you are certain to take what you attack is because you attack a place the enemy does not or cannot protect.

That you are certain of success in holding what you defend is because you defend a place the enemy must hasten to attack.

Therefore, against those skillful in attack, the enemy does not know where to defend, and against the experts in defense, the enemy does not know where to attack.

How subtle and insubstantial that the expert leaves no trace. How divinely mysterious that he is inaudible. Thus, he is master of his enemy's fate.

His offensive will be irresistible if he plunges into the enemy's weak points; he cannot be overtaken when he withdraws if he moves swiftly. Hence, if we wish to fight, the enemy will be compelled to an engagement even though he is safe behind high ramparts and deep ditches. This is because we attack a position he must relieve.

If we do not wish to fight, we can prevent him from engaging us even though the lines of our encampment be merely traced out on the ground. This is because we divert him from going where he wishes.

GAIN RELATIVE SUPERIORITY

Accordingly, by exposing the enemy's dispositions and remaining invisible ourselves, we can keep our forces concentrated, while the enemy's must be divided. We can form a single united body at one place, while the enemy must scatter his forces at ten places. Thus, it is ten to one when we attack him at one place, which means we are numerically superior. And if we are able to use many to strike few at the selected place, those we deal with will be in dire straits.

The spot where we intend to fight must not be made known. In this way, the enemy must take precautions at many places against the attack. The more places he must guard, the fewer his troops we shall have to face at any given point.

For if he prepares to the front, his rear will be weak; and if to the rear, his front will be fragile. If he strengthens his left, his right will be vulnerable; and if his right gets strengthened, there will be few troops on his left. If he sends reinforcements everywhere, he will be weak everywhere.

Numerical weakness comes from having to prepare against possible attacks; numerical strength from compelling the enemy to make these preparations against us.

PRACTICE GOOD INTELLIGENCE

Therefore, if one knows the place and time of the coming battle, his troops can march a thousand li and fight on the field. But if one knows neither the spot nor the time, then one cannot manage to have the left wing help the right wing or the right wing help the left; the forces in the front will be unable to support the rear, and the rear will be unable to reinforce the front. How much more so if the farthest portions of the troop deployments extend tens of li in breadth, and even the nearest troops are separated by several li!

Although I estimate the troops of Yue as many, of what benefit is this superiority in terms of victory?

Thus, I say that victory can be achieved. For even if the enemy is numerically stronger, we can prevent him from fighting.

Therefore, analyze the enemy's battle plan so as to have a clear understanding of its strong and weak points. Agitate the enemy so as to ascertain his pattern of movement. Lure him into the open so as to find out his vulnerable spots in disposition. Probe him and learn where his strength is abundant and where it is deficient.

Now, the ultimate in disposing one's troops is to conceal them without ascertainable shape. In this way, the most penetrating spies cannot pry nor can the wise lay plans against you.

BE FLEXIBLE

Even though we show people the victory gained by using flexible tactics in conformity to the changing situations, they do not comprehend this. People all know the tactics by which we achieved victory, but they do not know how the tactics were applied in the situation to defeat the enemy. Hence, no one victory is gained in the same manner as another. The tactics change in an infinite variety of ways to suit changes in the circumstances.

Now the laws of military operations are like water. The tendency of water is to flow from heights to lowlands. The law of successful operations is to avoid the enemy's strength and strike his weakness. Water changes its course in accordance with the contours of the land. The soldier works out his victory in accordance with the situation of the enemy.

Hence, there are neither fixed postures nor constant tactics in warfare. He who can modify his tactics in accordance with the enemy situation and thereby succeeds in winning may be said to be divine. Of the five elements, none is ever predominant; of the four seasons, none lasts forever; of the days, some are longer and others shorter; and of the moon, it sometimes waxes and sometimes wanes.

Chapter 7: Maneuvering

MANEUVER TO GAIN THE ADVANTAGE

Normally, in war, the general receives his commands from the sovereign. During the process from assembling the troops and mobilizing the people to deploying the army ready for battle, nothing is more difficult than the art of maneuvering for seizing favorable positions beforehand. What is difficult about it is to make the devious route the most direct and to turn disadvantage to advantage. Thus, by forcing the enemy to deviate and slow down his march by luring him with a bait, you may set out after he does and arrive at the battlefield before him. One able to do this shows the knowledge of artifice of deviation.

Thus, both advantage and danger are inherent in maneuvering for an advantageous position. One who sets the entire army in motion with impedimenta to pursue an advantageous position will be too slow to attain it. If he abandons the camp and all the impedimenta to contend for advantage, the baggage and stores will be lost.

It follows that when the army rolls up the armor and sets out speedily, stopping neither day nor night and marching at double speed for a hundred li to wrest an advantage, the commander of three divisions will be captured. The vigorous troops will arrive first and the feeble will straggle along behind, so that if this method is used, only one-tenth of the army will arrive. In a forced march of fifty li, the commander of the first and van division will fall, and using this method but half of the army will arrive. In a forced march of thirty li, but two-thirds will arrive. Hence, the army will be lost without baggage train, and it cannot survive without provisions, nor can it last long without sources of supplies.

DECEIVE YOUR OPPONENT

One who is not acquainted with the designs of his neighbors should not enter into alliances with them. Those who do not know the conditions of mountains and forests, hazardous defiles, and marshes and swamps cannot conduct the march of an army. Those who do not use local guides are unable to obtain the advantages of the ground.

Now, war is based on deception. Move when it is advantageous and change tactics by dispersal and concentration of your troops. When campaigning, he swift as the wind; in leisurely march, be majestic as the forest; in raiding and plundering, be fierce as fire; in standing, be firm as the mountains. When hiding, be as unfathomable as things behind the clouds; when moving, fall like a thunderclap. When you plunder the countryside, divide your forces. When you conquer territory, defend strategic points.

Weigh the situation before you move. He who knows the artifice of deviation will be victorious. Such is the art of maneuvering.

PRACTICE THE ART OF GOOD MANAGEMENT

The Book of Army Management says, "As the voice cannot be heard in battle, gongs and drums are used. As troops cannot see each other clearly in battle, flags and banners are used." Hence, in night fighting, usually use drums and gongs; in day fighting, banners and flags. Now, these instruments are used to unify the action of the troops. When the troops can be thus united, the brave cannot advance alone, nor can the cowardly retreat. This is the art of directing large masses of troops.

A whole army may be robbed of its spirit, and its commander deprived of his presence of mind. Now, at the beginning of a campaign, the spirit of soldiers is keen; after a certain period of time, it declines; and in the later stage, it may be dwindled to naught. A clever commander, therefore, avoids the enemy when his spirit is keen and attacks him when it is lost. This is the art of attaching importance to moods. In good order, he awaits a disorderly enemy; in serenity, a clamorous one. This is the art of retaining self-possession. Close to the field of battle, he awaits an enemy coming from afar; at rest, he awaits an exhausted enemy; with well-fed troops, he awaits hungry ones. This is the art of husbanding one's strength.

He refrains from intercepting an enemy whose banners are in perfect order, and desists from attacking an army whose formations are in an impressive array. This is the art of assessing circumstances.

Now, the art of employing troops is that when the enemy occupies high ground, do not confront him uphill, and when his back is resting on hills, do not make a frontal attack. When he pretends to flee, do not pursue. Do not attack soldiers whose temper is keen. Do not swallow a bait offered by the enemy. Do not thwart an enemy who is returning homeward. When you surround an army, leave an outlet free. Do not press a desperate enemy too hard. Such is the method of using troops.

Chapter 8: Variation of Tactics

TACTICS VARY WITH THE SITUATION

Generally in war, the general receives his commands from the sovereign, assembles troops, and mobilizes the people. When on grounds hard of access, do not encamp. On grounds intersected with highways, join hands with your allies. Do not linger on critical ground. In encircled ground, resort to stratagem. In desperate ground, fight a last-ditch battle.

There are some roads that must not be followed, some troops that must not be attacked, some cities that must not be assaulted, some ground that must not be contested, and some commands of the sovereign that must not be obeyed.

Hence, the general who thoroughly understands the advantages that accompany variation of tactics knows how to employ troops. The general who does not is unable to use the terrain to his advantage even though he is well acquainted with it. In employing the troops for attack, the general who does not understand the variation of tactics will be unable to use them effectively, even if he is familiar with the Five Advantages.

CAREFULLY CONSIDER ADVANTAGES AND DISADVANTAGES

And for this reason, a wise general in his deliberations must consider both favorable and unfavorable factors. By taking into account the favorable factors, he makes his plan feasible; by taking into account the unfavorable, he may avoid possible disasters.

What can subdue the hostile neighboring rulers is to hit what hurts them most. What can keep them constantly occupied is to make trouble for them, and what can make them rush about is to offer them ostensible allurements.

It is a doctrine of war that we must not rely on the likelihood of the enemy not coming, but on our own readiness to meet him; not on the chance of his not attacking, but on the fact that we have made our position invincible.

AVOID THE FAULTS OF LEADERSHIP

There are five dangerous faults that may affect a general:

- If reckless, he can be killed.
- If cowardly, he can be captured.
- If quick-tempered, he can be provoked to rage and make a fool of himself.
- If he has too delicate a sense of honor, he is liable to fall into a trap because of an insult.
- If he is of a compassionate nature, he may get bothered and upset.

These are the five serious faults of a general, ruinous to the conduct of war. The ruin of the army and the death of the general are inevitable results of these five dangerous faults. They must be deeply pondered.

Chapter 9: On the March

OCCUPY STRONG NATURAL POSITIONS

Generally, when an army takes up a position and sizes up the enemy situation, it should pay attention to the following:

When crossing the mountains, be sure to stay in the neighborhood of valleys; when encamping, select high ground facing the sunny side; when high ground is occupied by the enemy, do not ascend to attack. So much for taking up a position in mountains.

After crossing a river, you should get far away from it. When an advancing invader crosses a river, do not meet him in midstream. It is advantageous to allow half his force to get across and then strike. If you wish to fight a battle, you should not go to meet the invader near a river that he has to cross. When encamping in the river area, take a position on high ground facing the sun. Do not take a position at the lower reaches of the enemy. This relates to positions near a river.

In crossing salt marshes, your sole concern should be to get over them quickly, without any delay. If you encounter the enemy in a salt marsh, you should take position close to grass and water with trees to your rear. This has to do with taking up a position in salt marshes.

On level ground, take up an accessible position and deploy your main flanks on high grounds with front lower than the back. This is how to take up a position on level ground. These are principles for encamping in the four situations named. By employing them, the Yellow Emperor conquered his four neighboring sovereigns.

ALWAYS SEEK THE HIGH GROUND

Generally, in battle and maneuvering, all armies prefer high ground to low, and sunny places to shady. If an army encamps close to water and grass with adequate supplies, it will be free from countless diseases and this will spell victory. When you come to hills, dikes, or embankments, occupy the sunny side, with your main flank at the back. All these methods are advantageous to the army and can exploit the possibilities the ground offers.

When heavy rain falls in the upper reaches of a river and foaming water descends, do not ford, but wait until it subsides. When encountering "Precipitous Torrents," "Heavenly Wells," "Heavenly Prison," "Heavenly Net," "Heavenly Trap," and "Heavenly Cracks," you must march speedily away from them. Do not approach them. While we keep a distance from them, we should draw the enemy toward them. We face them and cause the enemy to put his back to them.

If in the neighborhood of your camp there are dangerous defiles or ponds and low-lying ground overgrown with aquatic grass and reeds or forested mountains with dense tangled undergrowth, they must be thoroughly searched, for these are possible places where ambushes are laid and spies are hidden.

MAKE AN ESTIMATE OF THE SITUATION

When the enemy is close at hand and remains quiet, he is relying on a favorable position. When he challenges battle from afar, he wishes to lure you to advance; when he is on easy ground, he must be in an advantageous position. When the trees are seen to move, it means the enemy is advancing; when many screens have been placed in the undergrowth, it is for the purpose of deception. The rising of birds in their flight is the sign of an ambuscade. Startled beasts indicate that a sudden attack is forthcoming.

Dust spurting upward in high, straight columns indicates the approach of chariots. When it hangs low and is widespread, it betokens that infantry is approaching. When it branches out in different directions, it shows that parties have been sent out to collect firewood. A few clouds of dust moving to and fro signify that the army is camping.

When the enemy's envoys speak in humble terms but the army continues preparations, that means it will advance. When their language is strong and the enemy pretentiously drives forward, these may be signs that he will retreat. When light chariots first go out and take positions on the wings, it is a sign that the enemy is forming for battle. When the enemy is not in dire straits but asks for a truce, he must be plotting. When his troops march speedily and parade in formations, he is expecting to fight a decisive battle on a fixed date. When half his force advances and half retreats, he is attempting to decoy you.

When his troops lean on their weapons, they are famished. When drawers of water drink before carrying it to camp, his troops are suffering from thirst. When the enemy sees an advantage but does not advance to seize it, he is fatigued.

When birds gather above his campsites, they are unoccupied. When at night the enemy's camp is clamorous, it betokens nervousness. If there is disturbance in the camp, the general's authority is weak.

If the banners and flags are shifted about, sedition is afoot. If the officers are angry, it means that men are weary. When the enemy feeds his horses with grain, kills the beasts of burden for food, and packs up the utensils used for drawing water, he shows no intention to return to his tents and is determined to fight to the death.

When the general speaks in meek and subservient tone to his subordinates, he has lost the support of his men. Too frequent rewards indicate that the general is at the end of his resources; too frequent punishments indicate that he is in dire distress. If the officers at first treat the men violently and later are fearful of them, it shows supreme lack of intelligence.

When envoys are sent with compliments in their mouths, it is a sign that the enemy wishes for a truce.

When the enemy's troops march up angrily and remain facing yours for a long time, neither joining battle nor withdrawing, then the situation demands great vigilance and thorough investigation.

In war, numbers alone confer no advantage. If one does not advance by force recklessly and is able to concentrate his military power through a correct assessment of the enemy situation and enjoys full support of his men, that would suffice. He who lacks foresight and underestimates his enemy will surely be captured by him.

GENERATE A FAIR AND HARMONIOUS RELATIONSHIP

If troops are punished before they have grown attached to you, they will be disobedient. If not obedient, it is difficult to employ them. If troops have become attached to you but discipline is not enforced, you cannot employ them either. Thus, soldiers must be treated in the first instance with humanity but kept under control by iron discipline. In this way, the allegiance of soldiers is assured.

If orders are consistently carried out and the troops are strictly supervised, they will be obedient. If orders are never carried out, they will be disobedient. And the smooth implementation of orders reflects a harmonious relationship between the commander and his troops.

Chapter 10: Terrain

KNOW THE BATTLEFIELD

Ground may be classified according to its nature as accessible, entangling, temporizing, constricted, precipitous, and distant.

Ground that both we and the enemy can traverse with equal ease is called accessible. On such ground, he who first takes high sunny positions and keeps his supply routes unimpeded can fight advantageously.

Ground easy to reach but difficult to exit is called entangling. The nature of this ground is such that if the enemy is unprepared and you sally out, you may defeat him. But if the enemy is prepared for your coming, and you fail to defeat him, then, return being difficult, disadvantages will ensue.

Ground equally disadvantageous for both the enemy and ourselves to enter is called temporizing. The nature of this ground is such that even though the enemy should offer us an attractive bait, it will be advisable not to go forth but march off. When his force is halfway out because of our maneuvering, we can strike him with advantage.

With regard to the constricted ground, if we first occupy it, we must block the narrow passes with strong garrisons and wait for the enemy. Should the enemy first occupy such ground, do not attack him if the pass in his hand is fully garrisoned, but only if it is weakly garrisoned.

With regard to the precipitous ground, if we first occupy it, we must take a position on the sunny heights and await the enemy. If he first occupies such ground, we should march off and not attack him.

When the enemy is situated at a great distance from us, and the terrain where the two armies deploy is similar, it is difficult to provoke battle and unprofitable to engage him.

These are the principles relating to six different types of ground. It is the highest responsibility of the general to inquire into them with the utmost care.

LEADERS MUST LEAD

There are six situations that cause an army to fail. They are: flight, insubordination, fall, collapse, disorganization, and rout. None of these disasters can be attributed to natural and geographical causes, but to the fault of the general.

1. Terrain conditions being equal, if a force attacks one ten times its size, the result is flight.
2. When the soldiers are strong and officers weak, the army is insubordinate.
3. When the officers are valiant and the soldiers ineffective, the army will fall.
4. When the higher officers are angry and insubordinate, and on encountering the enemy, rush to battle on their own account from a feeling of resentment, and the commander-in-chief is ignorant of their abilities, the result is collapse.
5. When the general is incompetent and has little authority, when his troops are mismanaged, when the relationship between the officers and men is strained, and when the troop formations are slovenly, the result is disorganization.
6. When a general unable to estimate the enemy's strength uses a small force to engage a larger one or weak troops to strike the strong, or fails to select shock troops for the van, the result is rout.

When any of these six situations exists, the army is on the road to defeat. It is the highest responsibility of the general that he examine them carefully.

KNOW THE SITUATION AND YOUR PEOPLE

Conformation of the ground is of great assistance in the military operations. It is necessary for a wise general to make correct assessments of the enemy's situation to create conditions leading to victory and to calculate distances and the degree of difficulty of the terrain. He who knows these things and applies them to fighting will definitely win. He who knows them not, and is, therefore, unable to apply them, will definitely lose.

Hence, if, in the light of the prevailing situation, fighting is sure to result in victory, then you may decide to fight even though the sovereign has issued an order not to engage.

If fighting does not stand a good chance of victory, you need not fight even though the sovereign has issued an order to engage.

Hence, the general who advances without coveting fame and retreats without fearing disgrace, whose only purpose is to protect his people and promote the best interests of his sovereign, is the precious jewel of the state.

If a general regards his men as infants, then they will march with him into the deepest valleys. He treats them as his own beloved sons and they will stand by him unto death. If, however, a general is indulgent toward his men but cannot employ them, cherishes them but cannot command them or inflict punishment on them when they violate the regulations, then they may be compared to spoiled children and are useless for any practical purpose.

KNOW YOURSELF AND YOUR OPPONENT

If we know that our troops are capable of striking the enemy but do not know that he is invulnerable to attack, our chance of victory is but half.

If we know that the enemy is vulnerable to attack but do not know that our troops are incapable of striking him, our chance of victory is again but half.

If we know that the enemy can be attacked and that our troops are capable of attacking him but do not realize that the conformation of the ground makes fighting impracticable, our chance of victory is once again but half.

Therefore, those experienced in war moves are never bewildered; when they act, they are never at a loss. Thus, the saying, "Know the enemy and know yourself, and your victory will never be endangered; know the weather and know the ground, and your victory will then be complete."

Chapter 11: The Nine Varieties of Ground

CHOOSE THE BATTLEGROUND

In respect to the employment of troops, ground may be classified as dispersive, frontier, key, open, focal, serious, difficult, encircled, and desperate.

When a chieftain is fighting in his own territory, he is in dispersive ground. When he has penetrated into hostile territory, but to no great distance, he is in frontier ground. Ground equally advantageous for us and the enemy to occupy is key ground. Ground equally accessible to both sides is open. Ground contiguous to three other states is focal. He who first gets control of it will gain the support of the majority of neighboring states. When an army has penetrated deep into hostile territory, leaving far behind many enemy cities and towns, it is in serious ground. Mountain forests, rugged steeps, marshes, fens, and all that is hard to traverse fall into the category of difficult ground. Ground to which access is constricted and from which we can retire only by tortuous paths so that a small number of the enemy would suffice to crush a large body of our men is encircled ground. Ground on which the army can avoid annihilation only through a desperate fight without delay is called a desperate one.

And, therefore, do not fight in dispersive ground; do not stop in the frontier borderlands.

Do not attack an enemy who has occupied key ground; in open ground, do not allow your communication to be blocked.

In focal ground, form alliances with neighboring states; in serious ground, gather in plunder.

In difficult ground, press on; in encircled ground, resort to stratagems; and in desperate ground, fight courageously.

SHAPE YOUR OPPONENT'S STRATEGY

In ancient times, those described as skilled in war knew how to make it impossible for the enemy to unite his van and his rear, for his large and small divisions to cooperate, for his officers and men to support each other, and for the higher and lower levels of the enemy to establish contact with each other.

When the enemy's forces were dispersed, they prevented him from assembling them; even when assembled, they managed to throw his forces into disorder. They moved forward when it was advantageous to do so; when not advantageous, they halted.

Should one ask, "How do I cope with a well-ordered enemy host about to attack me?" I reply, "Seize something he cherishes and he will conform to your desires."

Speed is the essence of war. Take advantage of the enemy's not being prepared, make your way by unexpected routes, and attack him where he has taken no precautions.

VICTORY IS THE ONLY OPTION

The general principles applicable to an invading force are that the deeper you penetrate into hostile territory, the greater will be the solidarity of your troops, and, thus, the defenders cannot overcome you.

Plunder fertile country to supply your army with plentiful food. Pay attention to the soldiers' well-being and do not fatigue them. Try to keep them in high spirits and conserve their energy. Keep the army moving and devise unfathomable plans.

Throw your soldiers into a position whence there is no escape, and they will choose death over desertion. For if prepared to die, how can the officers and men not exert their uttermost strength to fight? In a desperate situation, they fear nothing; when there is no way out, they stand firm. Deep in a hostile land, they are bound together. If there is no help for it, they will fight hard.

Thus, without waiting to be marshaled, the soldiers will be constantly vigilant; without waiting to be asked, they will do your will; without restrictions, they will be faithful; without giving orders, they can be trusted.

Prohibit superstitious practices and do away with rumors. Then nobody will flee even facing death. Our soldiers have no surplus of wealth, but it is not because they disdain riches; they have no expectation of long life, but it is not because they dislike longevity.

On the day the army is ordered out to battle, your soldiers may weep, those sitting up wetting their garments, and those lying down letting the tears run down their cheeks. But throw them into a situation where there is no escape and they will display the immortal courage of Zhuan Zhu and Cao Kuei.

Troops directed by a skillful general are comparable to the Shuai Ran. The Shuai Ran is a snake found in Mount Heng. Strike at its head, and you will be attacked by its tail; strike at its tail, and you will be attacked by its head; strike at its middle, and you will be attacked by both its head and its tail. Should one ask, "Can troops be made capable of such instantaneous coordination as the Shuai Ran?" I reply, "They can." For the men of Wu and the men of Yue are enemies, yet if they are crossing a river in the same boat and are caught by a storm, they will come to each other's assistance just as the left hand helps the right.

Hence, it is not sufficient to rely upon tethering of the horses and the burying of the chariots. The principle of military administration is to achieve a uniform level of courage. The principle of terrain application is to make the best use of both the high- and the low-lying grounds.

Thus, a skillful general conducts his army just as if he were leading a single man, willy-nilly, by the hand.

It is the business of a general to be quiet and thus ensure depth in deliberation; impartial and upright and, thus, keep a good management.

He should be able to mystify his officers and men by false reports and appearances and, thus, keep them in total ignorance. He changes his arrangements and alters his plans in order to make others unable to see through his strategies. He shifts his campsites and undertakes marches by devious routes so as to make it impossible for others to anticipate his objective.

He orders his troops for a decisive battle on a fixed date and cuts off their return route, as if he kicks away the ladder behind the soldiers when they have climbed up a height. When he leads his army deep into hostile territory, their momentum is trigger-released in battle. He drives his men now in one direction, then in another, like a shepherd driving a flock of sheep, and no one knows where he is going. To assemble the host of his army and bring it into danger—this may be termed the business of the general.

LEARN WINNING WAYS

The different measures appropriate to the nine varieties of ground and the expediency of advance or withdrawal in accordance with circumstances and the fundamental laws of human nature are matters that must be studied carefully by a general.

Generally, when invading a hostile territory, the deeper the troops penetrate, the more cohesive they will be; penetrating only a short way causes dispersion.

When you leave your own country behind and take your army across neighboring territory, you find yourself on critical ground.

When there are means of communication on all four sides, it is focal ground.

When you penetrate deeply into a country, it is serious ground.

When you penetrate but a little way, it is frontier ground.

When you have the enemy's strongholds on your rear, and narrow passes in front, it is encircled ground.

When there is no place of refuge at all, it is desperate ground.

Therefore, in dispersive ground, I would unify the determination of the army. In frontier ground, I would keep my forces closely linked. In key ground, I would hasten up my rear elements. In open ground, I would pay close attention to my defense. In focal ground, I would consolidate my alliances. In serious ground, I would ensure a continuous flow of provisions. In difficult ground, I would press on over the road. In encircled ground, I would block the points of access and egress. In desperate ground, I would make it evident that there is no chance of survival. For it is the nature of soldiers to resist when surrounded, to fight hard when there is no alternative, and to follow commands implicitly when they have fallen into danger.

One ignorant of the designs of neighboring states cannot enter into alliance with them. If ignorant of the conditions of mountains, forests, dangerous defiles, swamps, and marshes, he cannot conduct the march of an army. If he fails to make use of native guides, he cannot gain the advantages of the ground.

An army does not deserve the title of the invincible Army of the Hegemonic King if its commander is ignorant of even one of these nine varieties of ground. Now, when such an invincible army attacks a powerful state, it makes it impossible for the enemy to assemble his forces. It overawes the enemy and prevents his allies from joining him. It follows that one does not need to seek alliances with other neighboring states, nor is there any need to foster the power of other states, but only to pursue one's own strategic designs to overawe his enemy. Then one can take the enemy's cities and overthrow the enemy's state.

Bestow rewards irrespective of customary practice and issue orders irrespective of convention and you can command a whole army as though it were but one man.

Set the troops to their tasks without revealing your designs. When the task is dangerous, do not tell them its advantageous aspect. Throw them into a perilous situation and they will survive; put them in desperate ground and they will live. For when the army is placed in such a situation, it can snatch victory from defeat.

Now, the key to military operations lies in cautiously studying the enemy's designs. Concentrate your forces in the main direction against the enemy and from a distance of a thousand li you can kill his general. This is called the ability to achieve one's aim in an artful and ingenious manner.

Therefore, on the day the decision is made to launch war, you should close the passes, destroy the official tallies, and stop the passage of all emissaries. Examine the plan closely in the temple council and make final arrangements.

If the enemy leaves a door open, you must rush in. Seize the place the enemy values without making an appointment for battle with him. Be flexible and decide your line of action according to the situation on the enemy side.

At first, then, exhibit the coyness of a maiden until the enemy gives you an opening; afterward be swift as a running hare, and it will be too late for the enemy to oppose you.

Chapter 12: Attack by Fire

BE DISRUPTIVE AND INTRUSIVE

There are five ways of attacking with fire. The first is to burn soldiers in their camp; the second, to burn provision and stores; the third, to burn baggage trains; the fourth, to burn arsenals and magazines; and the fifth, to burn the lines of transportation.

To use fire, some medium must be relied upon. Materials for setting fire must always be at hand. There are suitable seasons to attack with fire, and special days for starting a conflagration. The suitable seasons are when the weather is very dry; the special days are those when the moon is in the constellations of the Sieve, the Wall, the Wing, or the Crossbar; for when the moon is in these positions, there are likely to be strong winds all day long.

Now, in attacking with fire, one must respond to the five changing situations: When fire breaks out in the enemy's camp, immediately coordinate your action from without. If there is an outbreak of fire but the enemy's soldiers remain calm, bide your time and do not attack. When the force of the flames has reached its height, follow it up with an attack, if that is practicable; if not, stay where you are. If fires can be raised from outside the enemy's camps, it is not necessary to wait until they are started inside. Attack with fire only when the moment is suitable. If the fire starts from up-wind, do not launch attack from down-wind. When the wind continues blowing during the day, then it is likely to die down at night.

Now, the army must know the five different fire-attack situations and wait for appropriate times.

Those who use fire to assist their attacks can achieve tangible results; those who use inundations can make their attacks more powerful. Water can intercept and isolate an enemy but cannot deprive him of the supplies or equipment.

CONSOLIDATE YOUR GAINS

Now, to win battles and capture lands and cities but to fail to consolidate these achievements is ominous and may be described as a waste of resources and time. And, therefore, the enlightened rulers must deliberate upon the plans to go to battle, and good generals carefully execute them.

EXERCISE RESTRAINT

If not in the interests of the state, do not act. If you are not sure of success, do not use troops. If you are not in danger, do not fight a battle.

A sovereign should not launch a war simply out of anger, nor should a general fight a war simply out of resentment. Take action if it is to your advantage; cancel the action if it is not. An angered man can be happy again, just as a resentful one can feel pleased again, but a state that has perished can never revive, nor can a dead man be brought back to life.

Therefore, with regard to the matter of war, the enlightened ruler is prudent, and the good general is full of caution. Thus, the state is kept secure and the army preserved.

Chapter 13: Employment of Secret Agents

BUDGET ADEQUATE FUNDS

Generally, when an army of 100,000 is raised and dispatched on a distant war, the expenses borne by the people together with the disbursements made by the treasury will amount to 1,000 pieces of gold per day. There will be continuous commotion both at home and abroad; people will be involved with convoys and exhausted from performing transportation services, and 700,000 households will be unable to continue their farmwork.

Hostile armies confront each other for years in order to struggle for victory in a decisive battle; yet if one who begrudges the expenditure of 100 pieces of gold in honors and emoluments remains ignorant of his enemy's situation, he is completely devoid of humanity. Such a man is no leader of the troops; no capable assistant to his sovereign; no master of victory.

ESTABLISH AN ACTIVE INTELLIGENCE SYSTEM

Now, the reason that the enlightened sovereign and the wise general conquer the enemy whenever they move and their achievements surpass those of ordinary men is that they have foreknowledge. This "foreknowledge" cannot be elicited from spirits, nor from gods, nor by analogy with past events, nor by any deductive calculations. It must be obtained from the men who know the enemy situation.

Hence, there are five sorts of spies: native, internal, converted, doomed, and surviving.

When all these five sorts of spies are at work and none knows their method of operation, it would be divinely intricate and constitutes the greatest treasure of a sovereign.

1. Native spies are those we employ from the enemy's country people.
2. Internal spies are enemy officials whom we employ.
3. Converted spies are enemy spies whom we employ.
4. Doomed spies are those of our own spies who are deliberately given false information and told to report it.
5. Surviving spies are those who return from the enemy camp to report information.

Hence, of all those in the army close to the commander, none are more intimate than the spies; of all rewards, none more liberal than those given to spies; of all matters, none are more confidential than those relating to spying operations.

He who is not sage cannot use spies. He who is not humane and generous cannot use spies. And he who is not delicate and subtle cannot get the truth out of them. Truly delicate indeed!

There is no place where espionage is not possible. If plans relating to spying operations are prematurely divulged, the spy and all those to whom he spoke of them should be put to death.

Generally, whether it be armies that you wish to strike, cities that you wish to attack, or individuals whom you wish to assassinate, it is necessary to find out the names of the garrison commander, the aides-de-camp, the ushers, the gatekeepers, and the bodyguards. You must instruct your spies to ascertain these matters in minute detail.

It is essential to seek out enemy spies who have come to conduct espionage against you and bribe them to serve you. Courteously exhort them and give your instructions, then release them back home. Thus, converted spies are recruited and used. It is through the information brought by the converted spies that native and internal spies can be recruited and employed. It is owing to their information, again, that the doomed spies, armed with false information, can be sent to convey it to the enemy. Lastly, it is by their information that the surviving spies can come back and give information as scheduled. The sovereign must have full knowledge of the activities of the five sorts of spies. And to know these depends upon the converted spies. Therefore, it is mandatory that they be treated with the utmost liberality.

In ancient times, the rise of the Shang Dynasty was due to Yi Zhi, who had served under the Xia. Likewise, the rise of the Zhou Dynasty was due to Lu Ya, who had served under the Yin. Therefore, it is only the enlightened sovereign and the wise general who are able to use the most intelligent people as spies and achieve great results. Spying operations are essential in war; upon them the army relies to make its every move.

Translated by Pan Jiabin and Liu Ruixiang
Peoples Republic of China

Index

timing of strikes
against, 146
ConAgra, 75
Concord, battle of, 10
Considerate behavior,
275–77
Consolidation strategy, 246
Container Store, 187, 204
Continuity programs, 148
Coordination. *See under*
Communication;
Efforts; Resources;
Timing
Coors, 149–50
Core competencies, 303,
304
Core values, 150
Cost, 139–40, 168–69, 243
Costco, 144, 150, 197,
238–39
Counsel, seeking, 288–91
Courage, 277–79
Couzens, Lansky, Fealk,
Ellis, Roeder & Lazar,
375
Cowardice, 80, 81, 383,
413
Craft, knowing, 19–21, 399
Creativity, 154, 282–86
Crecy, battle of, 152
Creech, Bill, 10
Crest toothpaste, 36
Critical mass, 65–67, 360.
See also Mass
CRM (customer relation-
ship management), 8,
15
Cryptography, 231
Cumulative implementa-
tion, 344
Cumulative initiatives, 66
Customers
centering business on,
171–72
complaints from, 168,
219
data and stories on, 213
focus on, 118
identifying wants of,
237
listening to, 156–57,
218–19, 222

loyalty of, 83–84, 126,
148, 187
as the North Star,
218–20
satisfaction with em-
ployees' work, 153
talking to, 222, 252
target, 251

Danner, 79
Darwin, Charles, 283
Davidoff, Mark, 383–84
Daymon Associates,
372–73
D-Day (Normandy) inva-
sion, 101–2, 210
Debenhams, 238
Decentralization, 41, 70,
99–100, 121, 134
Deception, 67–69, 410–11
Decision making, 212, 226,
337, 339, 392–93
bottom up *vs.* top
down, 170–71
fact-based, 218
Defense
adapted for business, 63
location and, 108–9
preparing adequate,
77–79
De Geus, Arnie, 35
De Jomini, Henri, 386
Dell, 120, 139, 178, 307
Dell, Michael, 139, 209,
216
DeLorean, John, 156
Delta Airlines, 144
Deming, W. Edwards,
104–5
Denton, Harold, 226, 271
De Vries, Kets, 35
Discipline, 335, 380
allegiance built
through, 92–94,
389–90
practicing, 280–82
Disney, 113, 115, 163
Disruptiveness, 110–11,
123–25, 221, 324,
427–28
Distribution, clarity of,
149–50

Dixon, Norman, 20, 29
Doctrine, 5, 389, 395
Domino's Pizza, 253, 327
Doner, Steve, 248
Doyle, Arthur Conan, 386
Dr. Pepper, 88
Dunkirk, battle of, 211
Dunlap, Al, 80
Du Picq, Ardant, 42, 93,
115, 321

Edsel, 103
Efforts
coordination of, 114–16
extraordinary, 325–26
redoubling, 254–57
Eloquent ignorance,
290–91
E-mail, efficient use of, 233
Emeril Lagasse, 250
Emotions, 83, 108–9, 168,
202–3, 263, 266, 346
Employees. *See* People
Empowerment, 159–60
Encirclement, 63
Enemies. *See also* Compe-
tition; Opponents
dislocating, 324–25
identifying, 358
practical tips for over-
coming, 376–77
Energy, use of, 41–48,
404–6
Enigma code, 231
Enterprise Rent-A-Car, 24
Environmental Dictionary
(King), 310
Eruzione, Mike, 254
ESPN, 10
Estimating the situation,
88–92, 415–17
The Exceptional Executive
(Levinson), 59, 335
Execution, 137–257. *See
also* Alignment; Flex-
ibility; People; Simplic-
ity; Strengths
Experience, 225, 246–50
Express Scripts, 60
Externally focused strate-
gic turns, 10
External restraint, 127–28

Fabian, 63
Facebook, 79
Failure, 210, 257
Family, 153, 255
Family positions, 315–16
Feather, William, 230
FedEx, 64, 124, 142
Feelers, 263
"F" exercise, 319–20
Fighting, 40–81. *See also*
Attacks; Battles; Energy,
use of; Maneuvering
the most important
fight, 165–70
variation of tactics,
74–81
weakness and strength
in, 49–61
winning without, 23–
25, 305–9, 375–76,
399–400, 403
Finickiness, 168–70
Firings, 80–81, 192, 341
Fites, Donald, 78
The Five Pillars of TQM
(Creech), 10
Five why's, 295
Flanking, 49, 63, 146, 150
Fleming, Ian, 386
Flexibility, 3, 382, 385, 409
for execution, 207–33
for managers, 82–136
translation and com-
mentary, 59–61
Flickr, 243
Focus, 360–61
Folgers, 239–40
Follow through, 362
Force
applying extraordi-
nary, 44–46, 66–67,
381–82, 404–5
economy of, 32
Ford, Betty, 279
Ford, Gerald, 271
Ford Motor Company, 8,
29, 58, 102–3, 239
Fosbury, Dick (Fosbury
Flop), 286, 307, 308
*The Foundations of Strat-
egy* (Johnstone), 51